I0762593

OF STROKES AND SHADES

THE SECRETS OF DIGITAL ART BY LAURA H. RUBIN

3dtotalPublishing

ONE TREE PLANTED FOR EVERY BOOK SOLD

We at 3dtotal Publishing donate 50% of our profits to charity. For every book sold, we give to reforesting charities to plant new trees. This is just one part of our annual donation to a large number of the most effective charities, covering causes such as humanitarian work, animal welfare, and the protection of existing rainforests. We also aim to be a carbon-neutral publisher with carbon-neutral products, which means that by buying from 3dtotal Publishing, you are helping to balance the environmental damage caused by the publishing, shipping, and retail industries, as well as supporting many other causes.

See **3dtotal.com/charity** for full details.

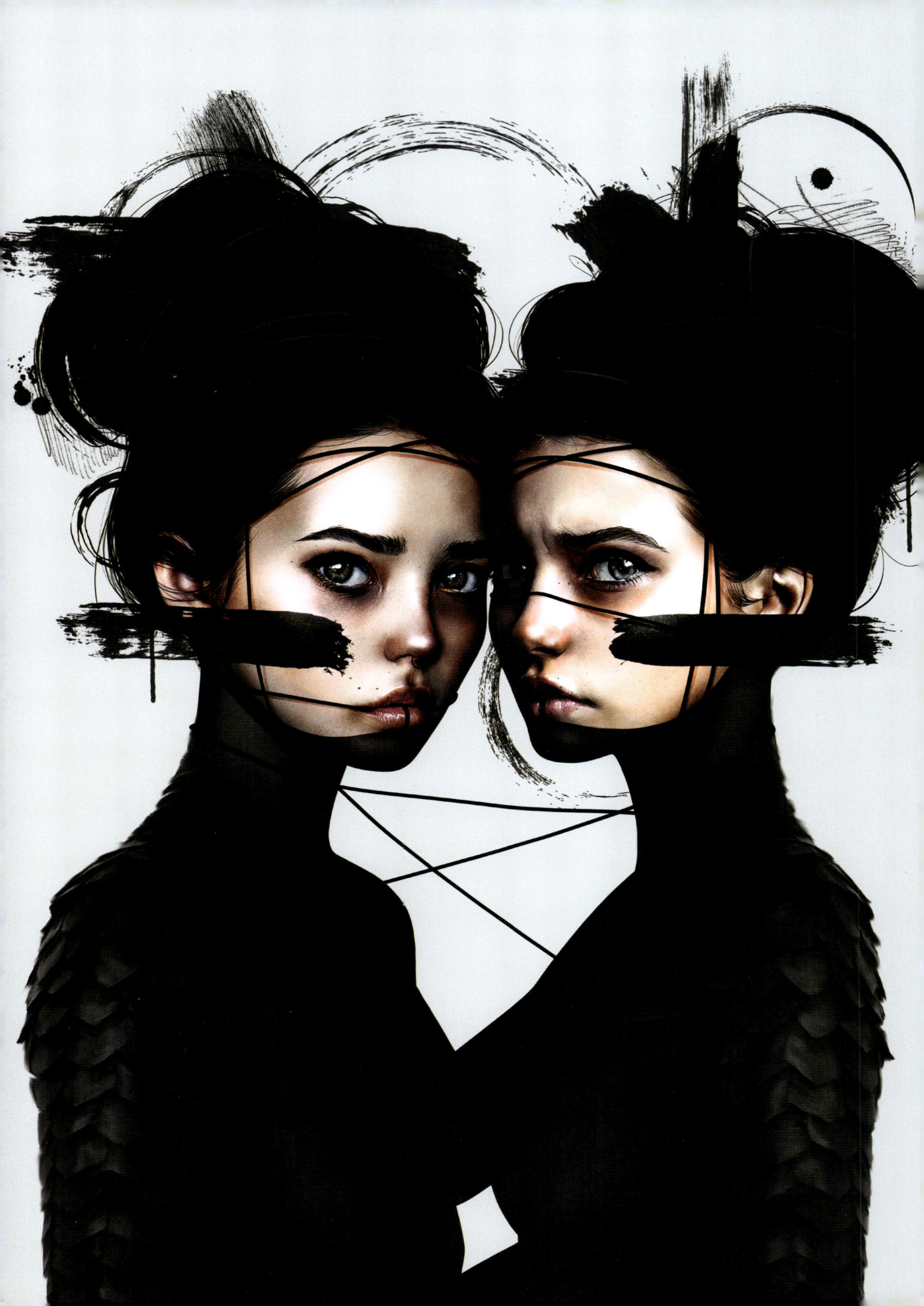

3dtotal Publishing

Correspondence: publishing@3dtotal.com
Website: www.3dtotal.com

First published in the United Kingdom, 2023, by 3dtotal Publishing.

Address: 3dtotal.com Ltd,
29 Foregate Street, Worcester
WR1 1DS, United Kingdom.

Hard cover ISBN: 978-1-912843-60-2

Printing and binding: Gutenberg Press Ltd (Malta) www.gutenberg.com.mt

Visit www.3dtotalpublishing.com for a complete list of available book titles.

Managing Director: Tom Greenway
Studio Manager: Simon Morse
Lead Editor: Samantha Rigby
Lead Designer: Joseph Cartwright
Editorial Project Manager: Rhiannon Joseph

Unsplash images by: Anne Nygard, Buscher, Francois Hoang, Rafaella Mendes Diniz, Rikonavt, Stephane Yaich, Tamara Schipchinskaya

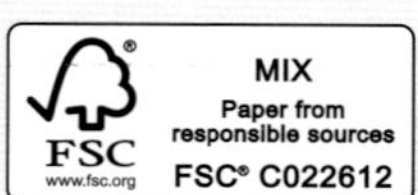

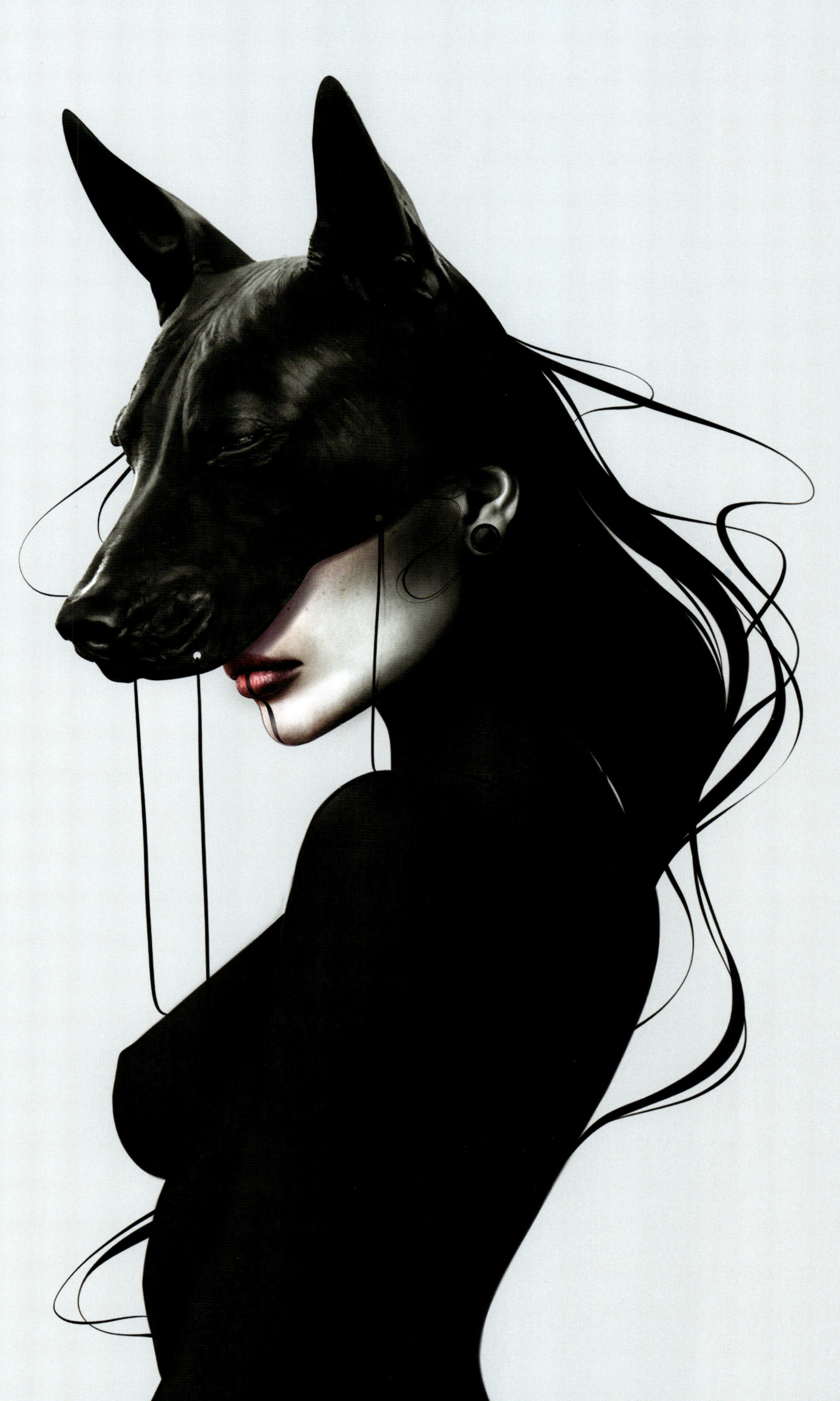

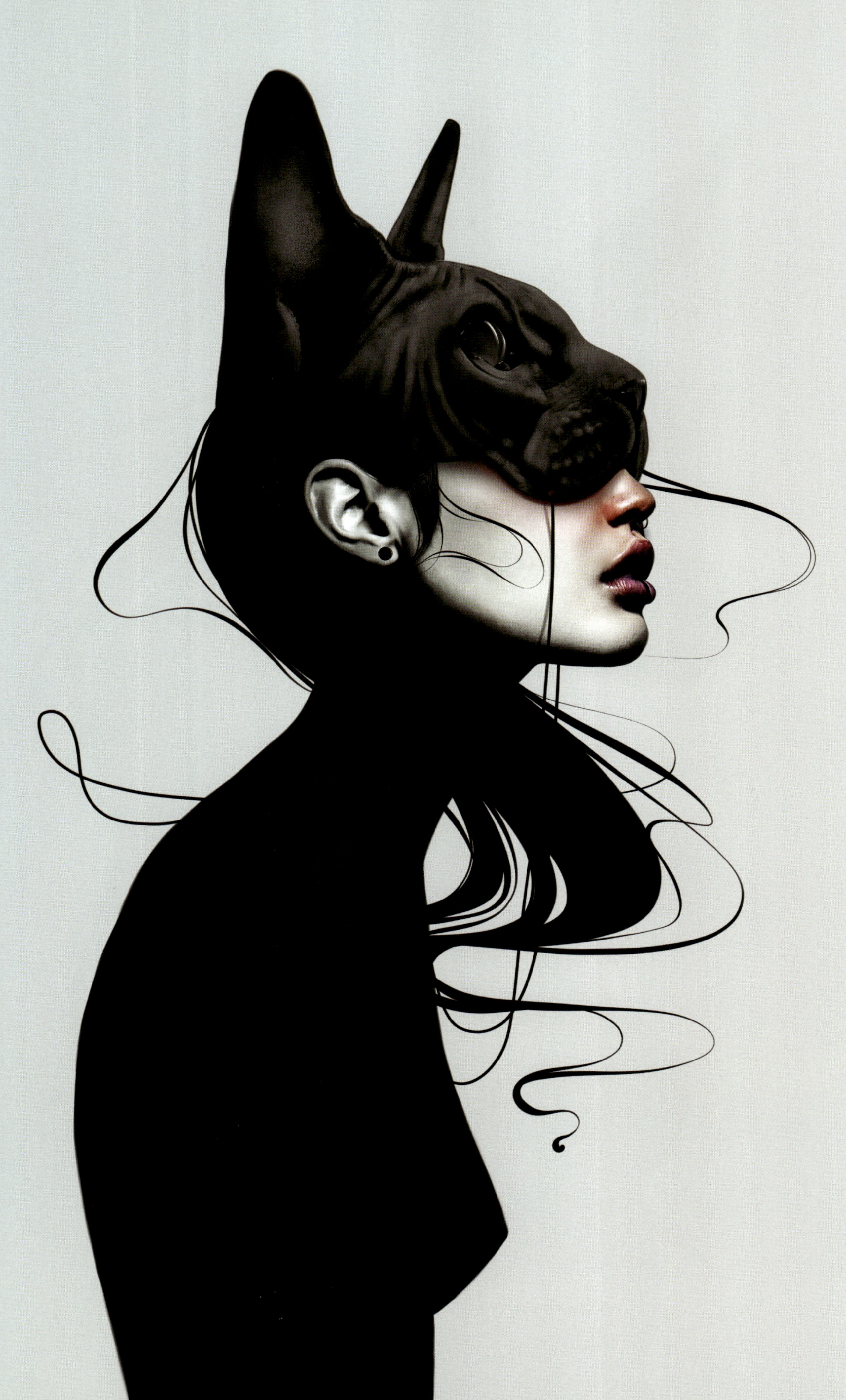

CONTENTS

8 INTRODUCTION

10 ARTISTIC JOURNEY

30 SKETCHBOOK

40 ARTWORK & BEHIND THE SCENES

64 CHARACTER DESIGN

72 TOOLS

76 THE PERFECT PORTRAIT

86 CREATING AN IMAGE IN PROCREATE

128 CHEAT SHEET

134 QUESTIONS & ANSWERS

140 GALLERY

150 THANK YOU

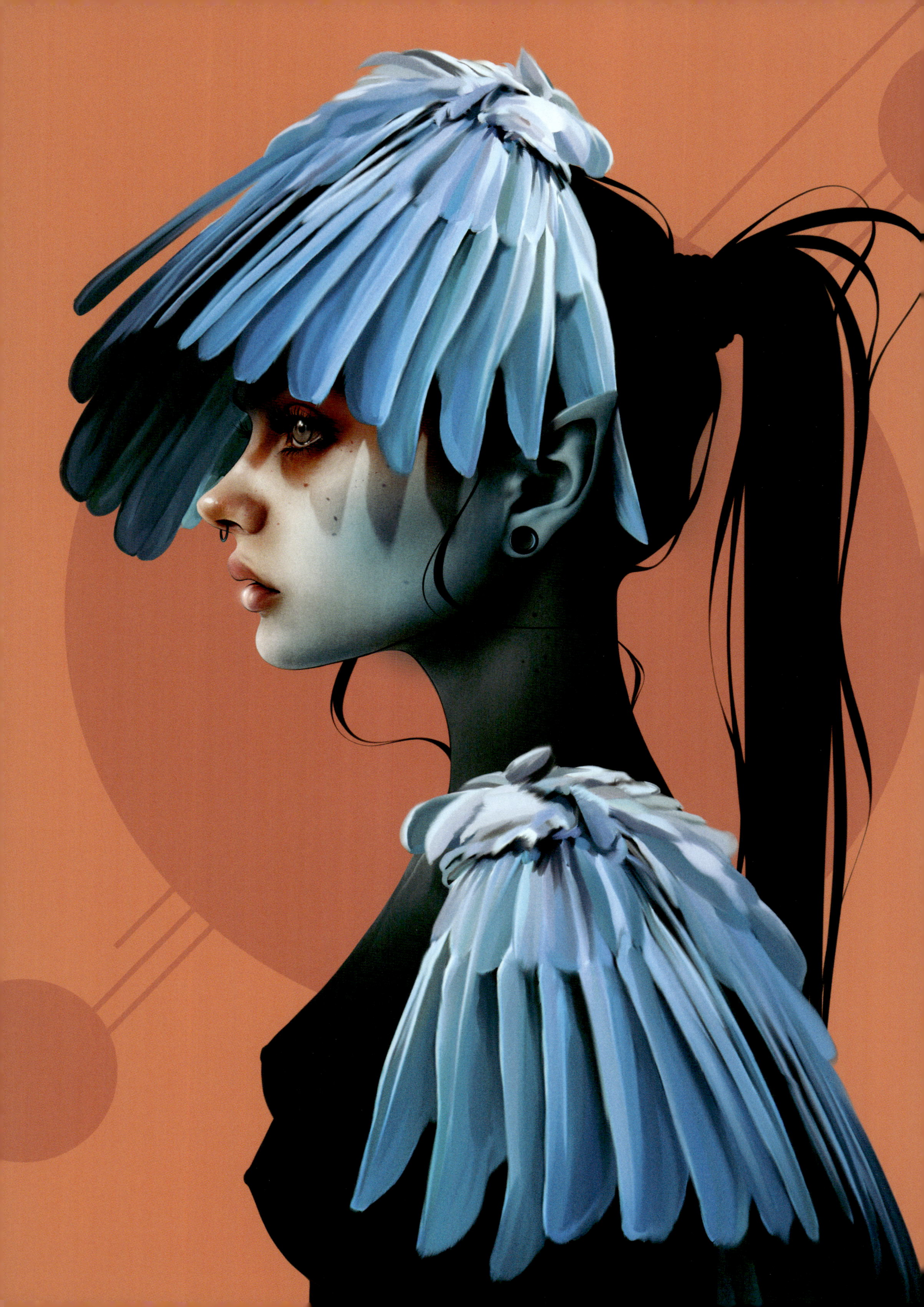

INTRODUCTION

Becoming a full-time artist was one of my biggest dreams that eventually turned into a reality. A few years ago, when I decided to draw more regularly and share the results on social media, I would never have guessed that it would have led me on such an exciting journey! Thanks to everyone who has followed me on this incredible path, I've been lucky enough to write a second book and share another snapshot of my artistic development with you all. To say I'm grateful would be an understatement.

Being an artist may sound easy and fun, but there are many questions involved and more than a few hurdles to jump over. What does it take to work as a successful artist? Is it even legal to draw and sell pictures of people? What do I have to consider if I want my pictures printed? And what the heck is PPI all about? These are some of the thoughts I'll do my best to answer throughout this book.

This is a tool for anyone who wants a deeper insight into my creative process, workflow, and artistic vision.

While the first section is dedicated to my career, daily routine, inspirations, sketchbook, and new illustrations from the past year, the second half is dedicated to the incredibly detailed process of creating a realistic portrait. In addition to these methods and procedures – brainstorming, image composition, mood, and lighting, to name a few – I also highlight all the technical aspects of my workflow in a comprehensive, step-by-step guide.

I hope to answer many of the questions I'm regularly asked by the art community, motivate some of you to try new stylistic approaches, and ignite the desire to further develop your own creative work.

ARTISTIC JOURNEY

“WE DON’T MAKE MISTAKES, JUST HAPPY LITTLE ACCIDENTS”

– Bob Ross

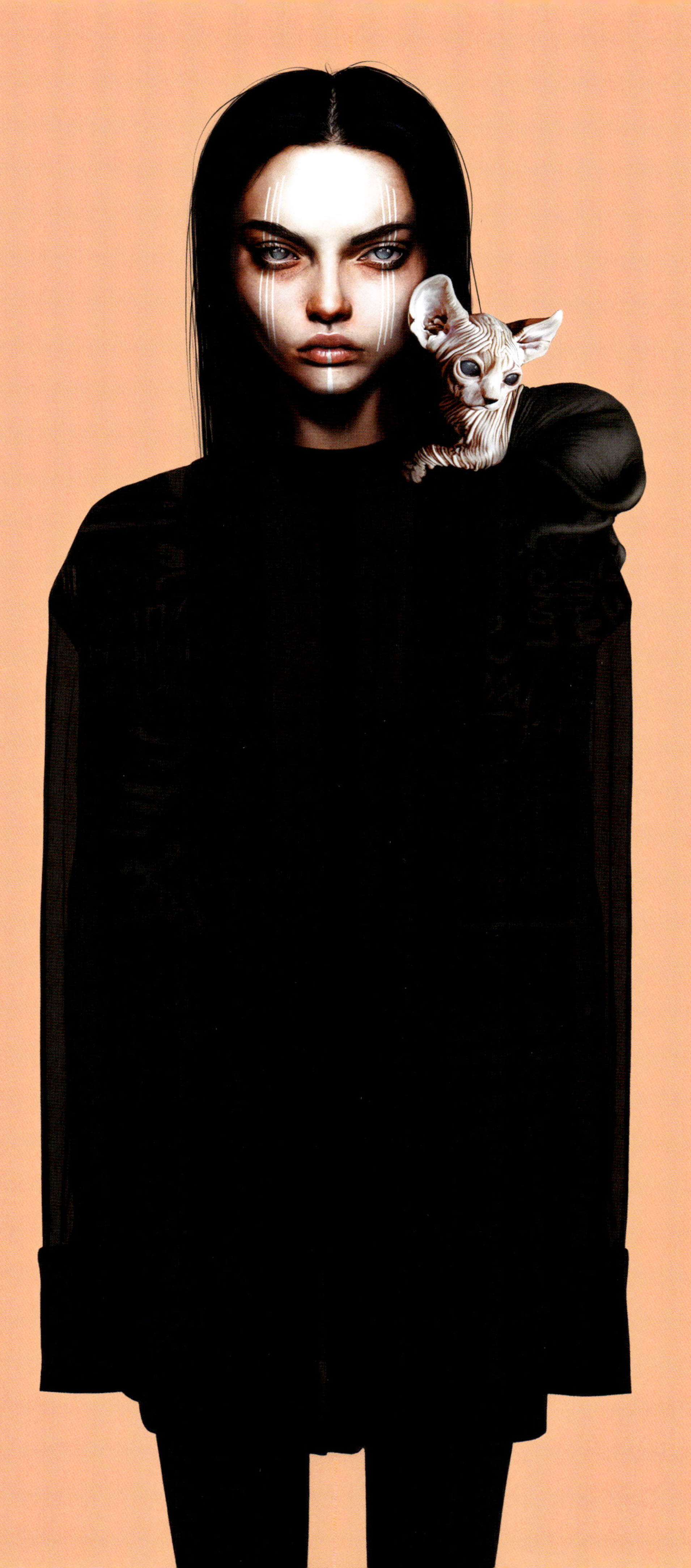

EARLY DAYS

For someone who's always been interested in drawing, I was surprisingly bad at it for a long time. I know that everyone has to start somewhere, but remember those kids from school who just seemed to be great at everything from the get-go? Well, I wasn't one of them. I had very little perseverance, and even less confidence in myself.

My dad, on the other hand, always believed in me. My parents split up when I was six years old, causing my mother and me to move three hours away from my father. As I was still afraid of taking the train by myself at that age, on weekends he had to pick me up and we'd travel to his home together.

Back then, I thought that my father and I didn't have much in common, other than loving sweets and being shy and quiet... which was the reason we never really knew how to talk to each other.

Since a six-year-old can be a handful during such a long train ride ("are we theeeere yet?!"), my dad invented a game to make the time go by faster. One of us would doodle an object on a piece of paper, and the other had to draw an object able to destroy the previous one, *ad infinitum*. Yes, I know this wasn't a terribly educational use of time, but my dad knew it would keep me entertained for hours. This is how we found a way to communicate with one another without having to actually talk much.

Later, when he realized I was getting more and more interested in drawing, he showed me one of his old sketchbooks. He attended an art school when he was younger and had kept his work from that time period. I was so impressed by his drawings that I wanted nothing more than to learn how to do it myself. However, that was easier said than done.

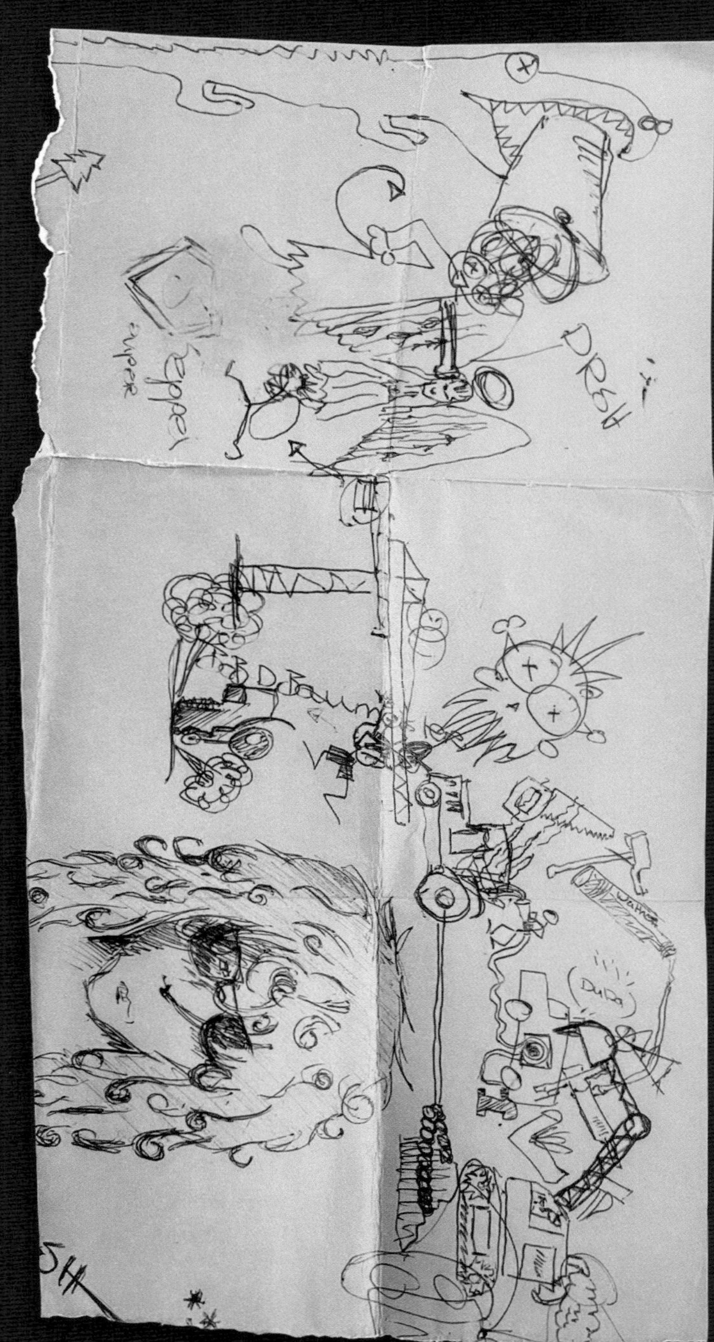

Some of our doodles. They look absolutely awful, but in our defense, it really isn't easy to draw in a shaking train.

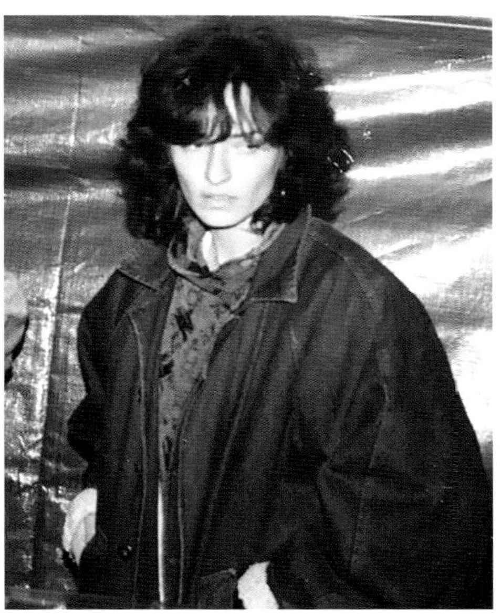

MY MOM

She helped my dad in his line of work, but more importantly spent a lot of time with me. Even though she never attended any art school, she was one of those prodigies who was just naturally great at drawing.

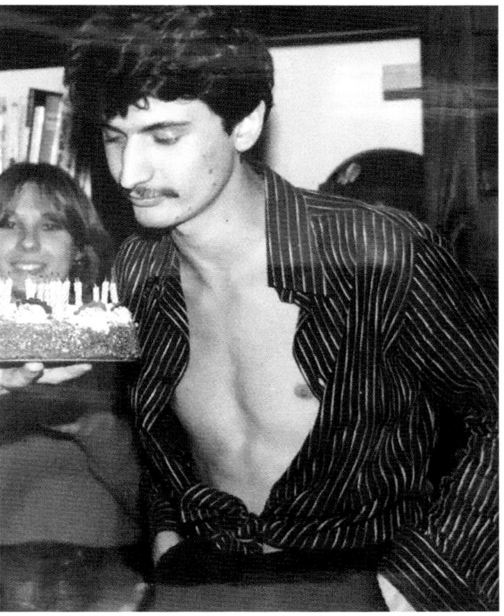

MY DAD

Although he was interested in art, he decided to become a mechanic. In the seventies, he was a racecar driver, and by the end of the eighties, he owned one of the most successful auto repair shops in Zurich.

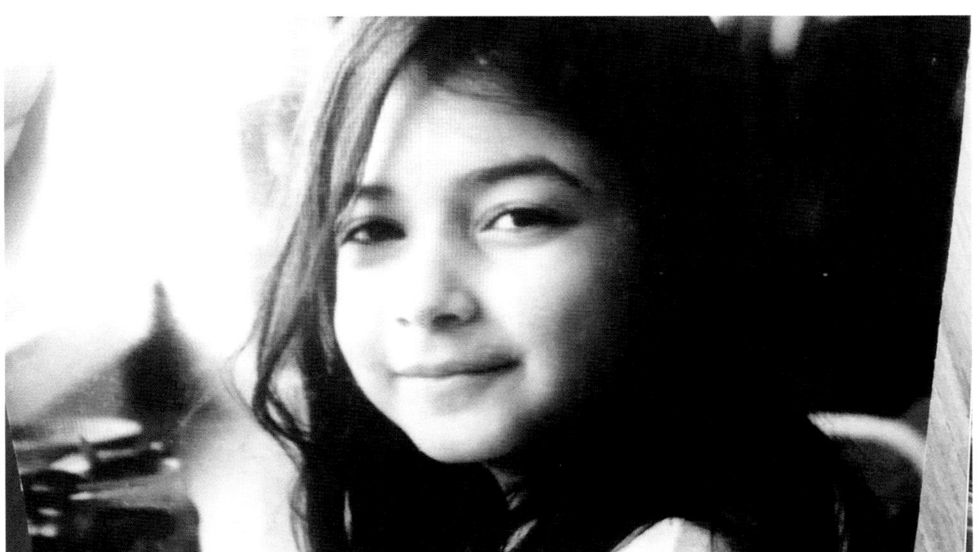

ME This was me in 1999 when I was six years old. The photo was taken not long after my parents split up.

ARTISTIC JOURNEY

1995

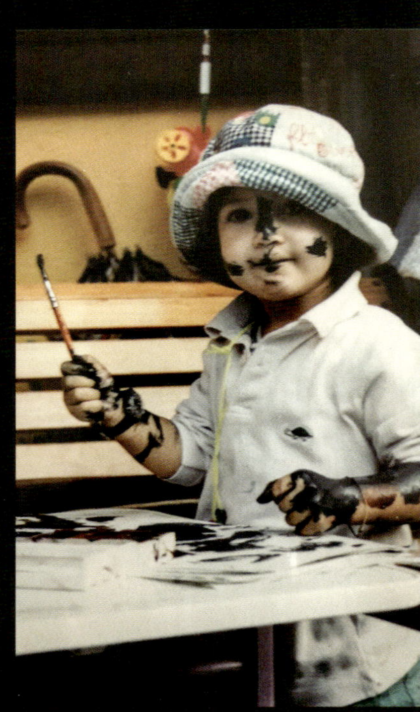

One of my first painting sessions from when I was two years old. I think I chose to paint with black because I wanted to use all the colors at the same time (ha!).

2008

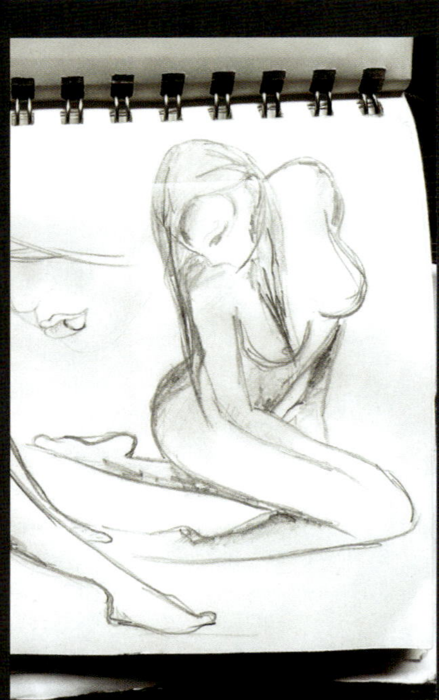

I was rarely patient enough to finish a sketch back then. I would often watch the making-of bonus features that came with animated movies... they made it look so easy.

2009

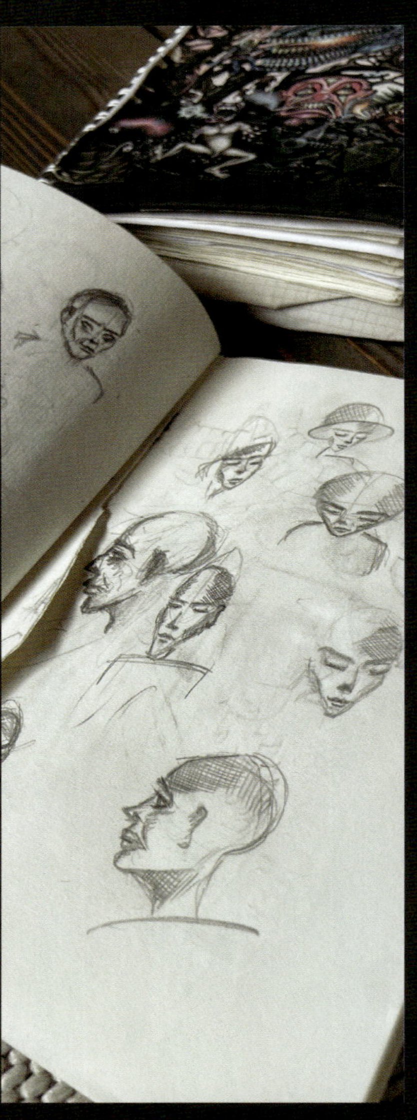

Some of my first proper attempts to draw a face. I was always incredibly disappointed by the results, which is why I often ripped pages out of my sketchbook and threw them away.

2010

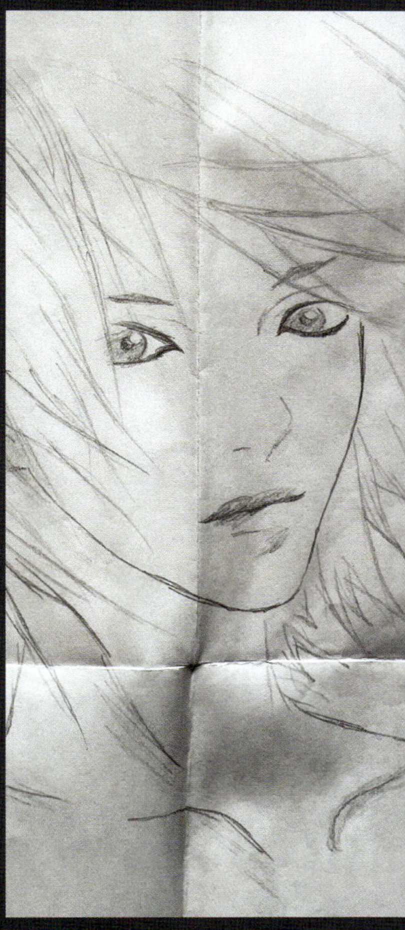

I discovered my preference for manga and anime. It was a little easier to draw faces in this style because there were fewer rules to follow.

2012

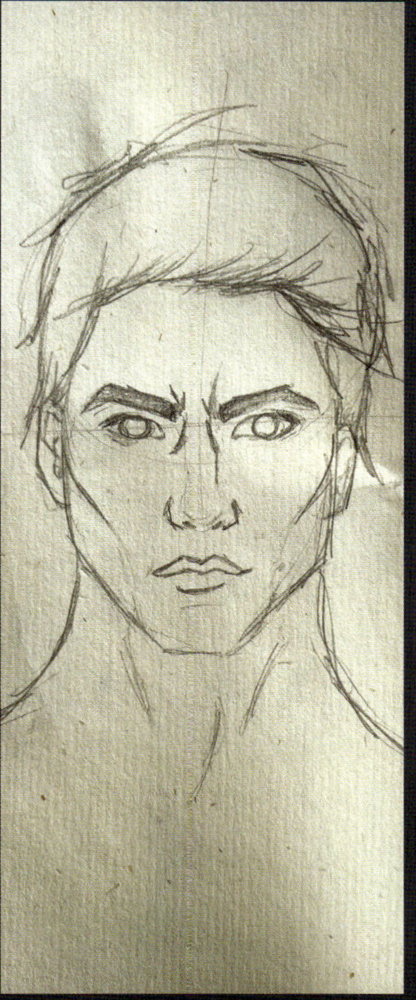

This was the year I began the Film & VFX course at the SAE Institute in Zurich. We had to create many storyboards, so I decided to learn the Loomis method, which teaches you how to draw characters from different angles and perspectives without having to rely on references. This was the first time I structured my art instead of just scribbling away.

2013

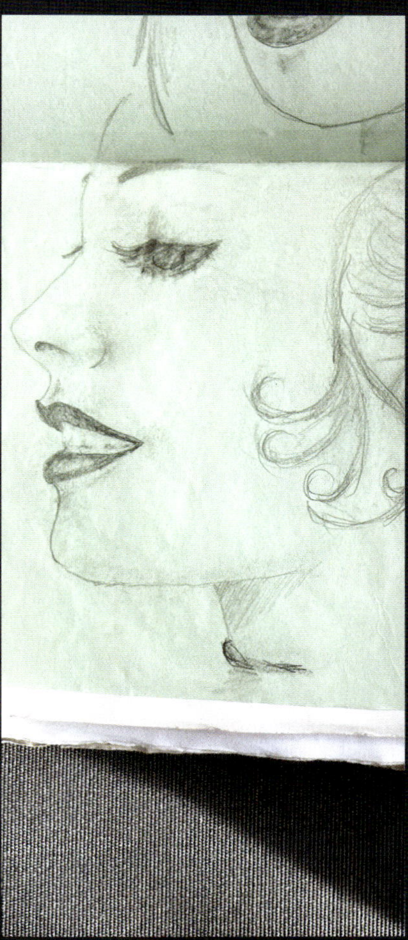

We only had very basic drawing lessons in college, so I bought a lot of books to supplement my knowledge and learn new techniques from different artists.

2014

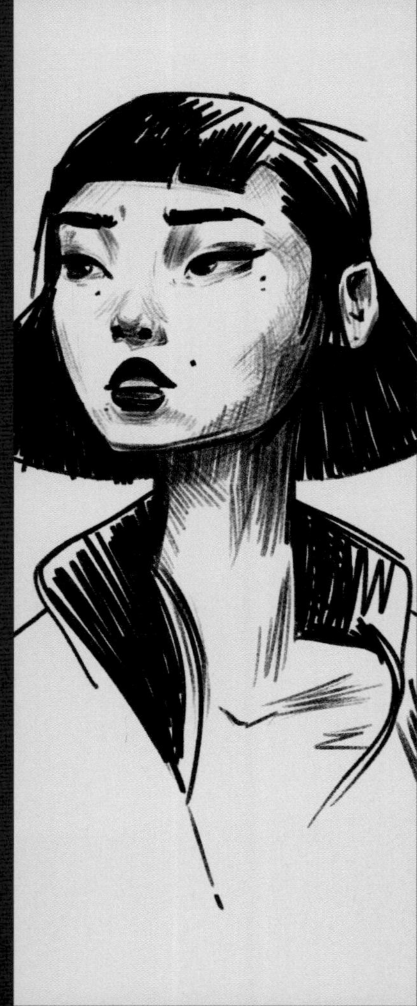

Around this time, I'd acquired a style that made it possible to design storyboards very quickly. I also started drawing with a tablet in school.

2014

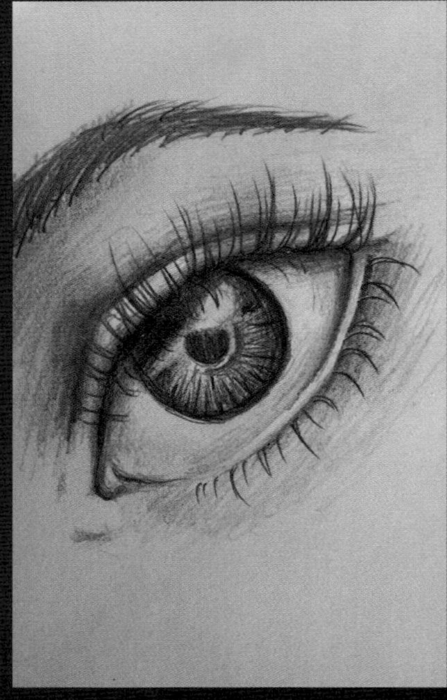

The start of my interest in realism. I decided to take a few extra classes relating to the subject. Due to the high cost of these classes, I was completely broke, so I was over the moon when I unexpectedly received the best present ever: a drawing tablet!

2015

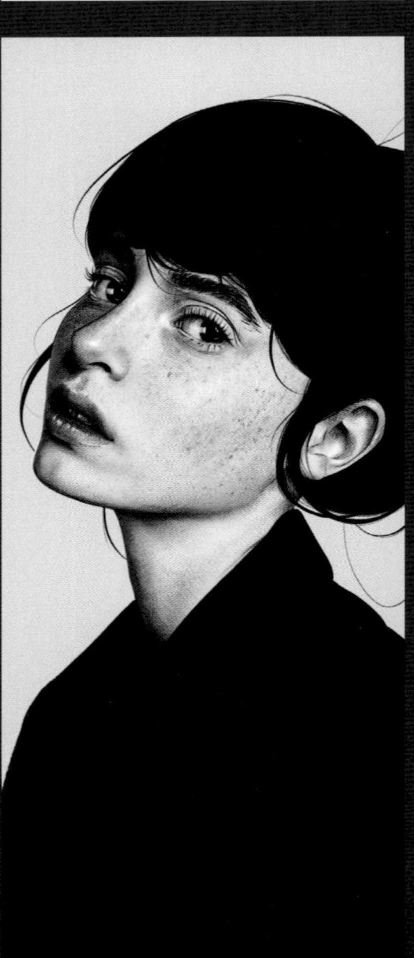

I began experimenting with strong contrasts in my work. I enjoyed the results so much that I painted entire areas black.

I hope that in the next few years I will continue to develop my work. Let's see where the road takes me. Thank you for being a part of it!

2016

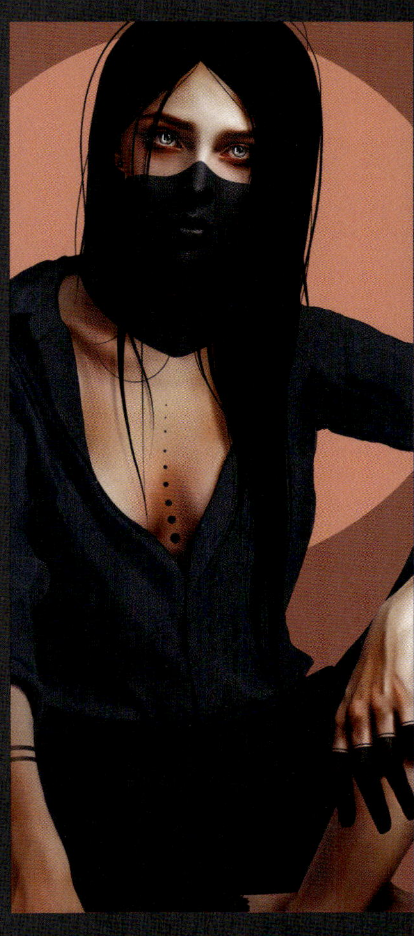

My teacher used to say that every artist must draw a self-portrait at least once in their life.

2017

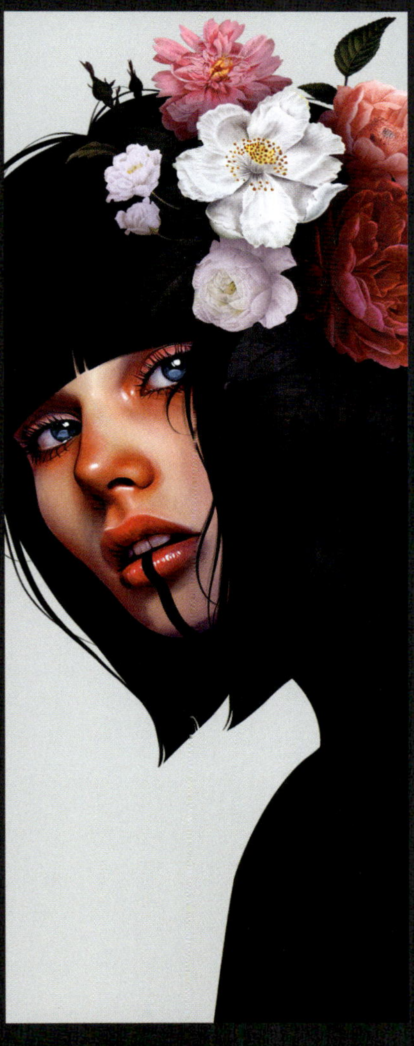

This was the first time I was completely happy with the work I was creating, and felt I'd found a style that really belonged to me.

2022

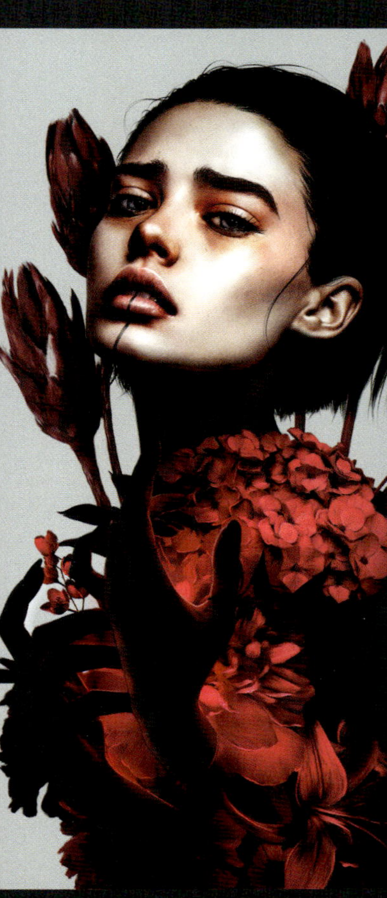

Today, I've backed away from making whole areas black. Instead, I paint the body and hair very dark but still incorporate detail.

HIGHER EDUCATION

After completing high school, I started living on my own and had no money to finance further schooling, so I looked for a job that didn't require a degree or experience and ended up at a call center. My sincere apologies to anyone I might have called in an attempt to sell useless junk!

I hated that job, and because I still wasn't making enough money, I was forced to sell a lot of my possessions... including most of my art supplies. Eventually, all I owned was a mattress, a rug, and a shelf with some knickknacks on it. At the time, I was grateful to still have a roof over my head, clothes to wear, and enough food to get by, but I was unhappy with my lack of higher education, so I decided things needed to change.

The stars aligned when a friend told me about the SAE Institute in Zurich, a school that specializes in creative media. Back then, the voice of reason in my head said, "Don't do this, it's way too expensive and there are very few jobs catering to that skill set in Switzerland." Of course, I ignored it. After sourcing two part-time jobs to cover the cost, I signed up for a course on Film & VFX. Living far away from the school meant a daily total of five hours commuting by train. It was then that I remembered the game my dad and I invented, and over time, I rediscovered my joy of drawing.

STUDYING AT THE SAE INSTITUTE WAS INCREDIBLY FUN; FOR THE FIRST TIME IN MY LIFE, I WAS ACTUALLY GOOD AT SOMETHING.

Our storyboarding teacher – who was one of the art directors for the game *Journey* – taught us all the basics, and we'd often visit restricted areas in museums to research and draw sculptures without being disturbed. These invaluable lessons provided me with a great set of foundational skills, and I still use many of the same techniques to this day.

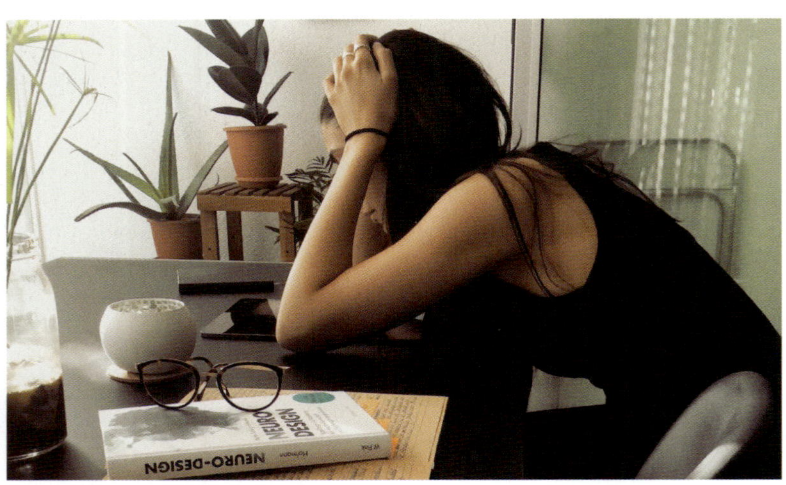

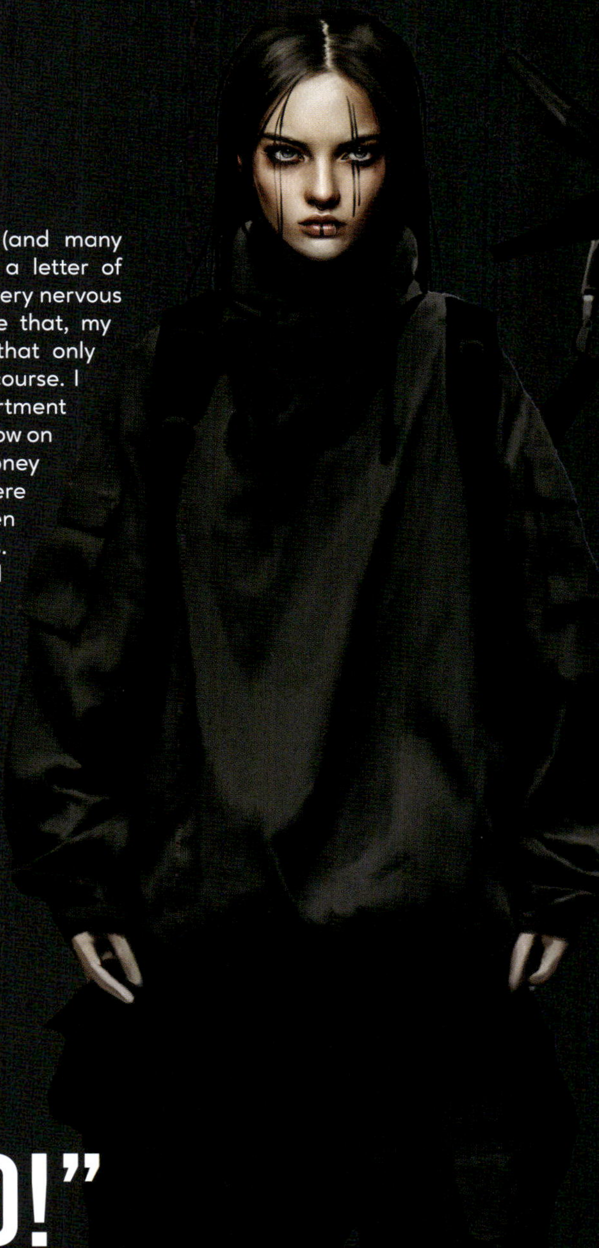

After three years of study (and many sleepless nights), I received a letter of completion in the mail. I was very nervous to open it – not long before that, my professor had informed us that only two people had passed the course. I remember standing in my apartment elevator, trying to figure out how on earth I was going to get the money to repeat the course. There was no way I could have been one of those two students. Agitated, I handed the sealed letter to my partner, ranting about how I should have tried harder. It wasn't until we reached our floor that I realized what he was saying over and over, waving the opened mail in my face:

"YOU PASSED!"

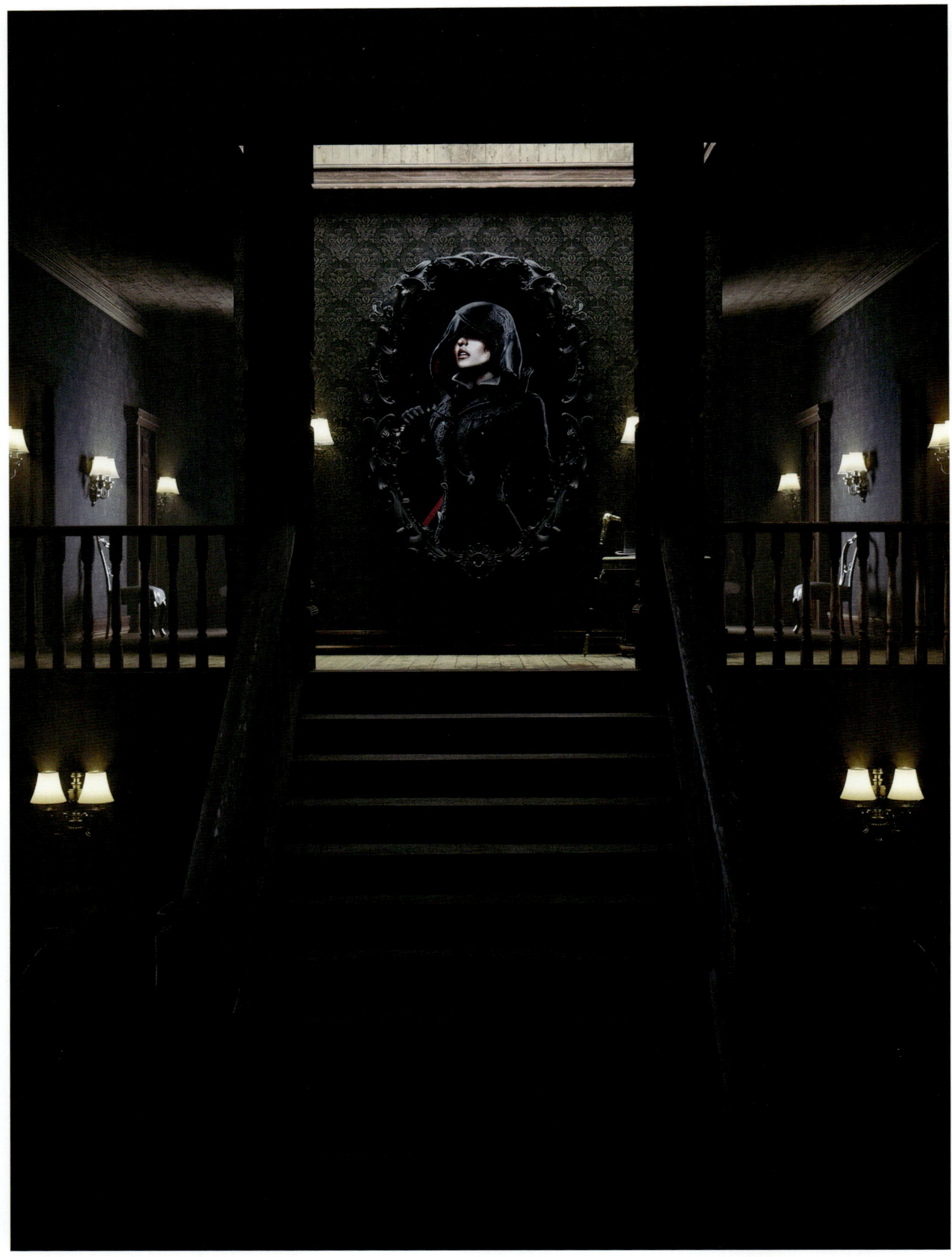

CLIENT: Ubisoft
PROJECT: *Assassin's Creed* 15th Anniversary
ROOM VISUALIZATION: neeon visual studio

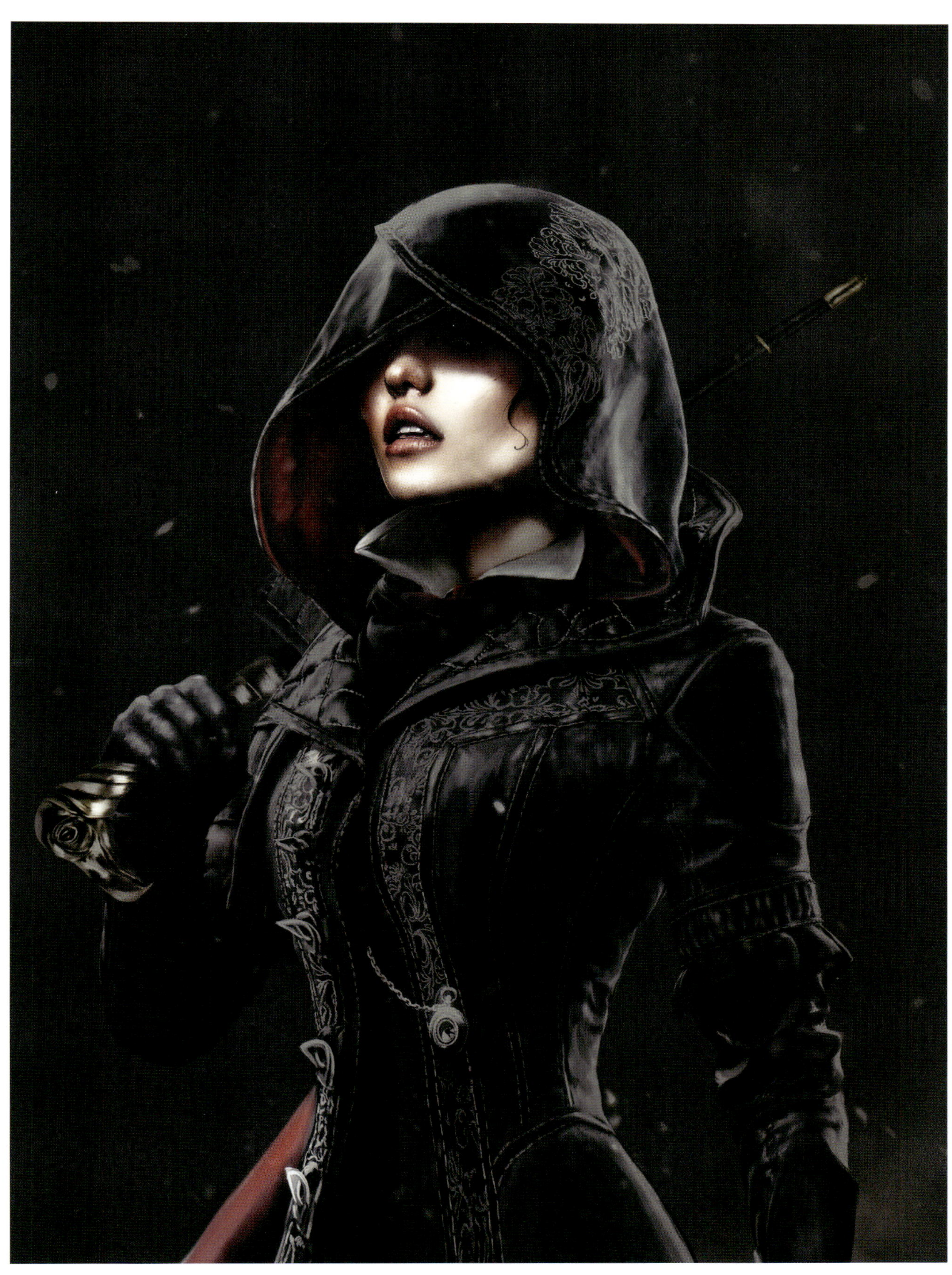

CHARACTER: **Evie Frye** was a master assassin of the British Assassin Brotherhood during the Victorian Age in *Assassin's Creed Syndicate.*

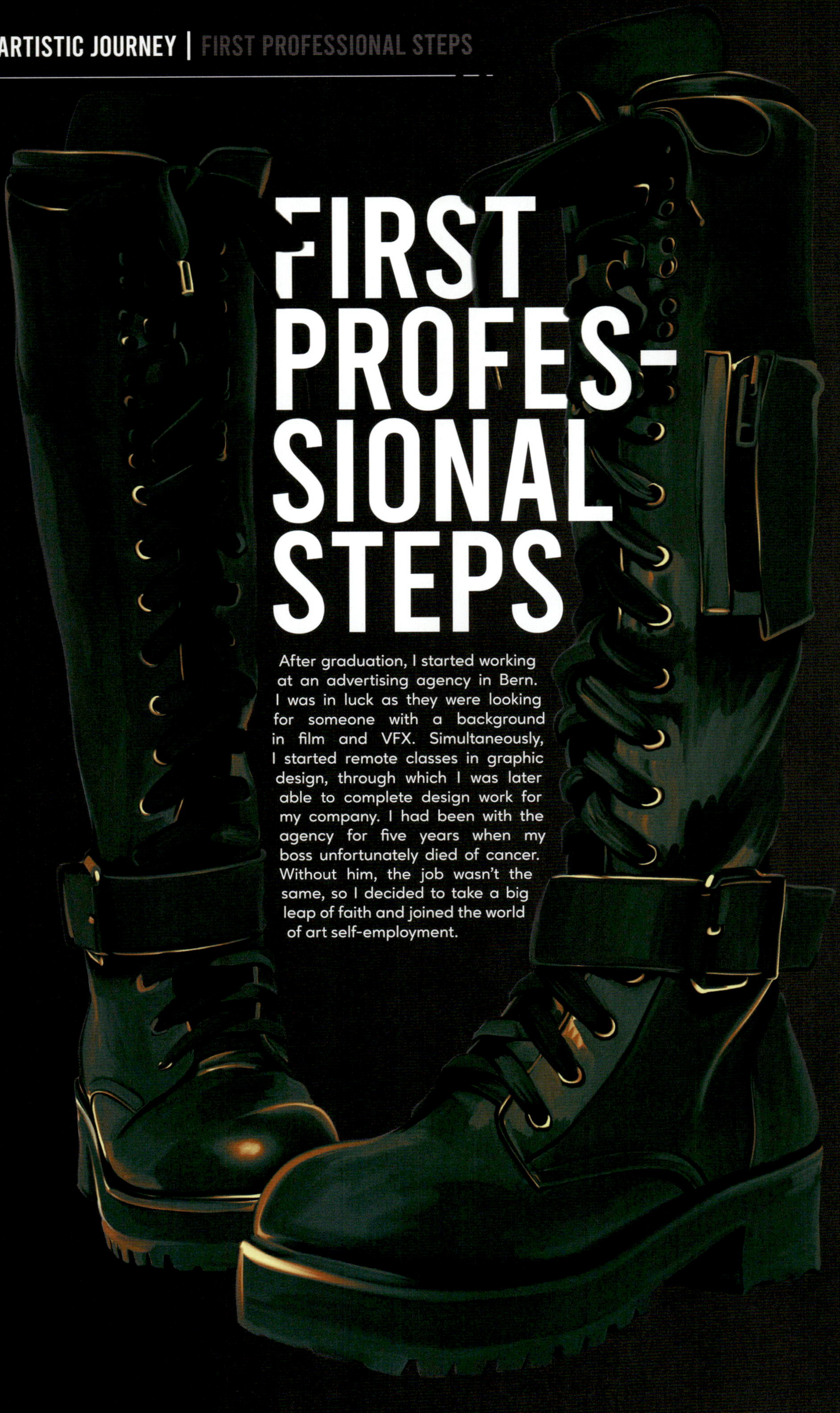

FIRST PROFESSIONAL STEPS

After graduation, I started working at an advertising agency in Bern. I was in luck as they were looking for someone with a background in film and VFX. Simultaneously, I started remote classes in graphic design, through which I was later able to complete design work for my company. I had been with the agency for five years when my boss unfortunately died of cancer. Without him, the job wasn't the same, so I decided to take a big leap of faith and joined the world of art self-employment.

SOCIAL MEDIA & ART

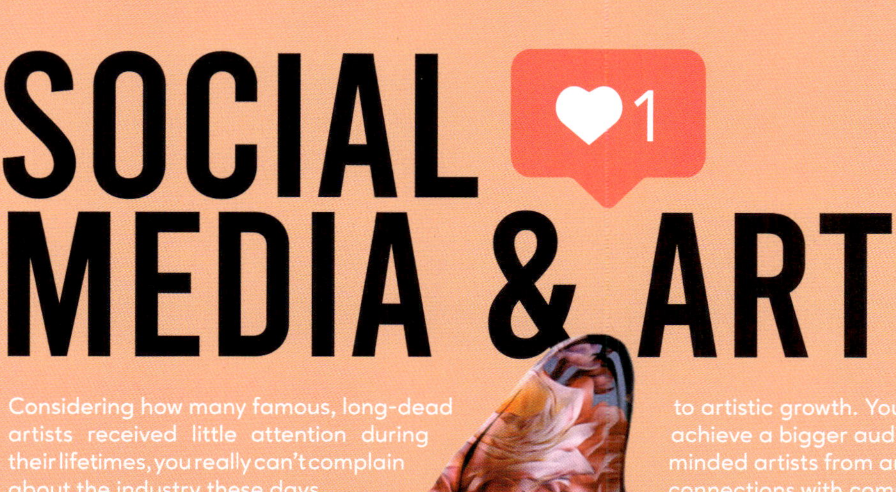

Considering how many famous, long-dead artists received little attention during their lifetimes, you really can't complain about the industry these days.

VAN GOGH ONLY SOLD ONE PAINTING IN HIS LIFETIME, AND IT WAS TO HIS BROTHER.

Today, the word "attention" means something completely different than it did a few decades ago. Thanks to social media, it's now a currency we all compete for, and cellphones and internet access have leveled the playing field for everyone. You don't need famous parents or rich friends; social media just requires you and your skills. My work mostly took off through Instagram, although I later started uploading to other platforms such as TikTok, YouTube, and Pinterest. However, because of the frequent changes to these social-media algorithms, content creators are often forced to leave their comfort zone. It isn't always pleasant, but it does lead to artistic growth. You can tap into recent trends to achieve a bigger audience reach, network with like-minded artists from around the world, or create new connections with companies.

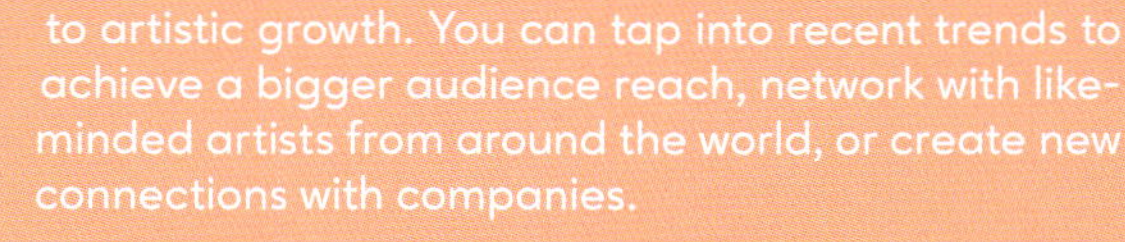

Although most of my clients found me through my social-media accounts, it's worthwhile to also find your footing outside the digital world. The internet is growing and changing fast. There is no guarantee that Instagram or TikTok will still be relevant or even exist a few years from now.

I recommend investing some time to work on popularity through traditional channels such as exhibitions or events.

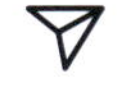

STUDIO

My workplace is simultaneously my home. After falling instantly in love with a Victorian-era house, my fiancé and I made the quick decision to move in. He is also self-employed, so we needed a bigger place that could house both our offices on one floor and the living area on another, and this place was perfect. Unfortunately, my office isn't quite finished yet but it's my own doing; I struggle to make any long-term commitments to artwork or furniture. When I became self-employed, I thought I'd prefer a studio away from my home, but then Covid-19 happened, and suddenly everyone worked from home. I realized then that I was saving a lot of time and money. No commute, no studio rental fee... but it also came with disadvantages.

It's very difficult to "unplug" as the work is always right there, so even on my days off, I frequently find myself sitting in my office and working anyway.

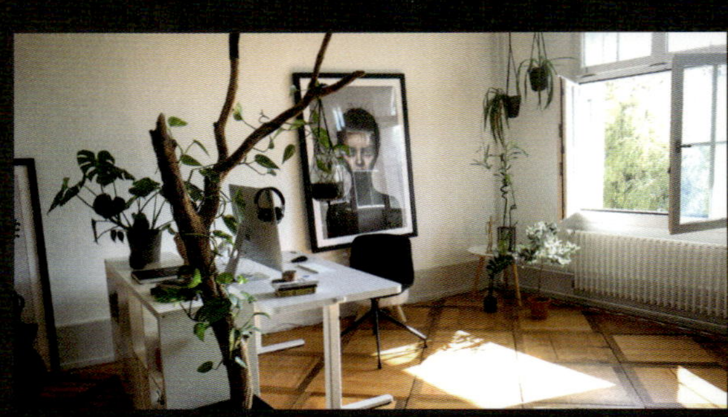

DAILY ROUTINE

As soon as I find myself without anything to do, the little voice in the back of my head says, "Maybe you should rework that painting or answer a few emails instead of lazing around!" That's why I always get up around 8am and exercise for about an hour. I then shower and eat breakfast with my better half. Around 10am, I start answering emails – this always takes up more time than I'd like, which is why I hired an assistant to help with inquiries.

At around 4pm, I'm done with most of the administrative work and can finally work on a new or existing painting. Before I switch gears, I take a little break.

I typically work until 10pm, at which point I leave my office. SometimesI draw a little while watching TV (tablet PCs make this really easy), but 12-hour workdays are pretty normal for me. I think that's okay when you're lucky enough to work in a profession you love.

8AM
GET UP & EXCERCISE

9AM
SHOWER & BREAKFAST

10AM
ANSWER EMAILS

4PM
BREAK

6PM
TIME TO DRAW

10PM
FREE TIME

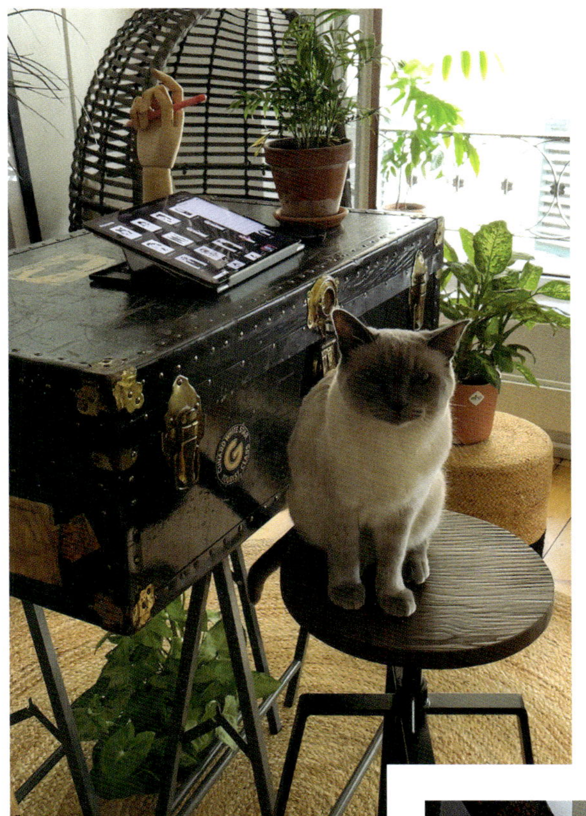

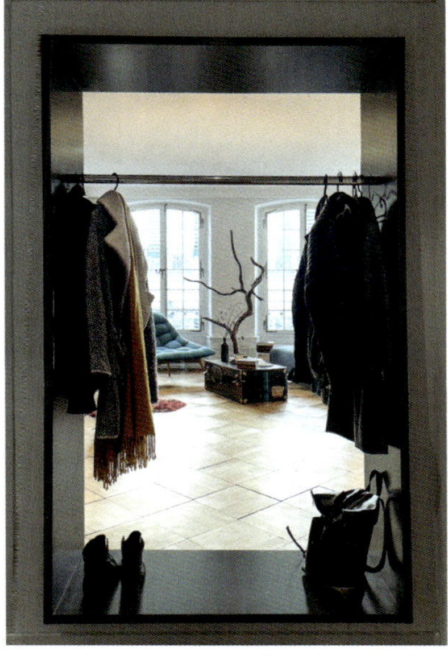

THE NARNIA ROOM

We call it that because you can enter the room through the wardrobe. It also has a perfectly functional regular door, but that's much less fun, so we usually take the wardrobe path.

I LOVE OLD STUFF

One of my work desks is a suitcase that's more than 100 years old, propped up on stilts. I'm not sure why, but I love old suitcases… I usually don't know what to do with them, but I NEED them!

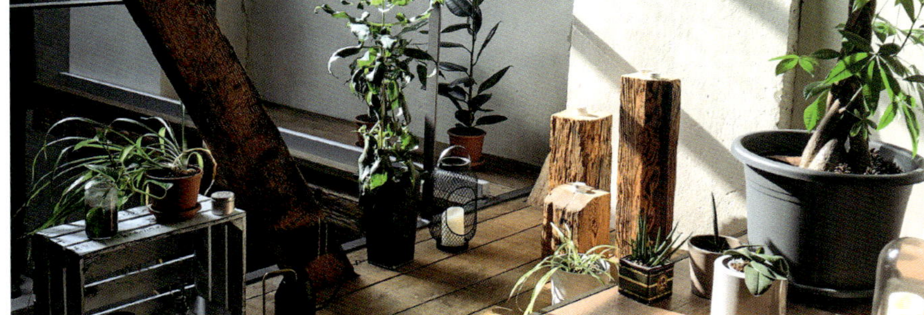

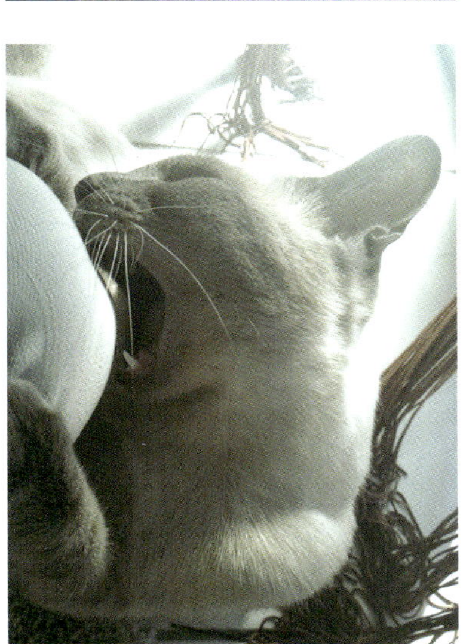

THIS IS BEANZ

The most unproductive employee ever. His hobbies include biting my knee, throwing things off shelves, and sleeping in my sweater (but only while I wear it).

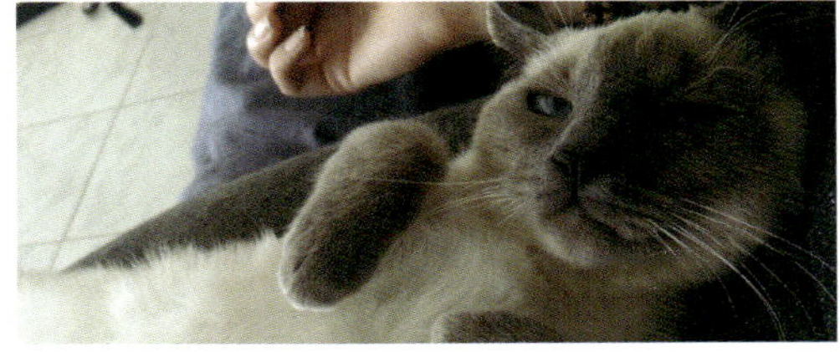

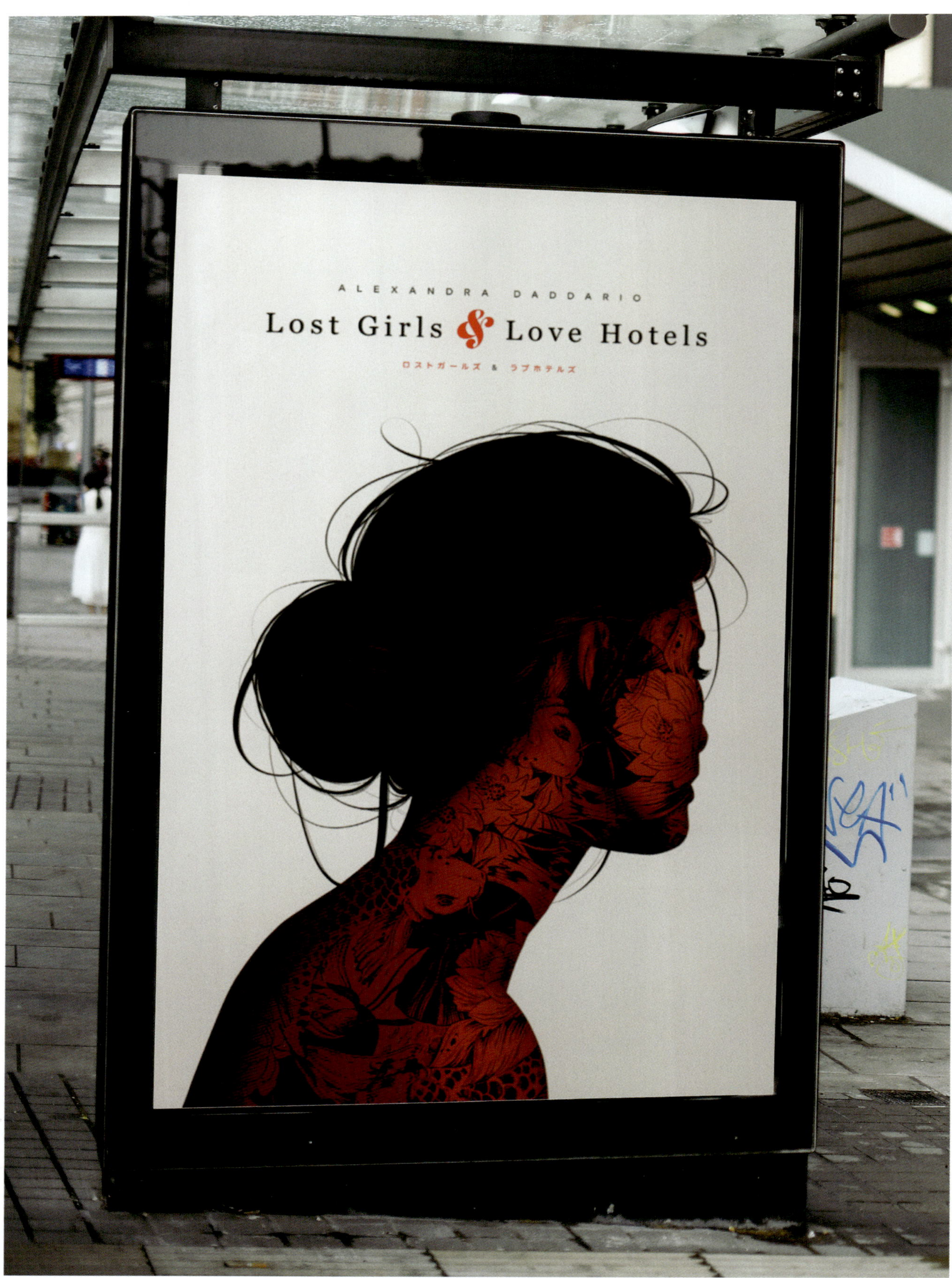

PROJECT: Artwork for the movie *Lost Girls & Love Hotels*
DIRECTOR: William Olsson
MAIN ACTRESS: Alexandra Daddario

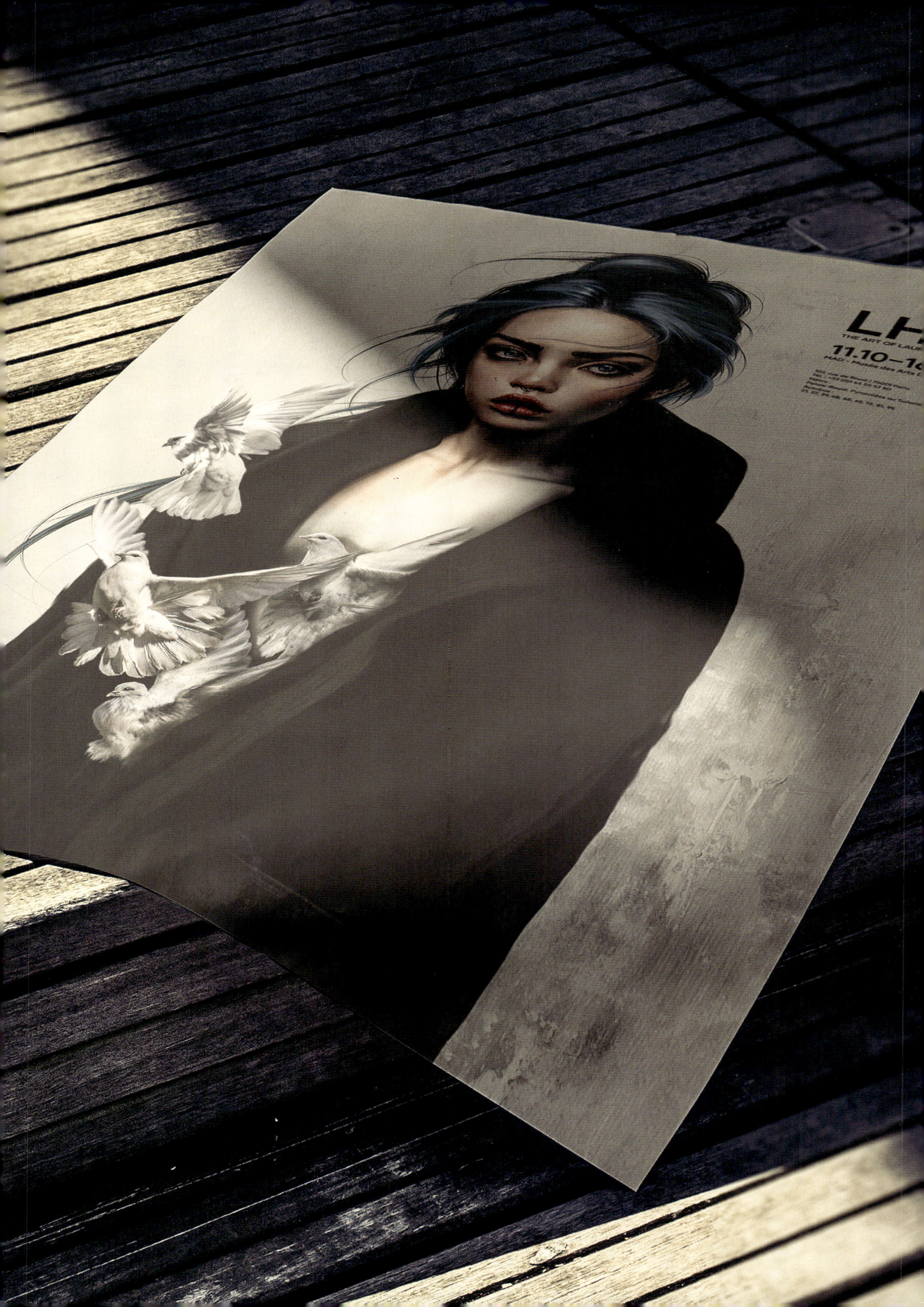
THE ART OF

IMPETUS

As I mentioned earlier, I'm not someone who's good with words. But I did find a way to communicate without having to use them: by drawing.

The reason my racecar-driving, mechanic father always picked me up by train was because he was the victim of a hit-and-run incident. He sustained such terrible injuries that it resulted in epilepsy, and now he has to live with medication that makes him shake so violently he can barely hold a pen.

I began researching neuroscience so that I could have proper discourse with doctors to find some alternate treatments, but nothing came of it. Despite all the meds, he still has episodes that can injure him severely.

For a long time, I couldn't handle seeing my dad suffer like that. He tried to keep his struggles hidden from me, but I knew what had happened every time a hospital or police station contacted me. Many people don't know how to deal with someone who's having a panic attack followed by a seizure, so they call the police because "a crazy person is crying and screaming in the streets." Not everything is as it seems at first glance. Not everyone is crazy just because they're not acting how we expect them to. I wish this was normalized, and that people would try to have more empathy for things they don't understand.

My utter helplessness in the situation makes me incredibly sad, and talking about it doesn't seem to help, so I work my feelings into my paintings.

Life isn't always fair. Terrible things can happen, and that's okay – it's normal, and so are the accompanying emotions. Unfortunately, many don't realize that and become bitter because it's easier to be angry than it is to deal with your grief and fears. That's why it's so important to find an outlet for your feelings.

MY OUTLET IS MY ART.

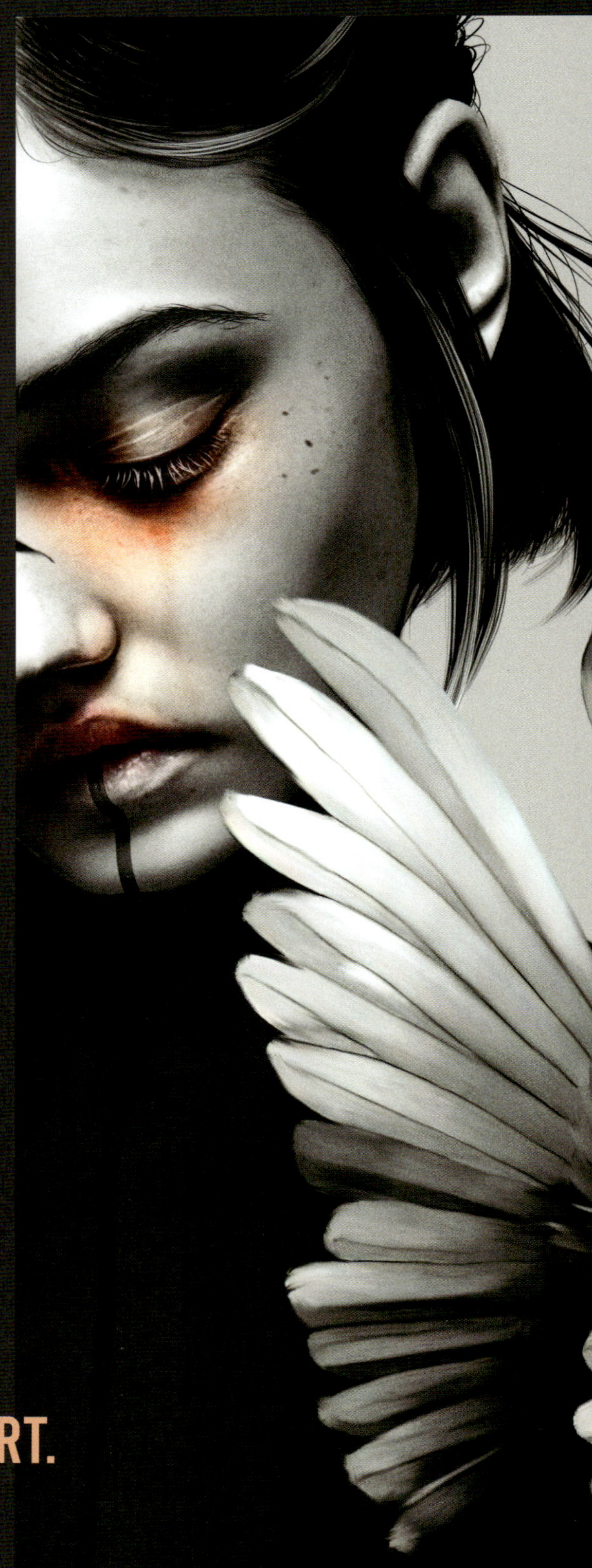

VISION

I think it's possible to find inspiration in anything, be it a bowl of nuts or the texture of a rock. It just depends on the extent of your imagination and how far you're willing to go to discover it. My inspirations are found in my hobbies. I love reading dystopian novels and tragedies, and every month I buy new books to learn about interesting topics like psychology, mythology, and philosophy. Constantly discovering new things gives me a much needed feeling of security. I'm also heavily influenced by certain video games. Sometimes it's nice to get lost in a new world where I don't have to be myself for a little while. Many of my paintings have Latin plant names because my house is filled to the corners with foliage. I like spending my time outside and taking pictures or videos of anything and everything that catches my eye. You could call photography a supplemental hobby to my art, often resulting in a lot of useable material for new brush textures or color combinations.

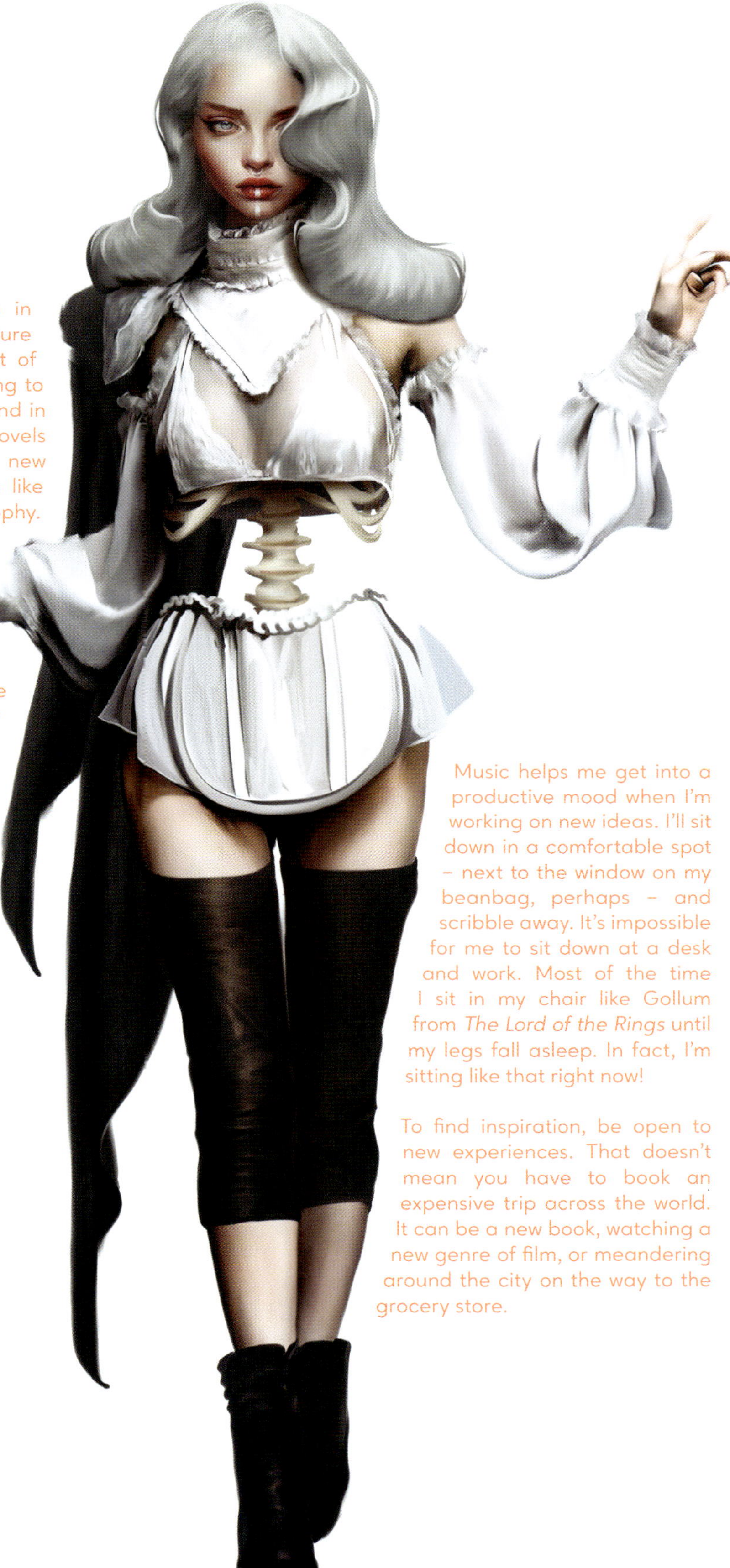

"TO FIND INSPIRATION, BE OPEN TO NEW EXPERIENCES."

Music helps me get into a productive mood when I'm working on new ideas. I'll sit down in a comfortable spot – next to the window on my beanbag, perhaps – and scribble away. It's impossible for me to sit down at a desk and work. Most of the time I sit in my chair like Gollum from *The Lord of the Rings* until my legs fall asleep. In fact, I'm sitting like that right now!

To find inspiration, be open to new experiences. That doesn't mean you have to book an expensive trip across the world. It can be a new book, watching a new genre of film, or meandering around the city on the way to the grocery store.

SKETCHBOOK

**“SUCCESS IS A
WORN DOWN PENCIL”**

– Robert Rauschenberg

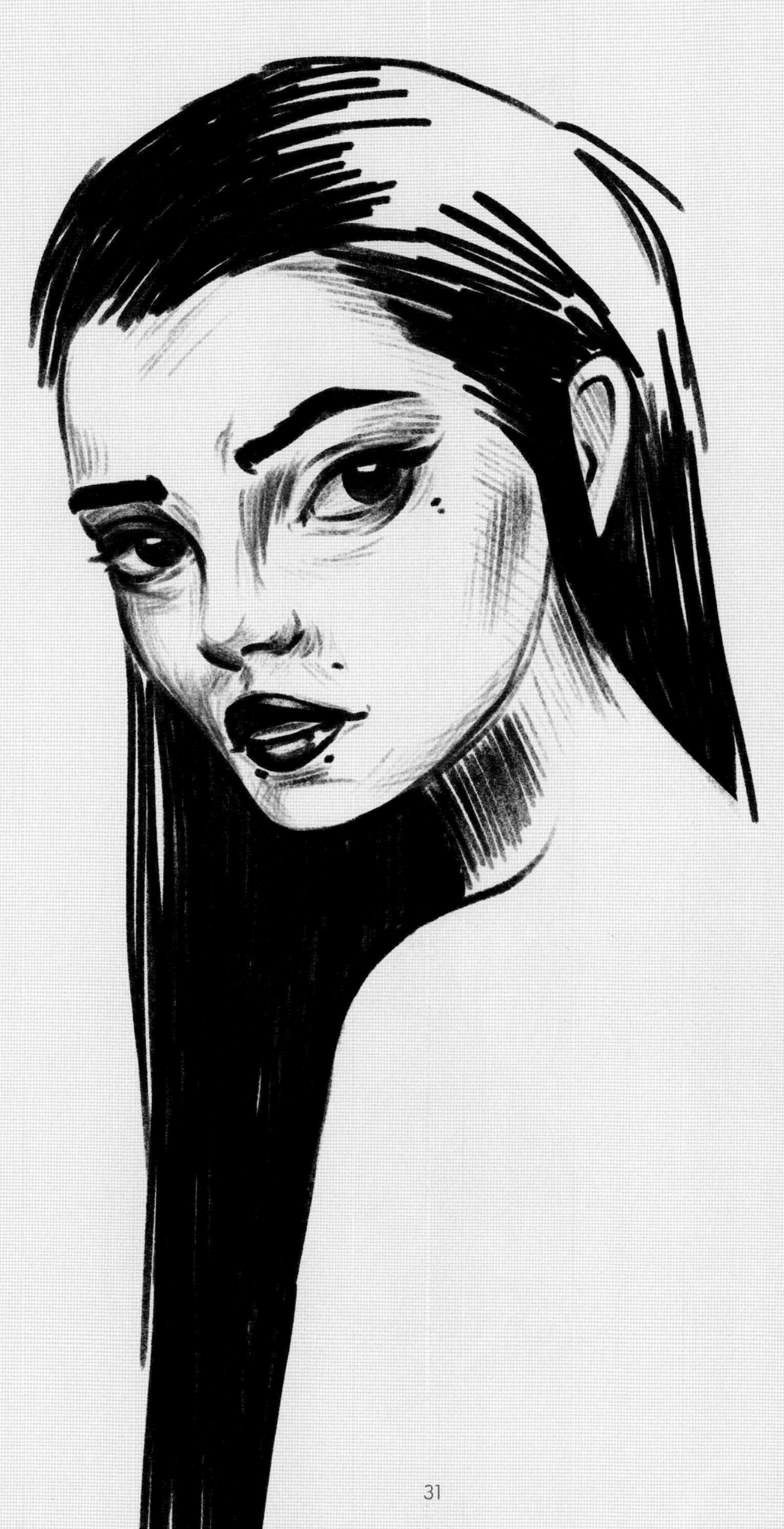

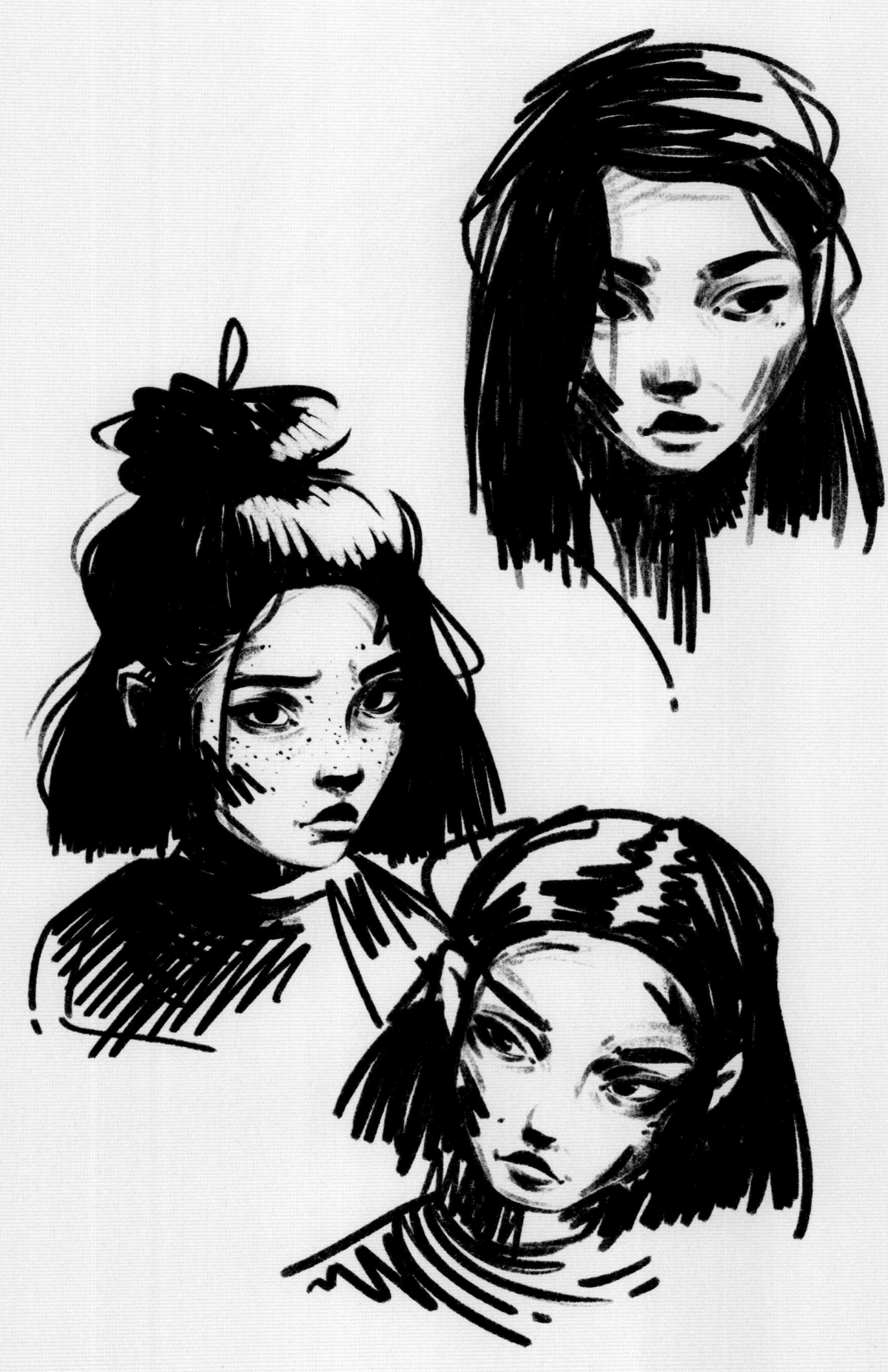

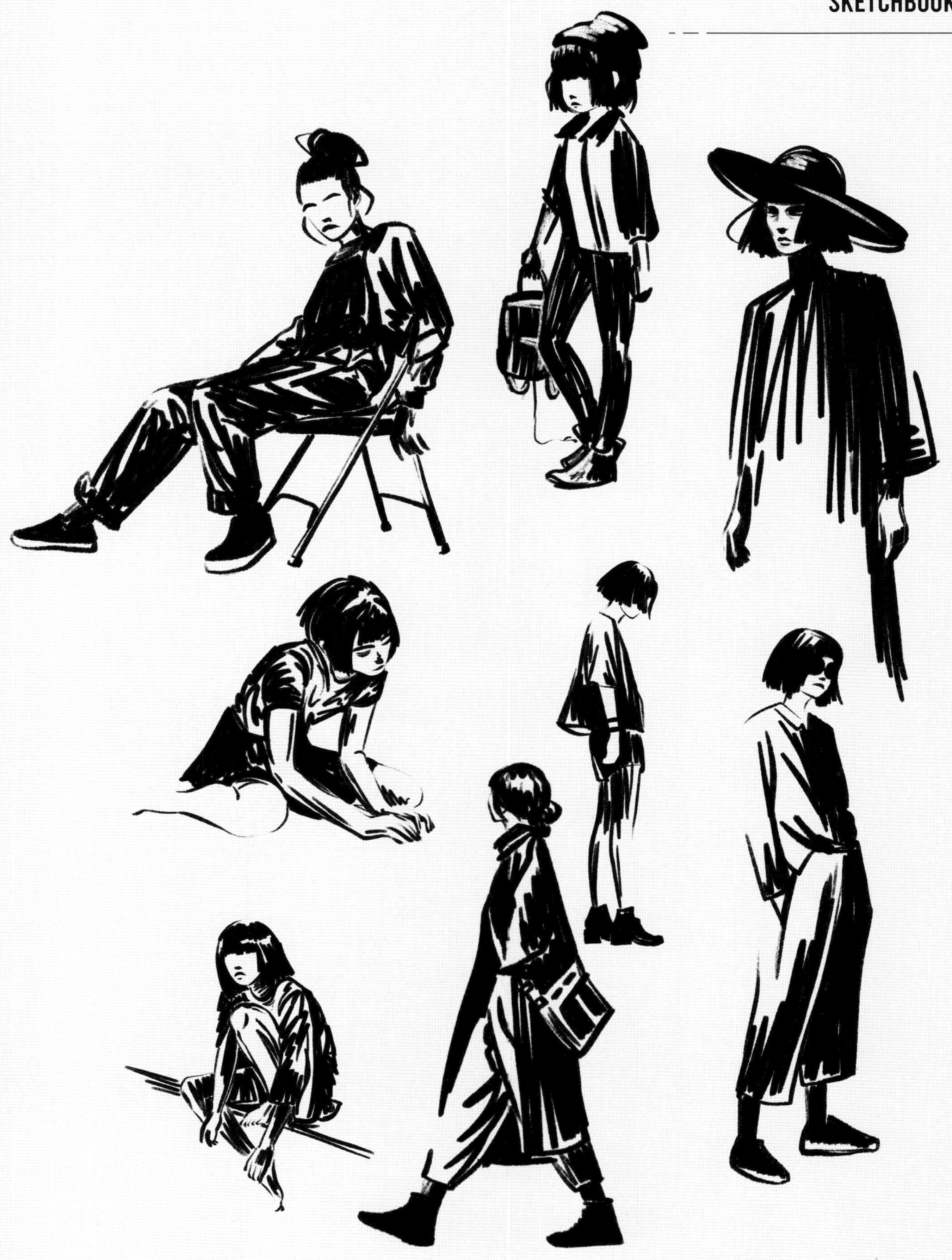

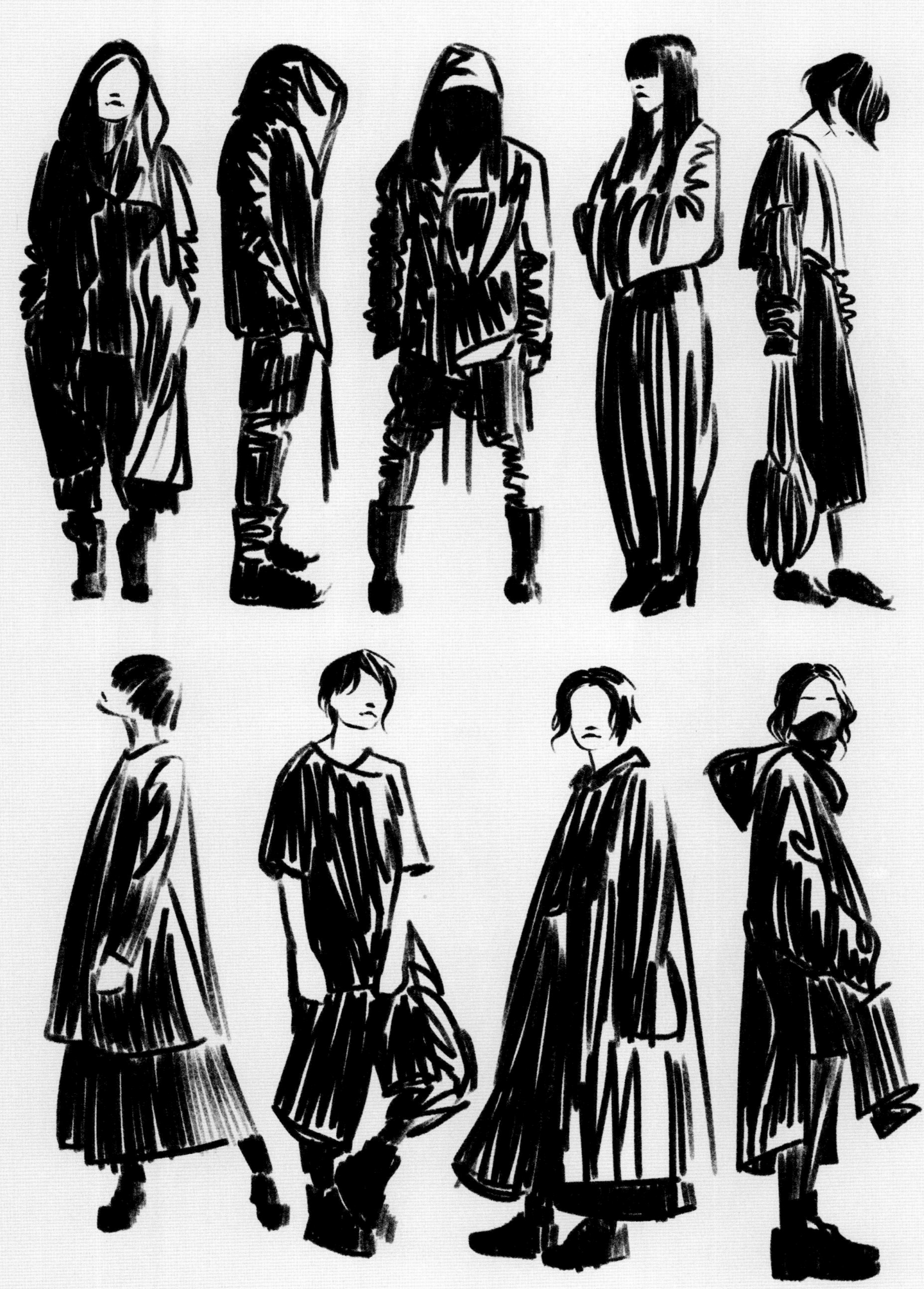

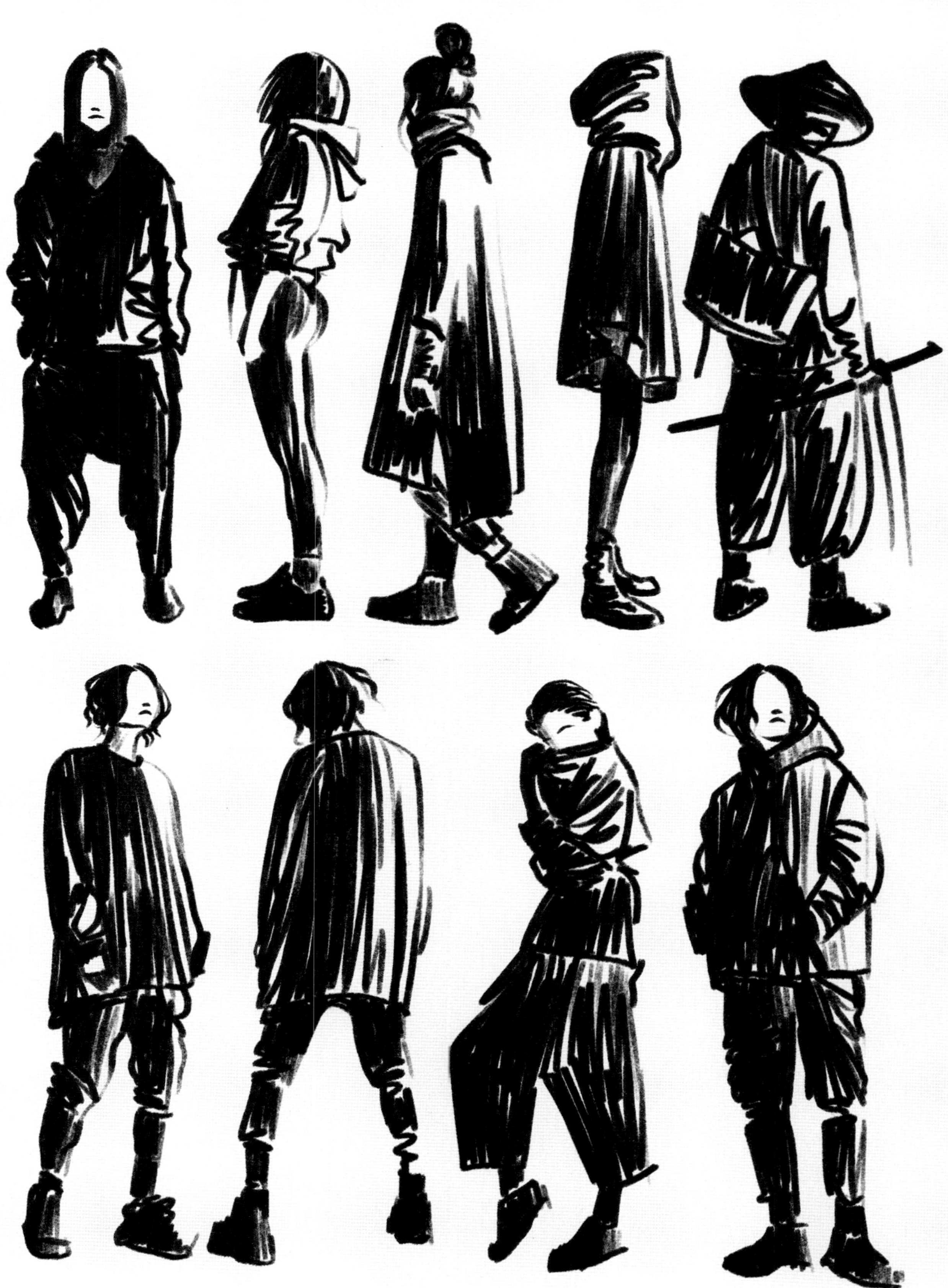

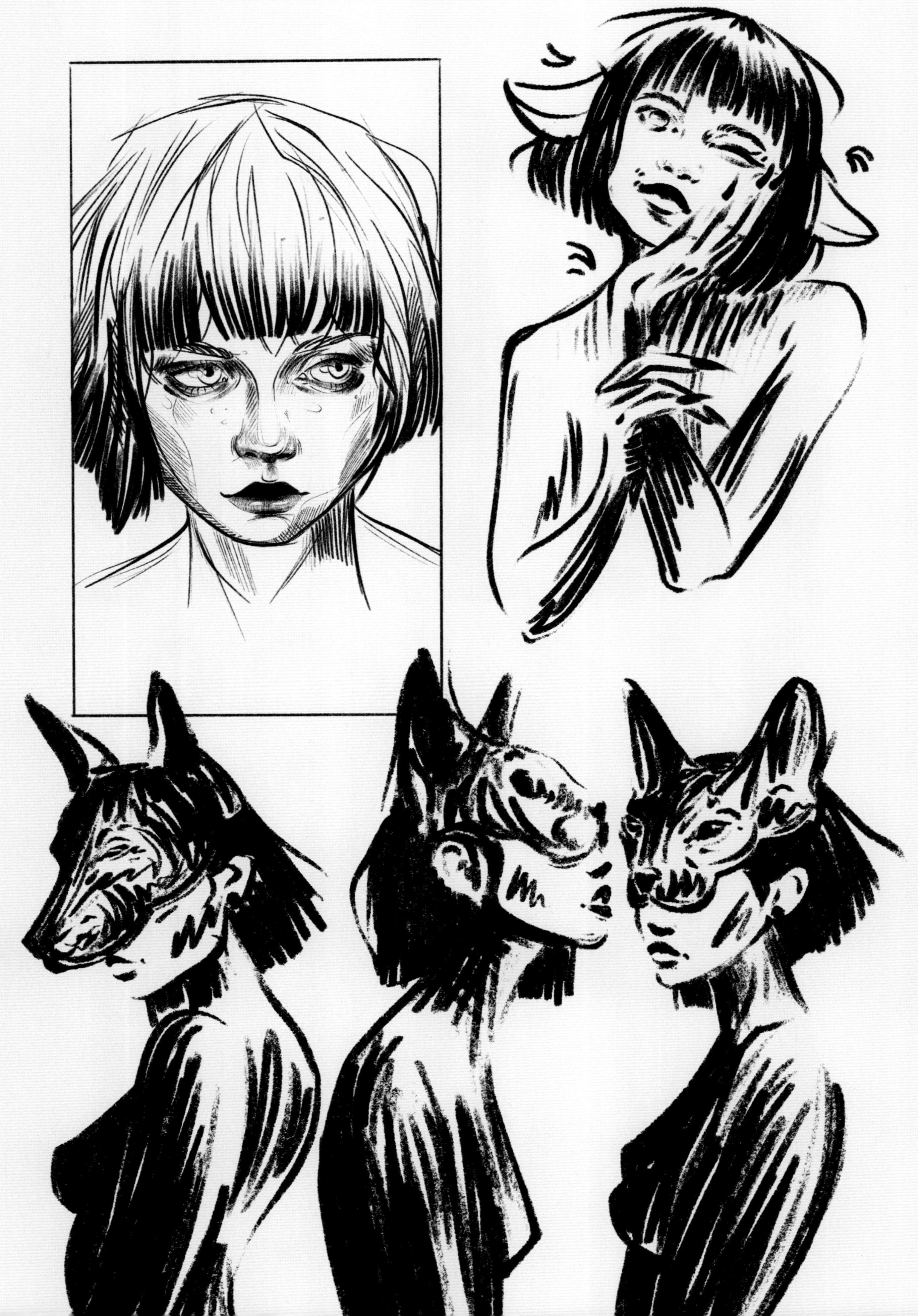

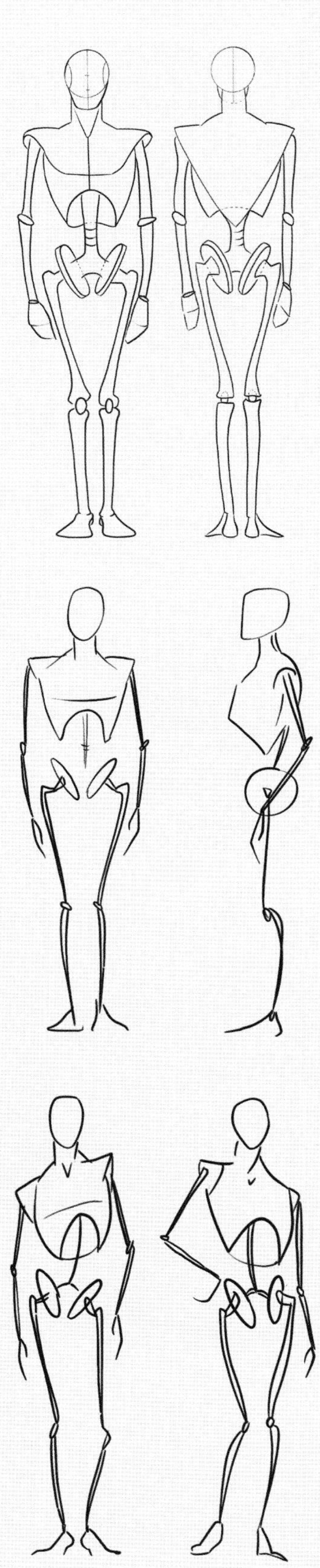

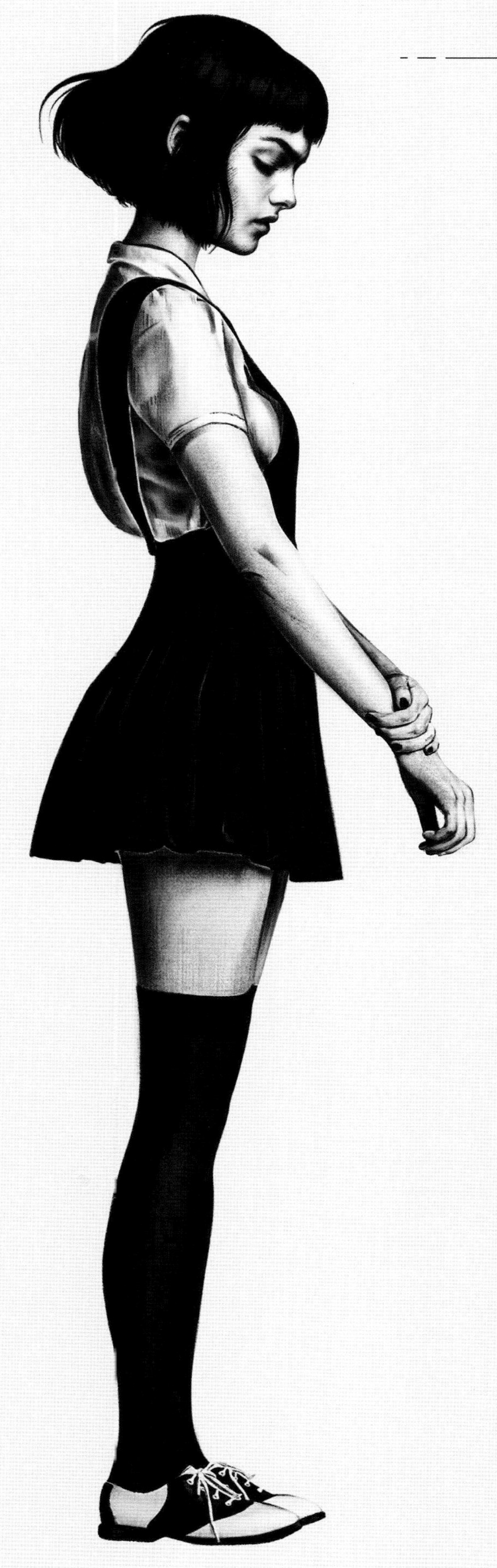

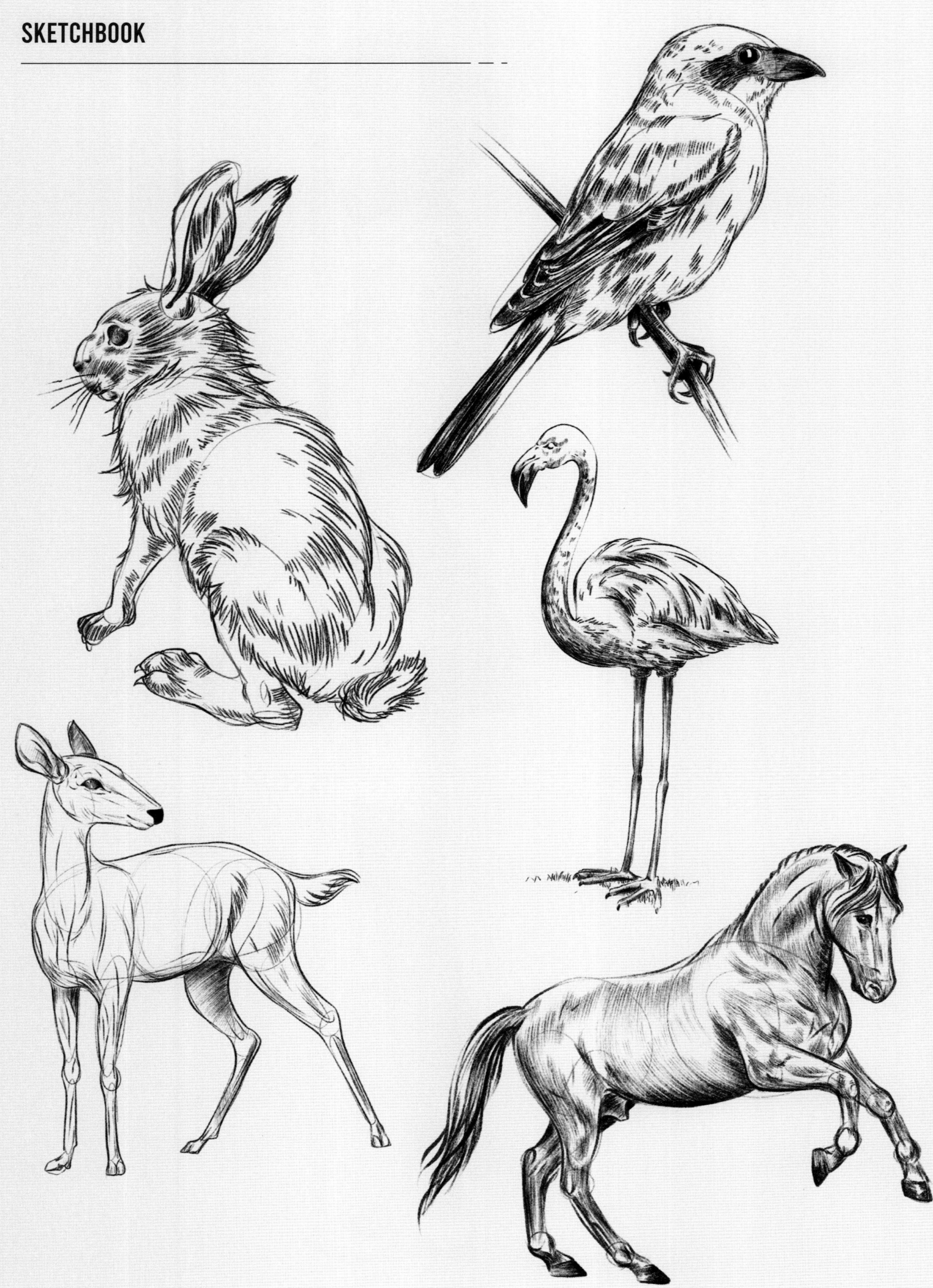

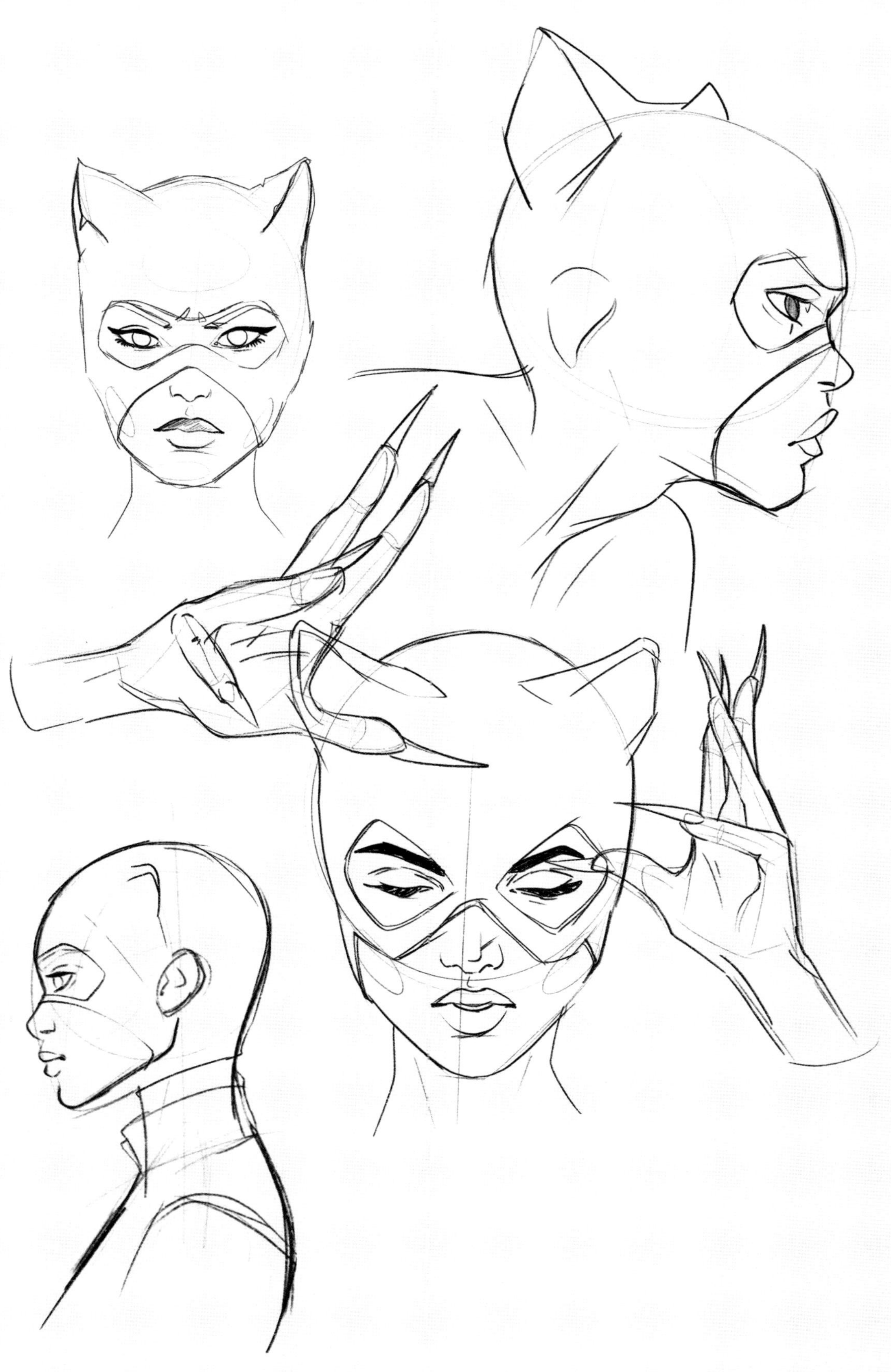

ARTWORKS & BEHIND THE SCENES

“PAINTING IS JUST ANOTHER WAY OF KEEPING A DIARY”

– Pablo Picasso

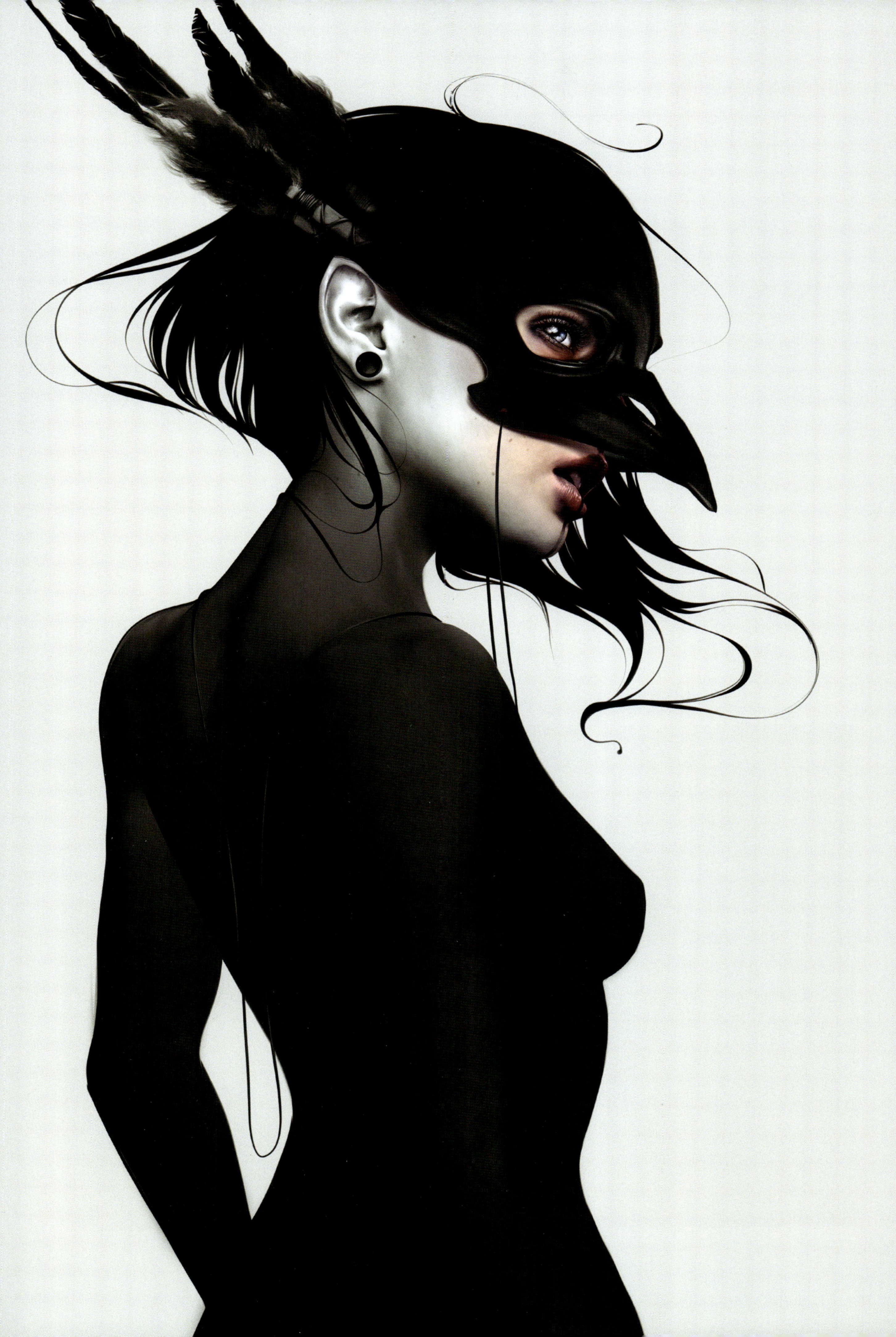

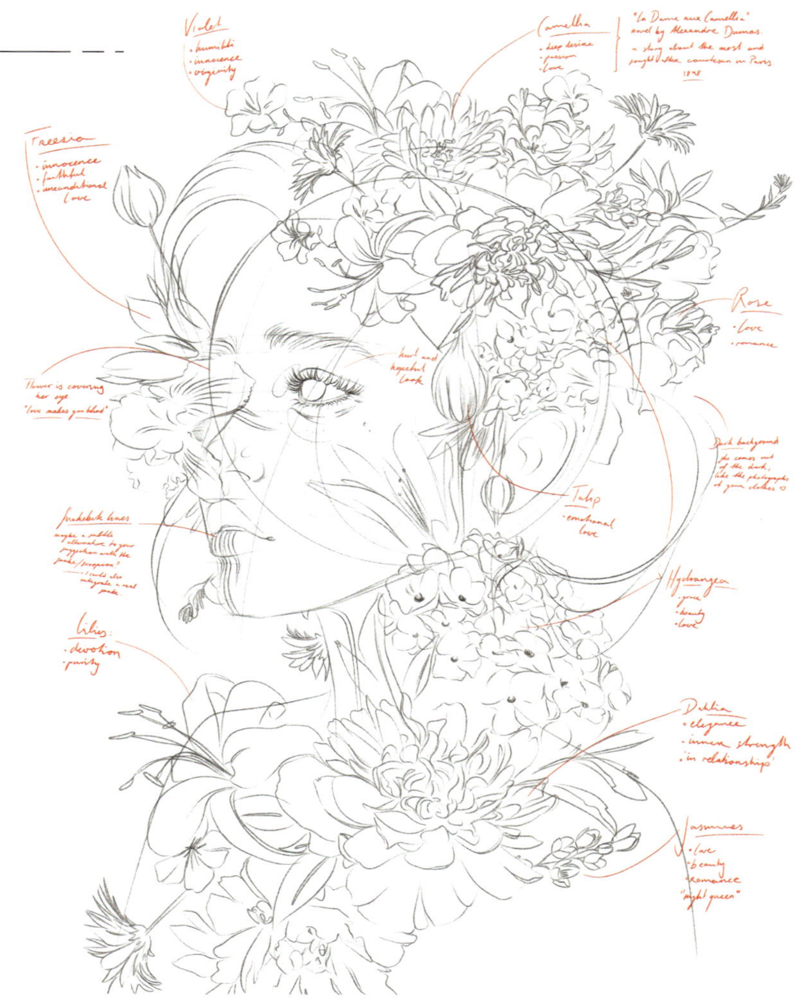

LOVE

Love is a collaborative piece I designed together with the fashion designer Nathaniel Gray. He created a beautiful and emotionally moving gown from our design. Gray's unique quality is that he intertwines his emotions with his artwork – his dresses aren't just something to wear, but rather artistic masterpieces. Collaborations with other artists are important, both to learn about their process and to forge new connections.

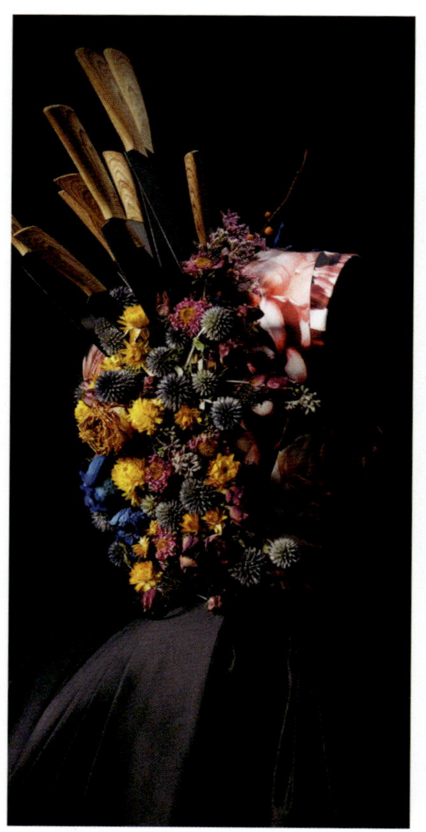

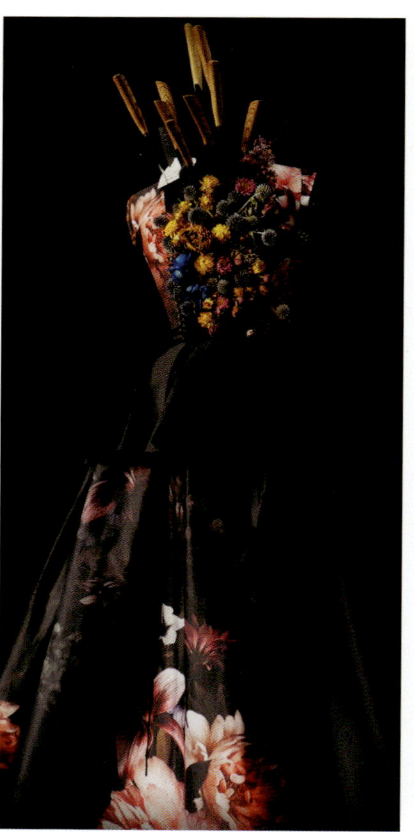

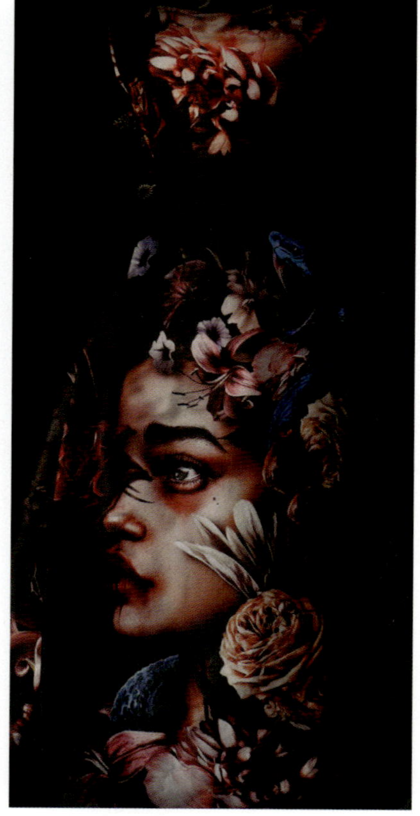

Design by Nathaniel Gray

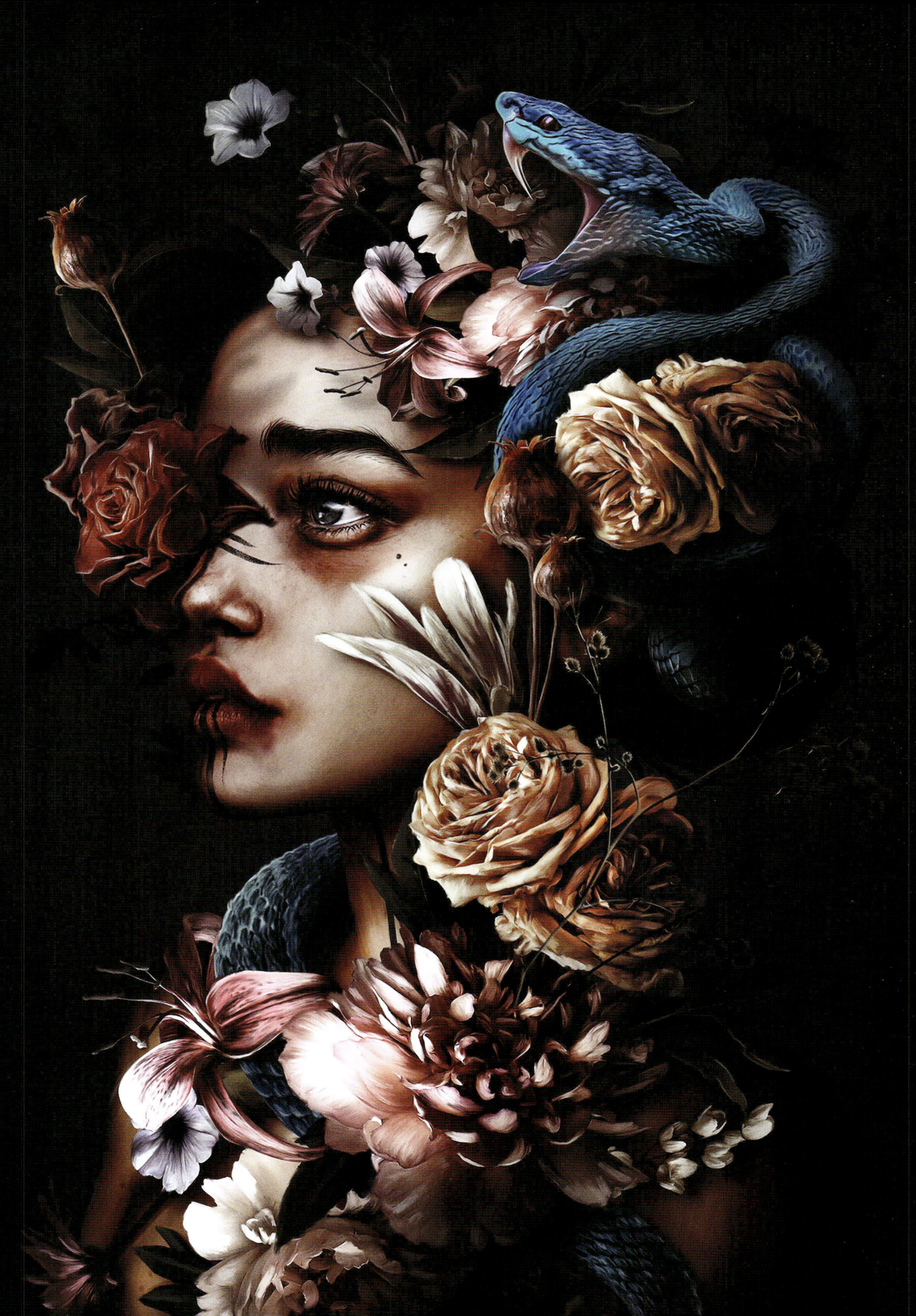

ERIS

According to Greek mythology, Eris is the goddess of discord and strife. In some versions, she is daughter to Nyx, one of the five primordial gods who emerged at the dawn of creation. Other accounts call her the sister of Ares, god of war. Eris' parallel in Roman mythology is Discordia. I absolutely love drawing mythological characters, even though it's not always easy to research their backstories, as Greek and Roman mythology often use the same names for different gods.

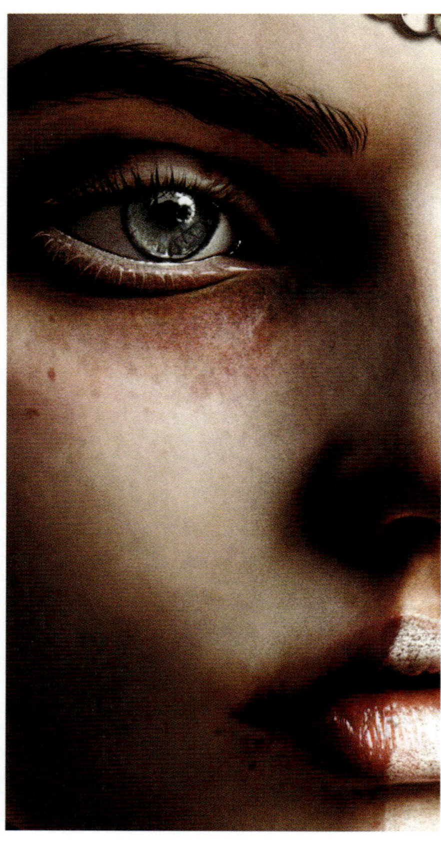

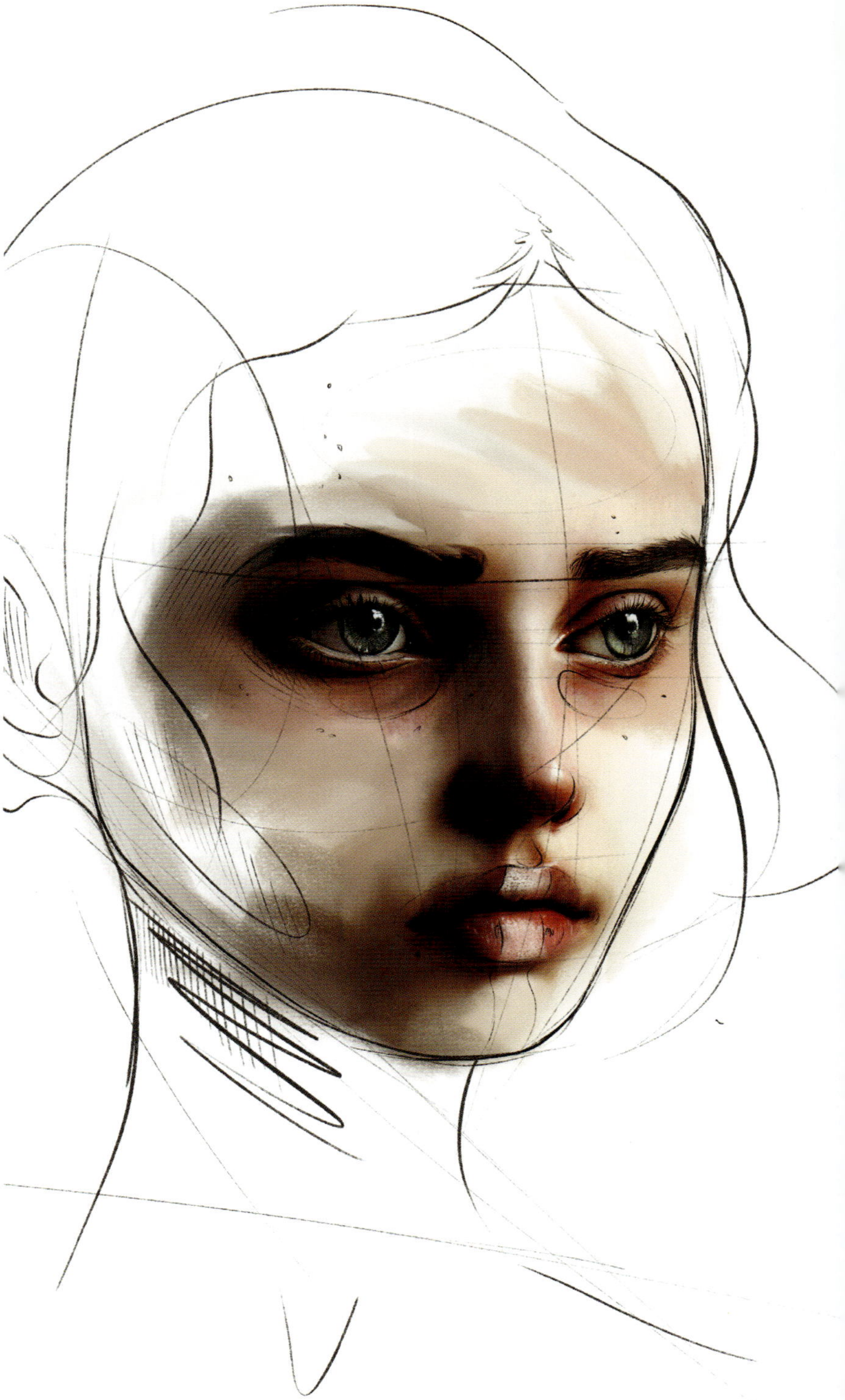

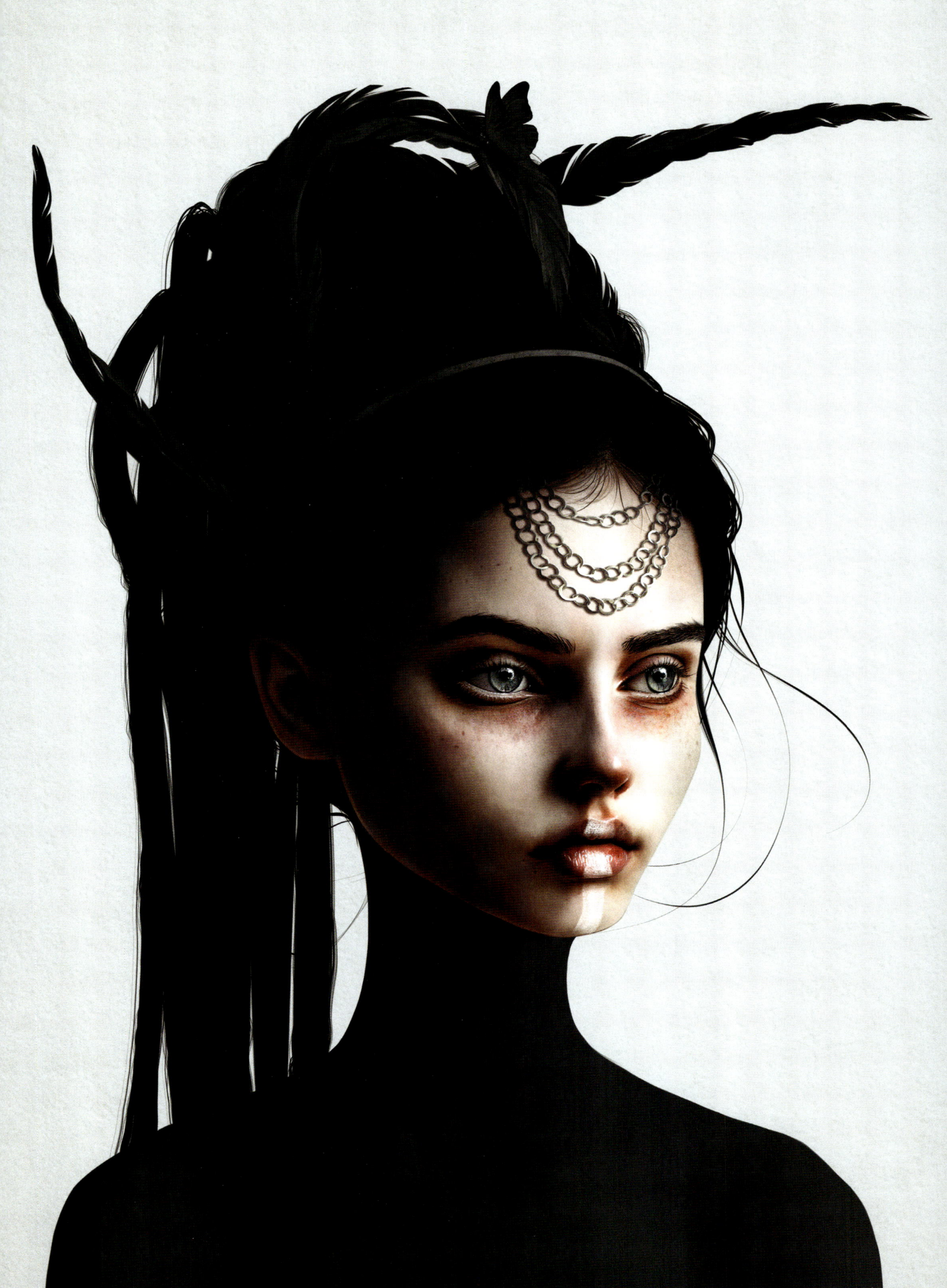

VIORED

A combination of the colors violet and red. The existence of this painting is accidental; I originally set out to study how to paint transparent clothing. During that process I happened to create this violet/red color and just had to try to integrate it into a portrait... and thus, *Viored* was born.

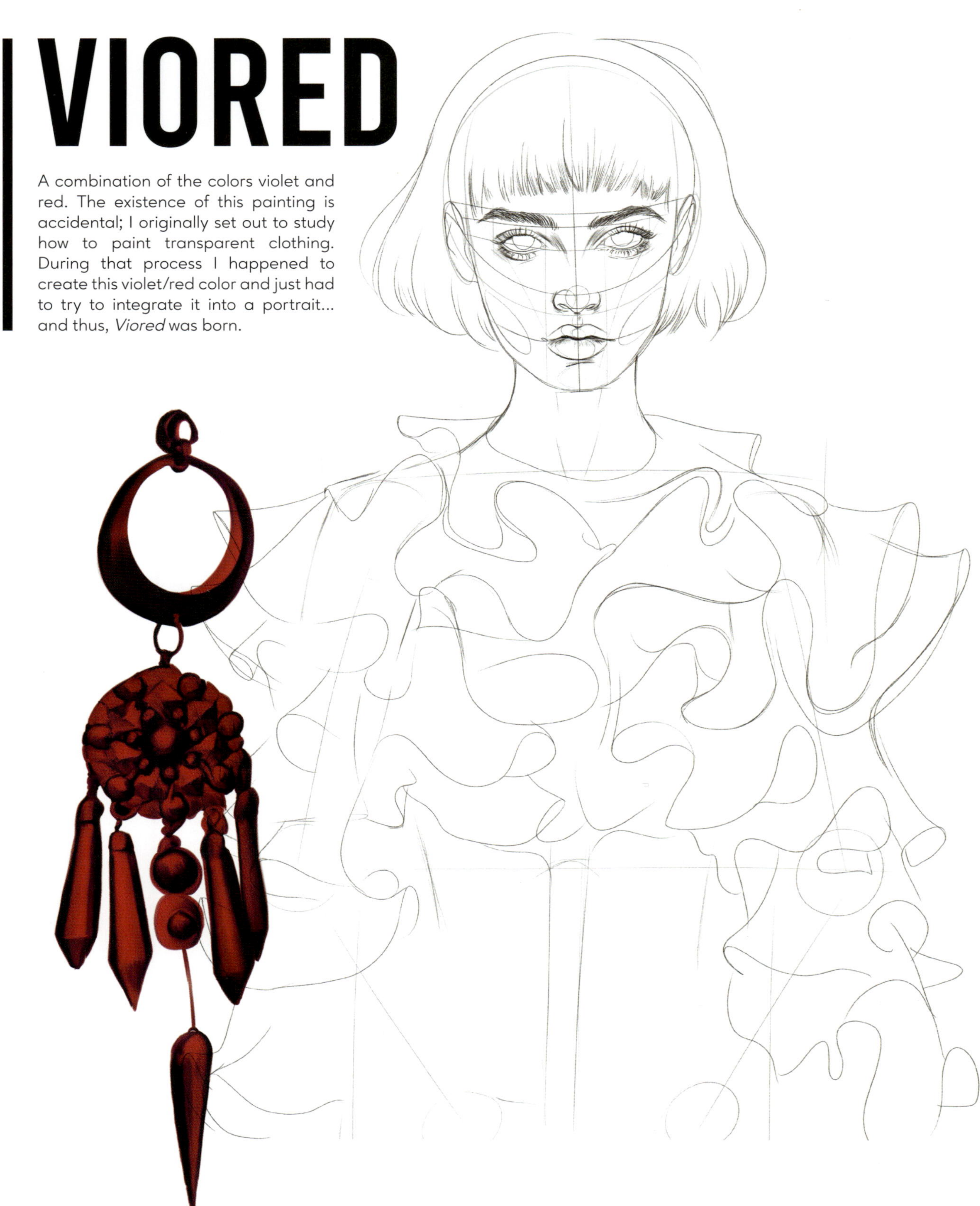

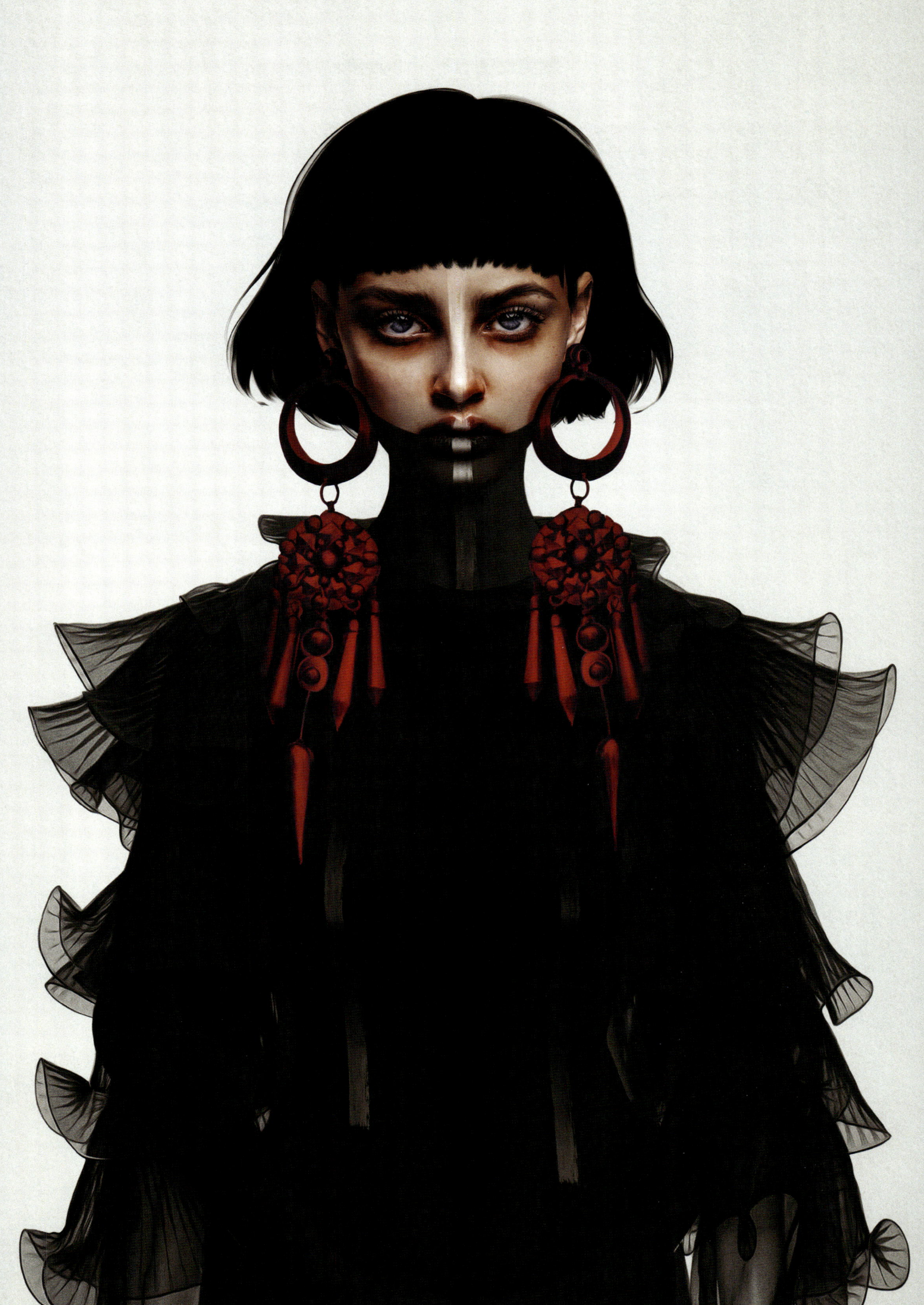

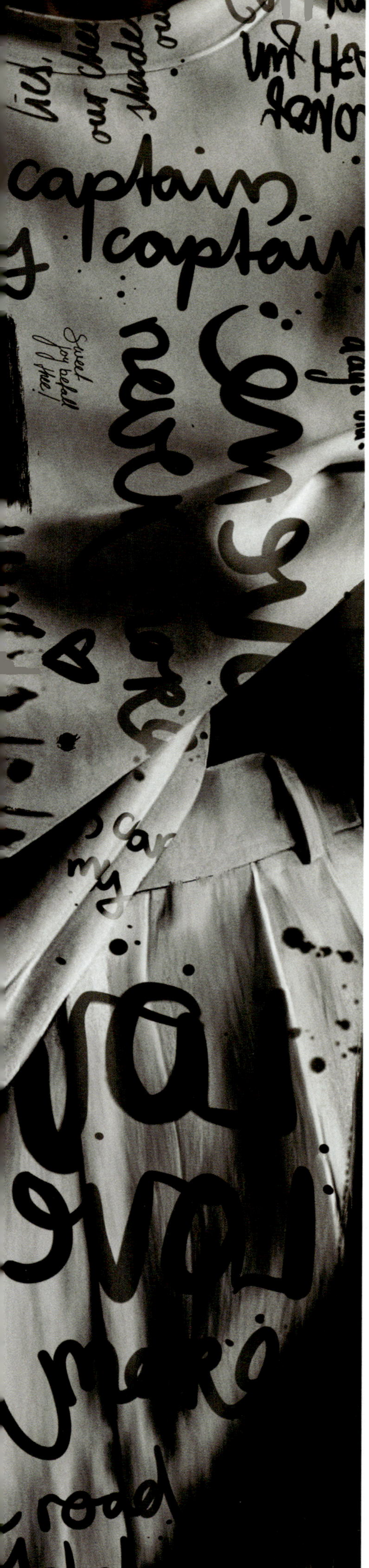

DRESSED IN POETRY

I tried to integrate some of my favorite poems into this painting. Among others, her clothing contains excerpts from the following poems:

THE RAVEN | EDGAR ALLAN POE
O CAPTAIN! MY CAPTAIN! | WALT WHITMAN
THE ROAD NOT TAKEN | ROBERT FROST
INFANT JOY | WILLIAM BLAKE
WE WEAR THE MASK | PAUL LAURENCE DUNBAR

FUN FACT:

As a reference for the proportions, I used a photo of the poet Edgar Allan Poe.

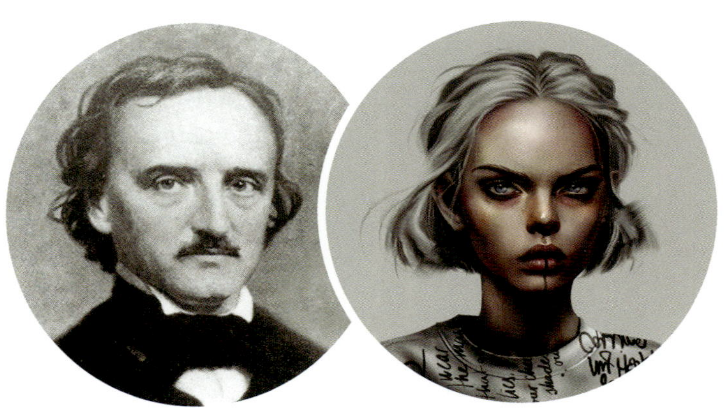

Above: Everett Collection/ Shutterstock.com.

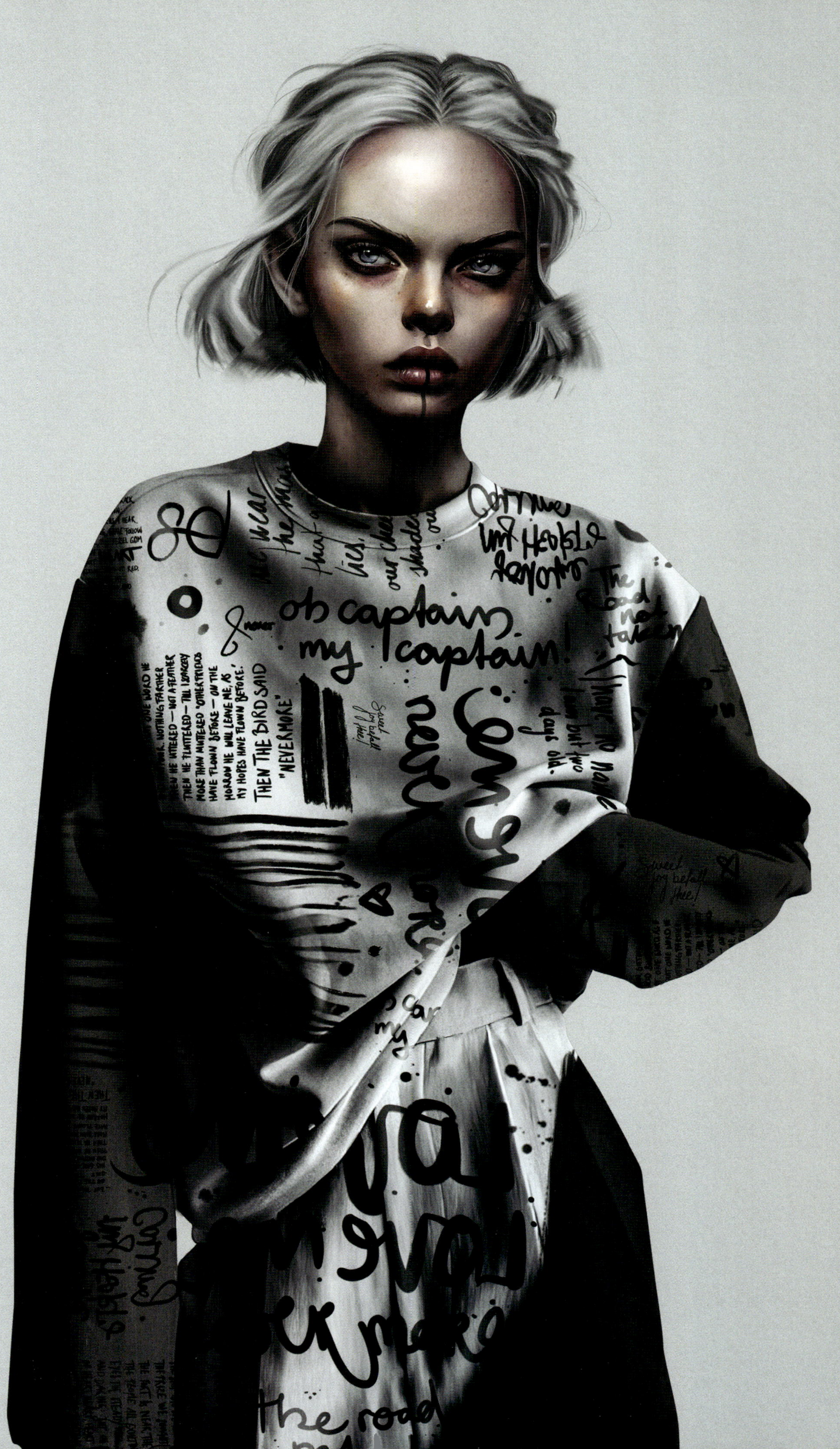

oh captain
my captain!
The Road not taken
I have no name
I am but two days old.
THEN THE 'BIRD SAID
"NEVERMORE"
the road

AQUA

Aqua is named for the zodiac sign Aquarius. It's the second of twelve zodiac images that I created in 2021. This piece became my favorite in the series, because I fell in love with the combination of her hair and skin color. For me, it was important to not directly depict any water in the image, but instead have the character embody the element, which was a formidable challenge.

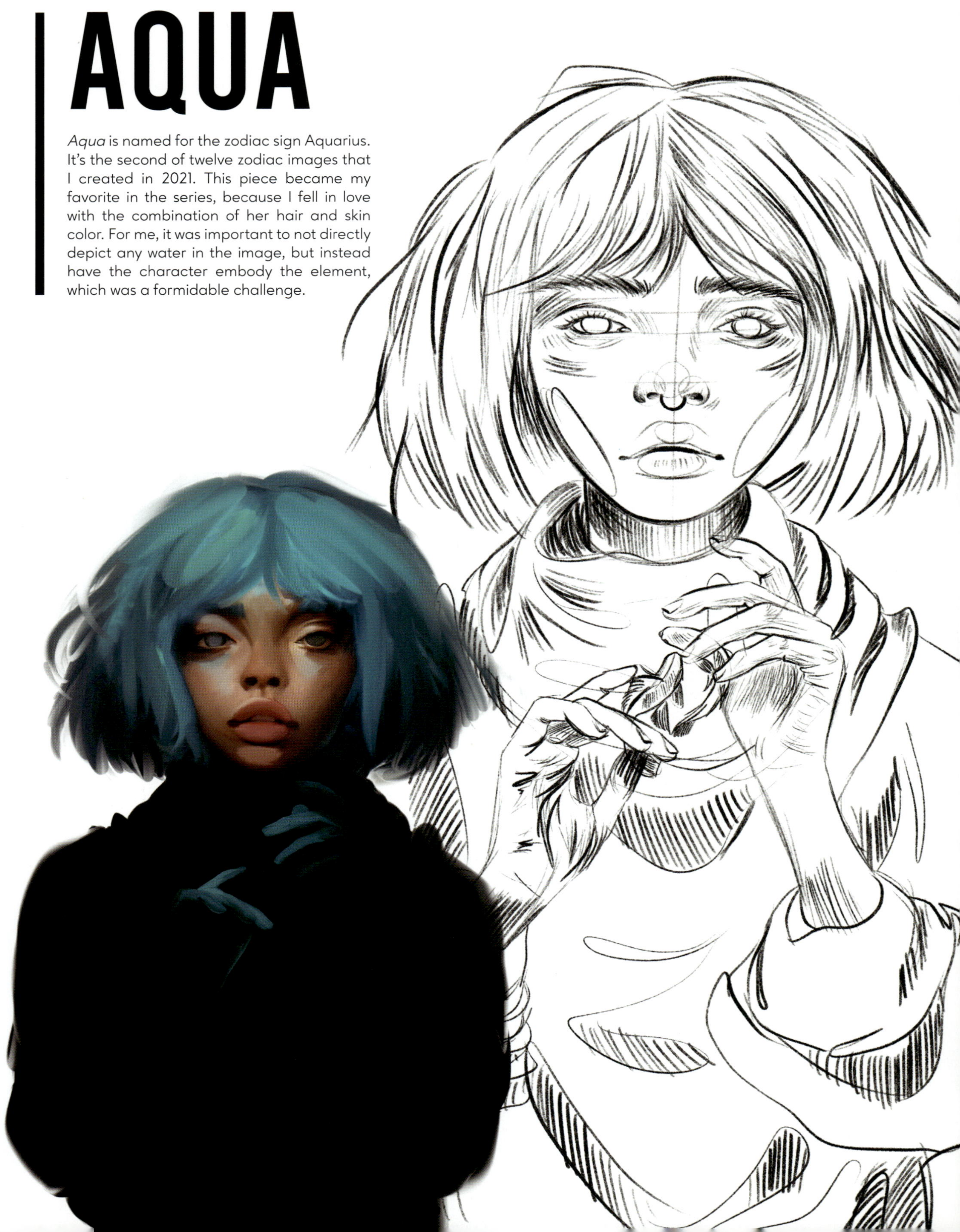

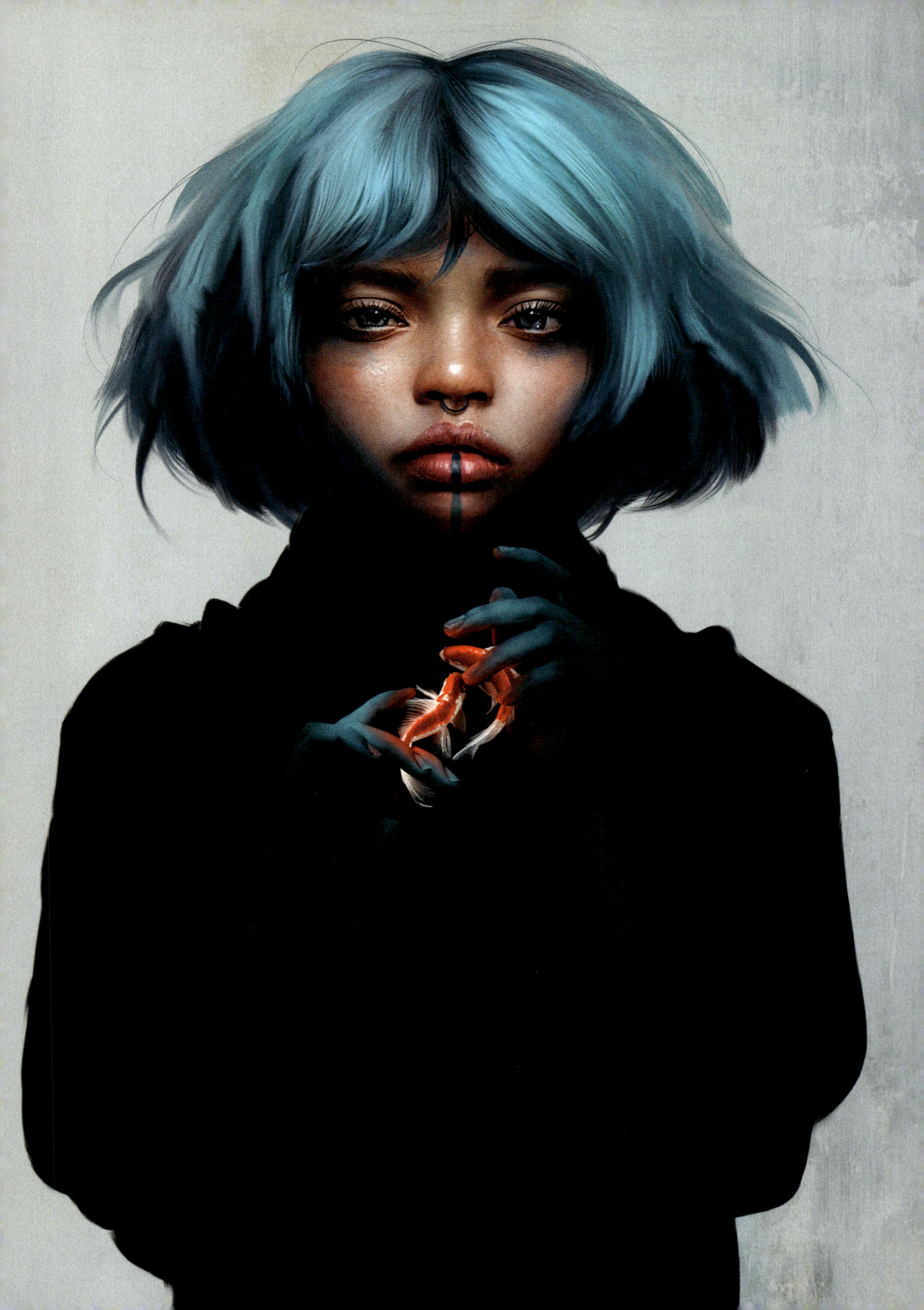

MISERY

Misery was a complex character to realize. I painted her roughly a week after Putin's army invaded Ukraine. My partner and I took part in demonstrations, donated clothes and other relief goods, and offered our home to refugees... but none of it was enough to express how absolutely wrong I consider the war to be.

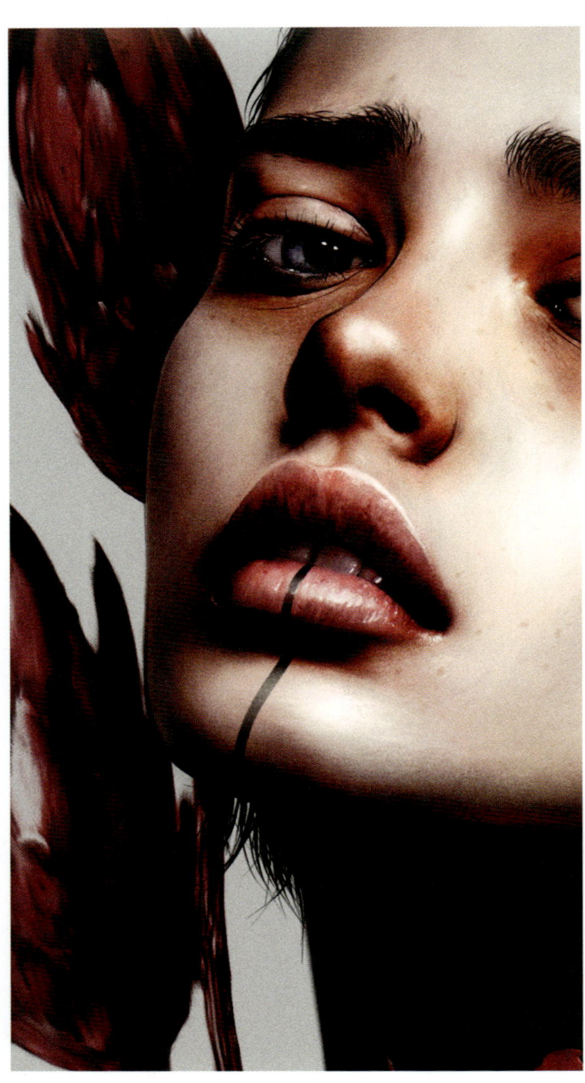

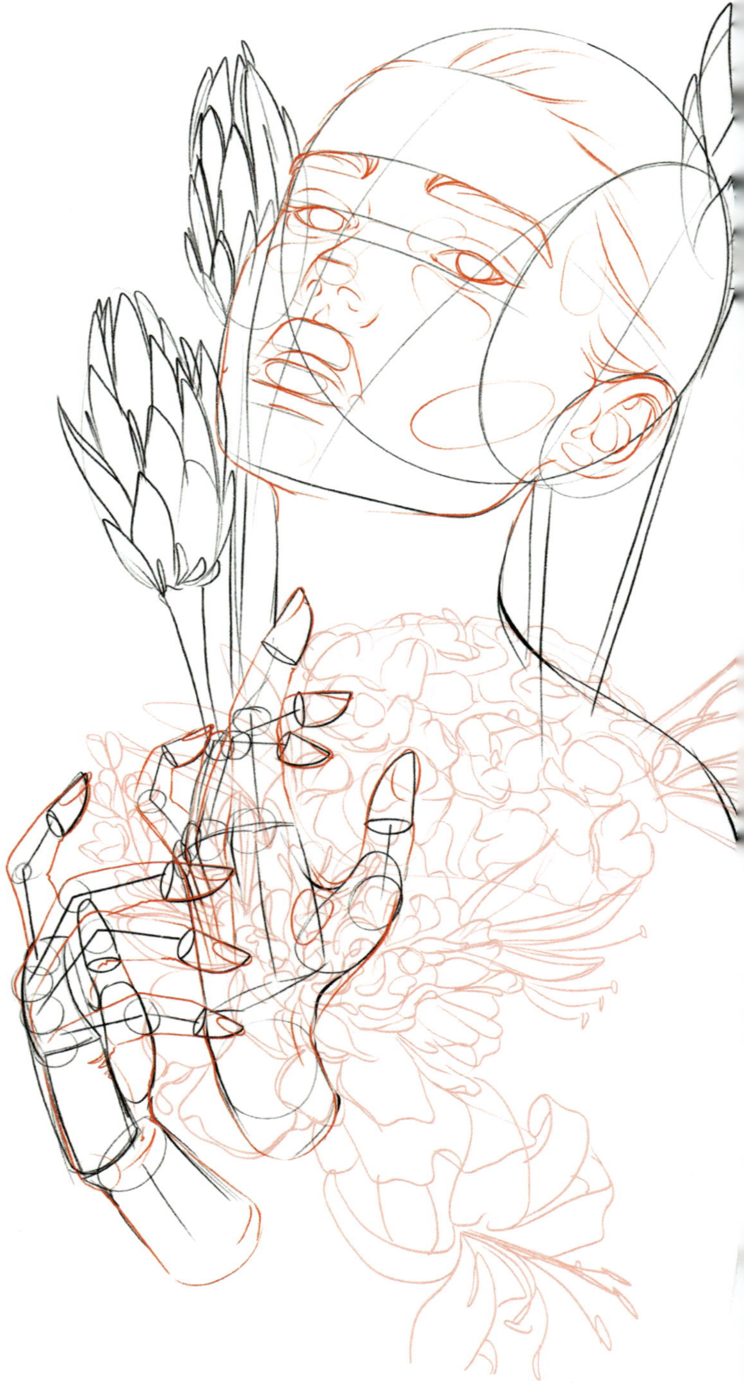

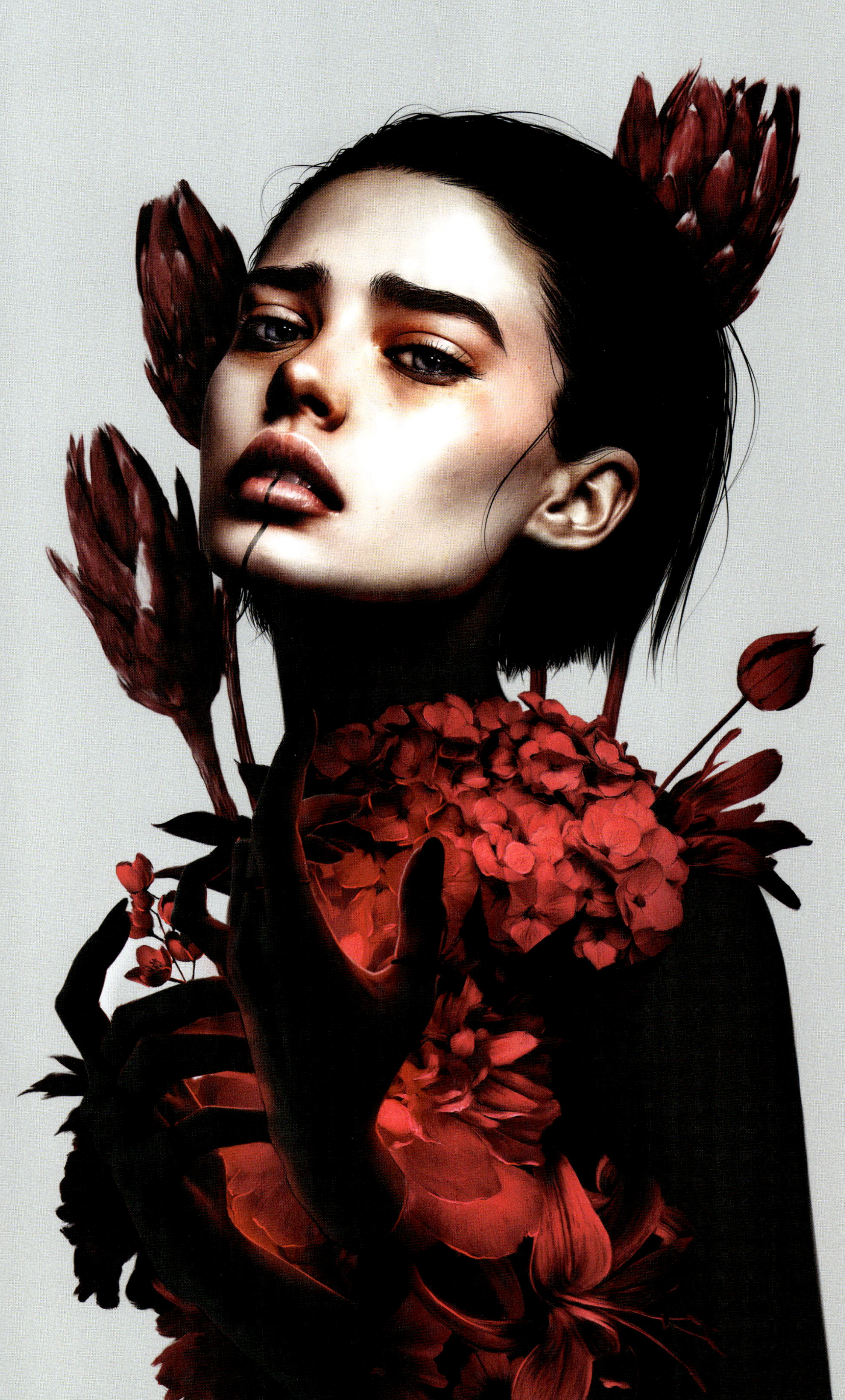

ALL THAT REMAINS

This painting shows how tempting yet unimportant opulence is when compared to the people who are always there for us.

The left character is crowned by a dead pheasant. In some Asian cultures, a pheasant represents professional success and financial wealth. The character wears nothing but the dead pheasant to signify she's lost all her wealth, but what remains is even more valuable.

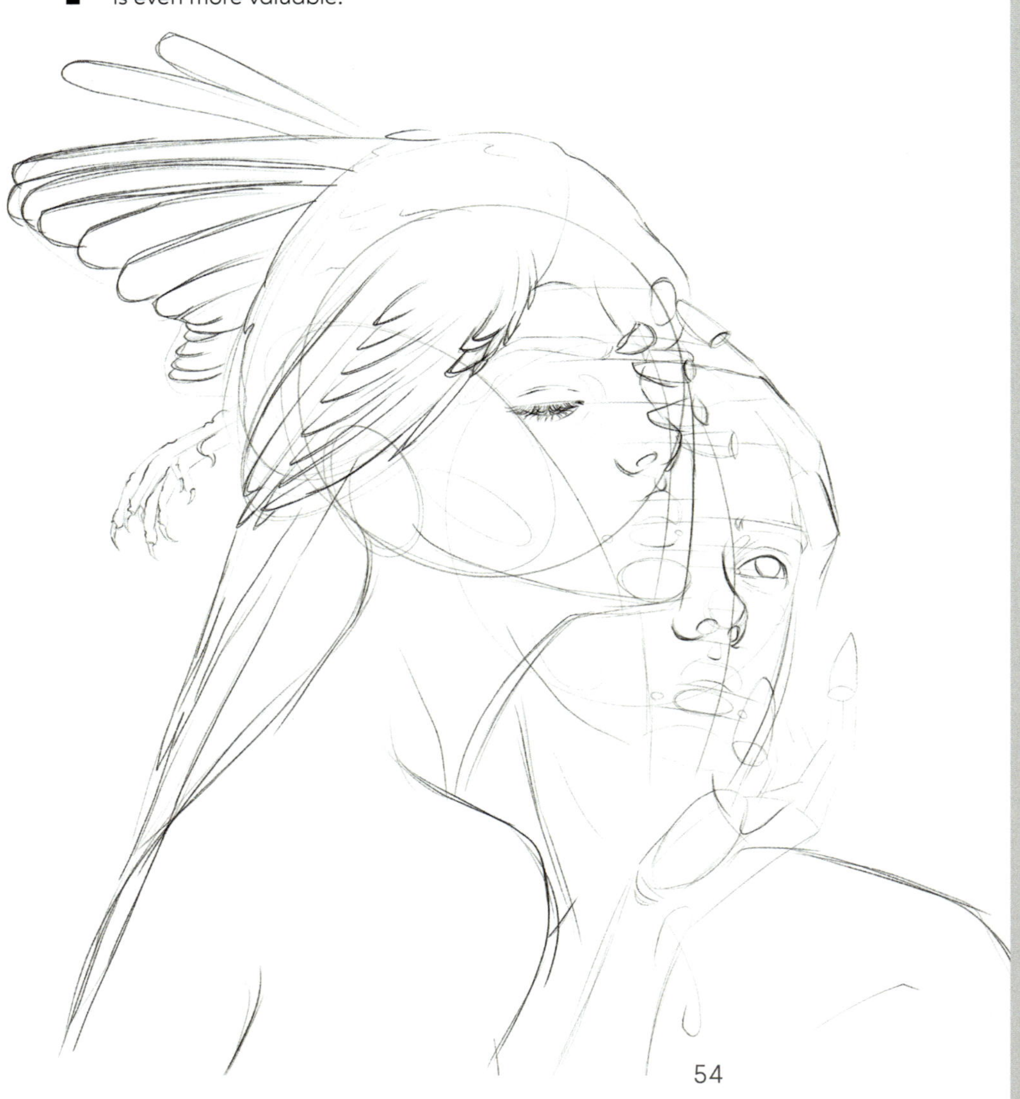

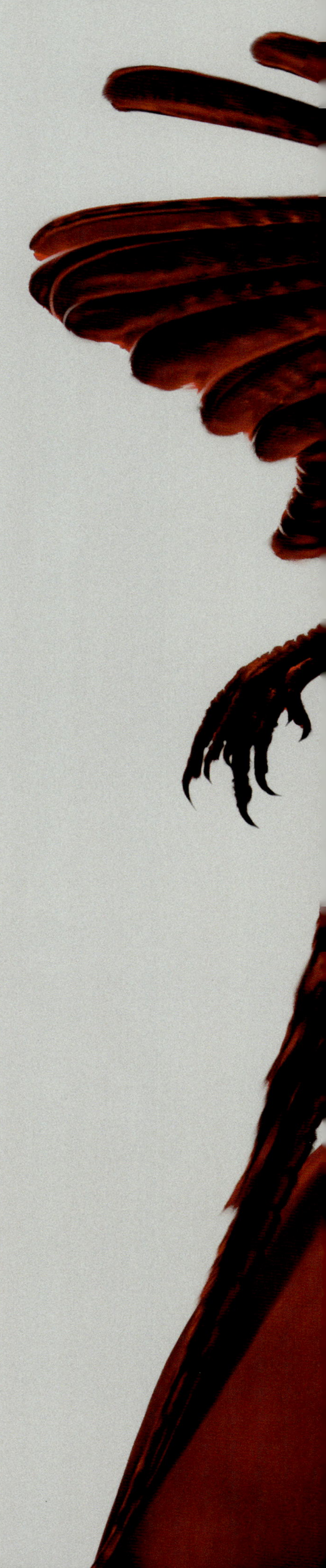

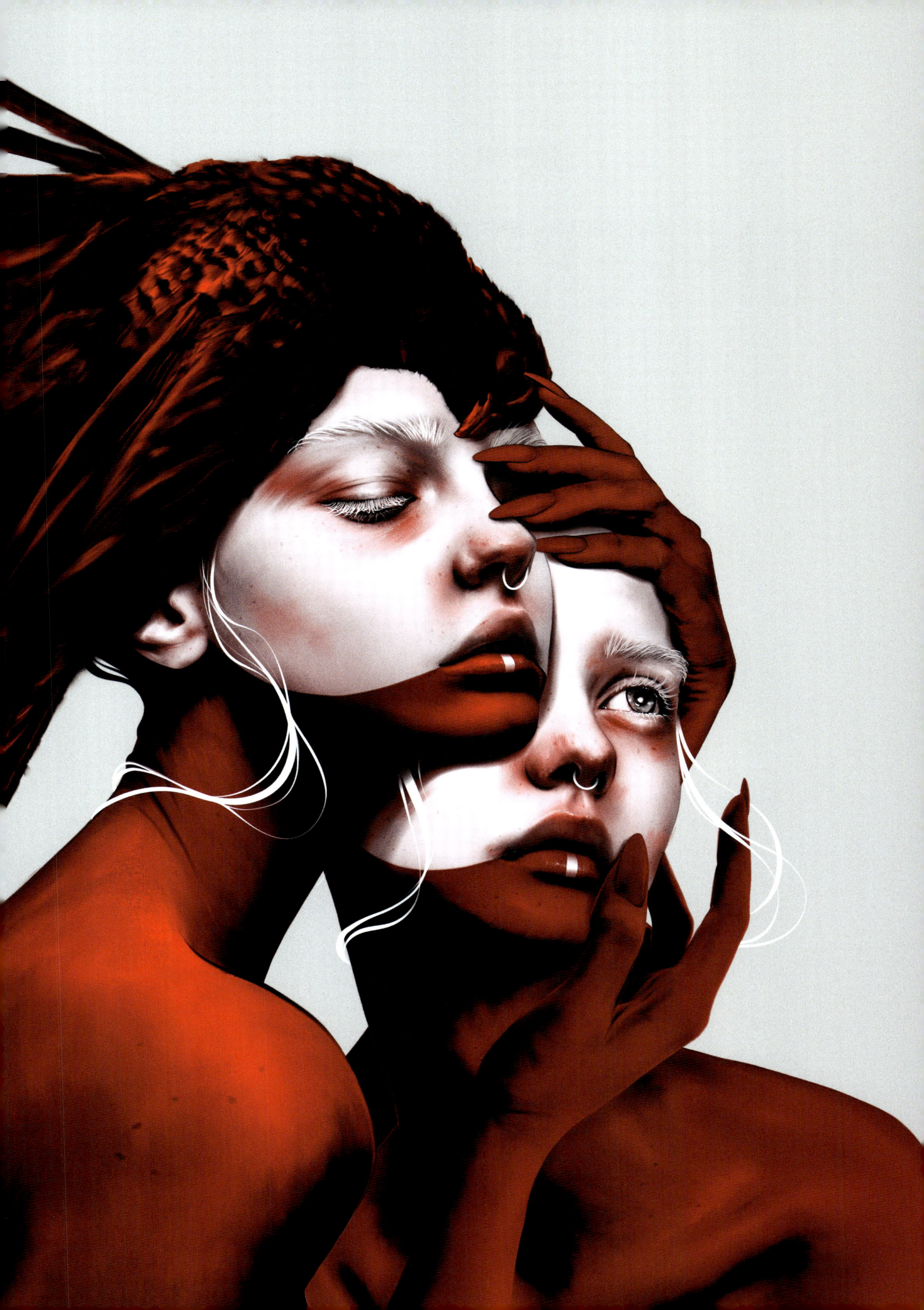

DIFFERENT

A continuation of the painting *All That Remains*. It touches on the theme of tempting, superfluous riches, but the variety of colors signifies the tolerance and acceptance we should extend to other people. No one should feel excluded for being different, and should instead be respected for their authenticity.

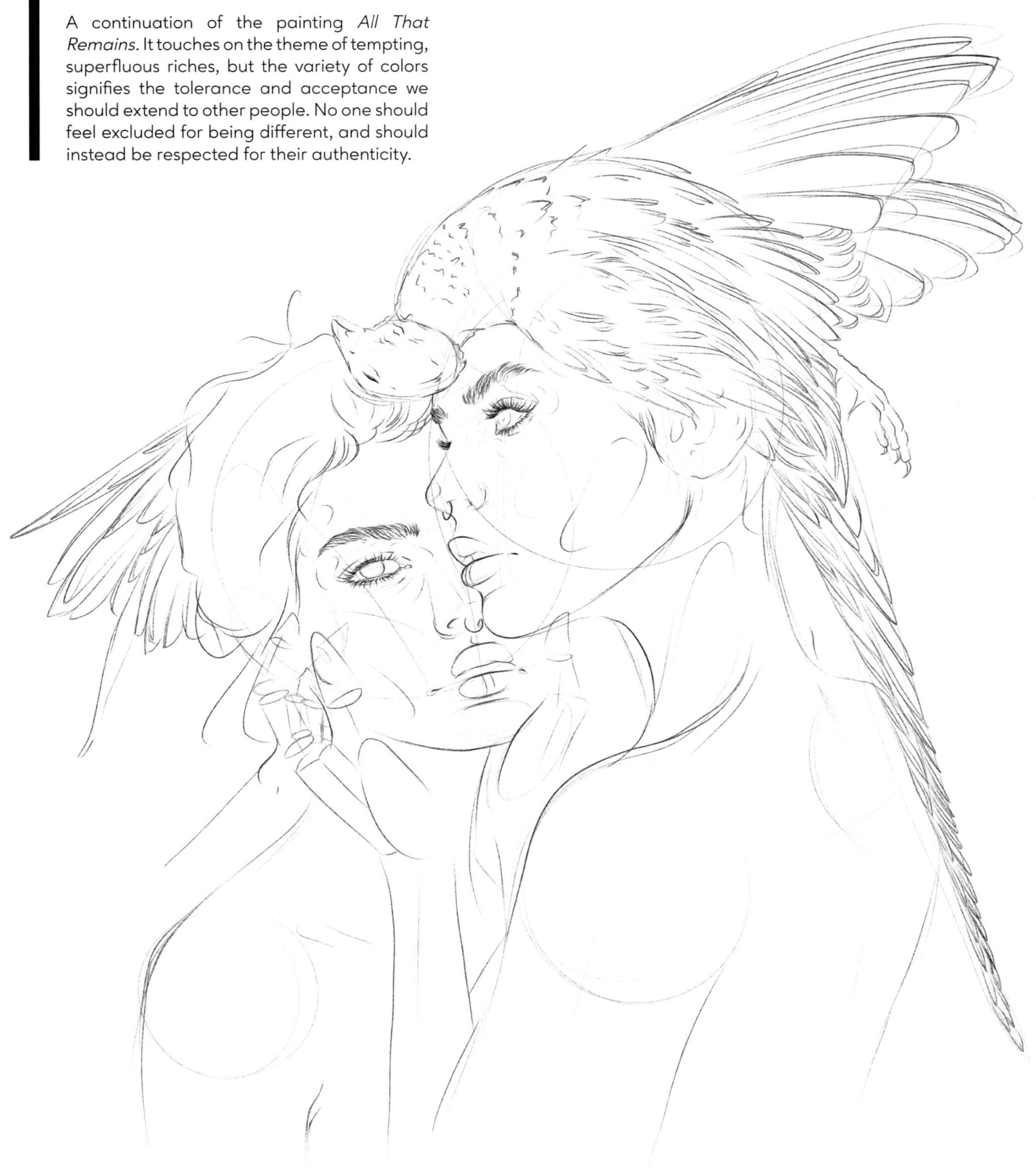

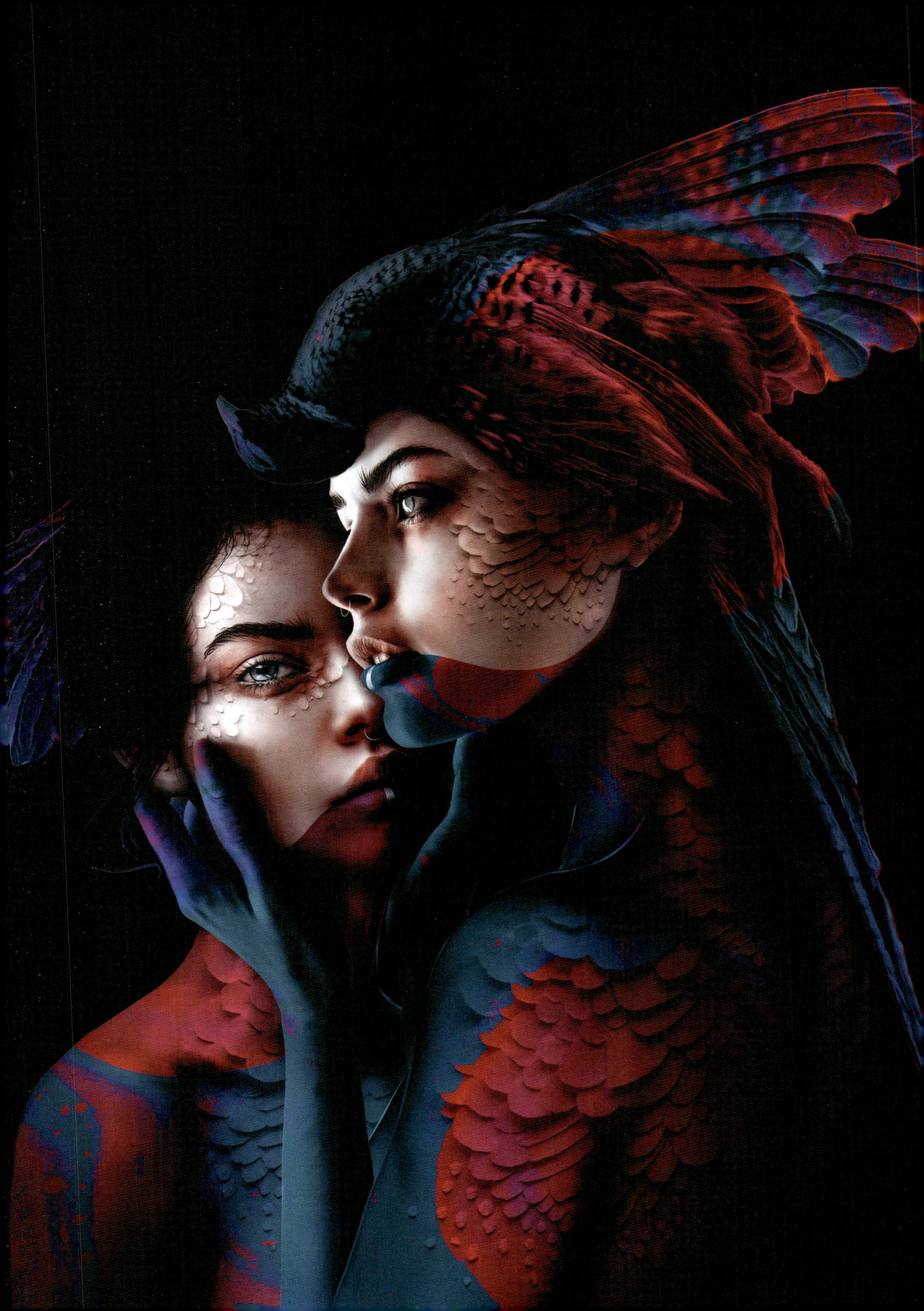

THROUGH MY EYES

Through My Eyes is a series of four paintings in which the characters all have masks covering their eyes. The messages I hoped to convey were kindness and understanding; I believe we should cultivate empathy instead of being so self-absorbed. The world would be a very different place if we imagined life from a factory-farm animal's point of view.

To see the rest of the series, turn to page 5, 6 and 41.

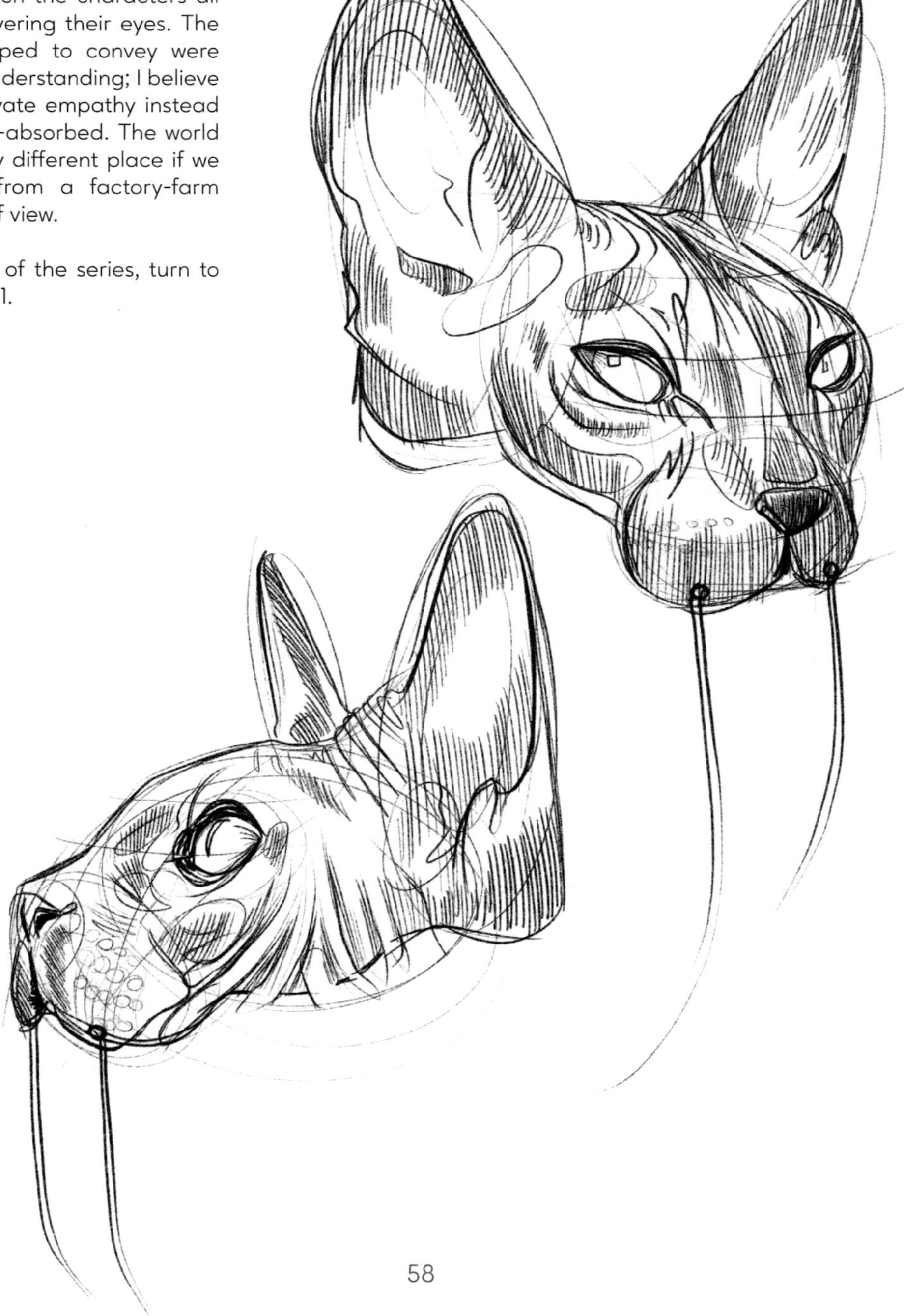

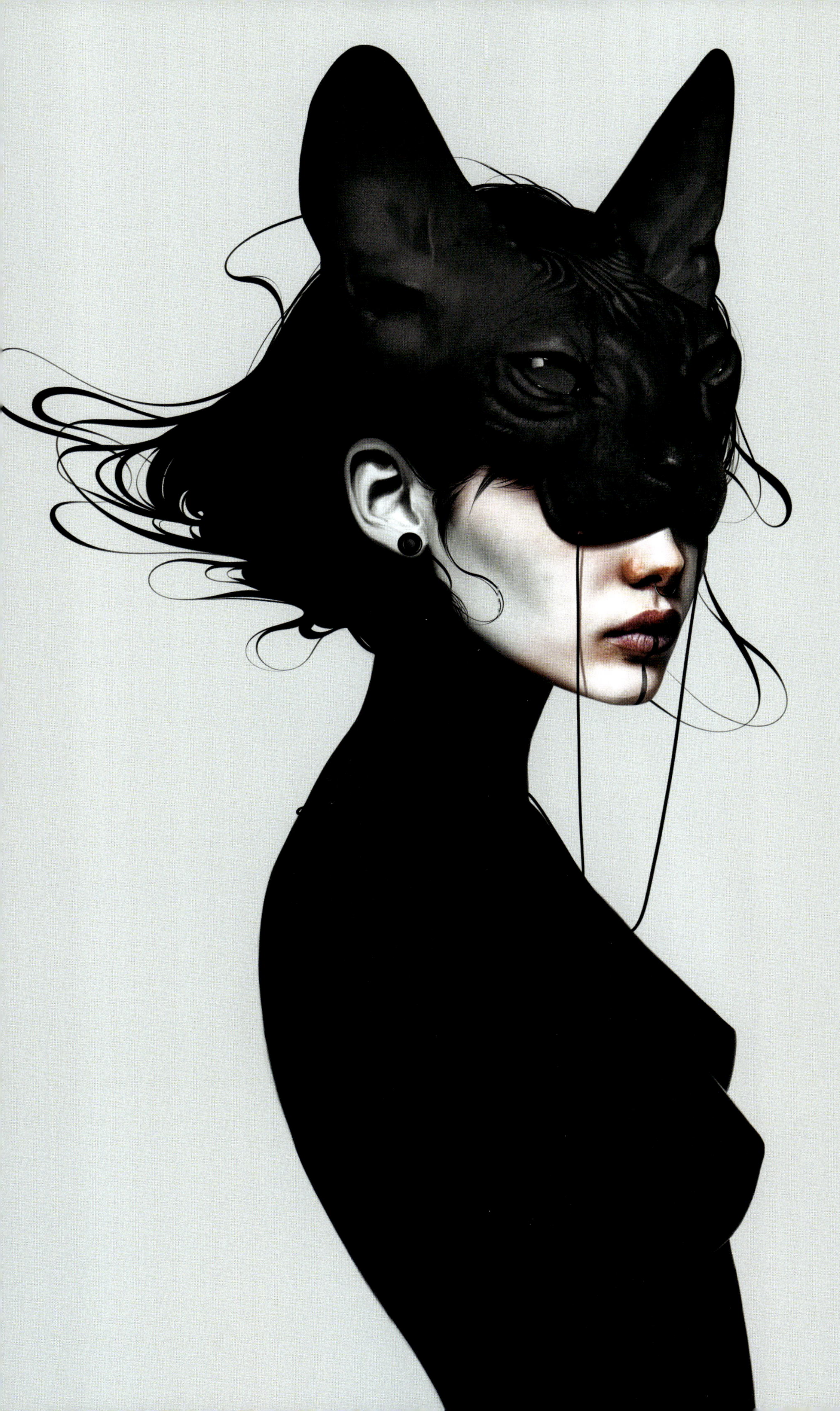

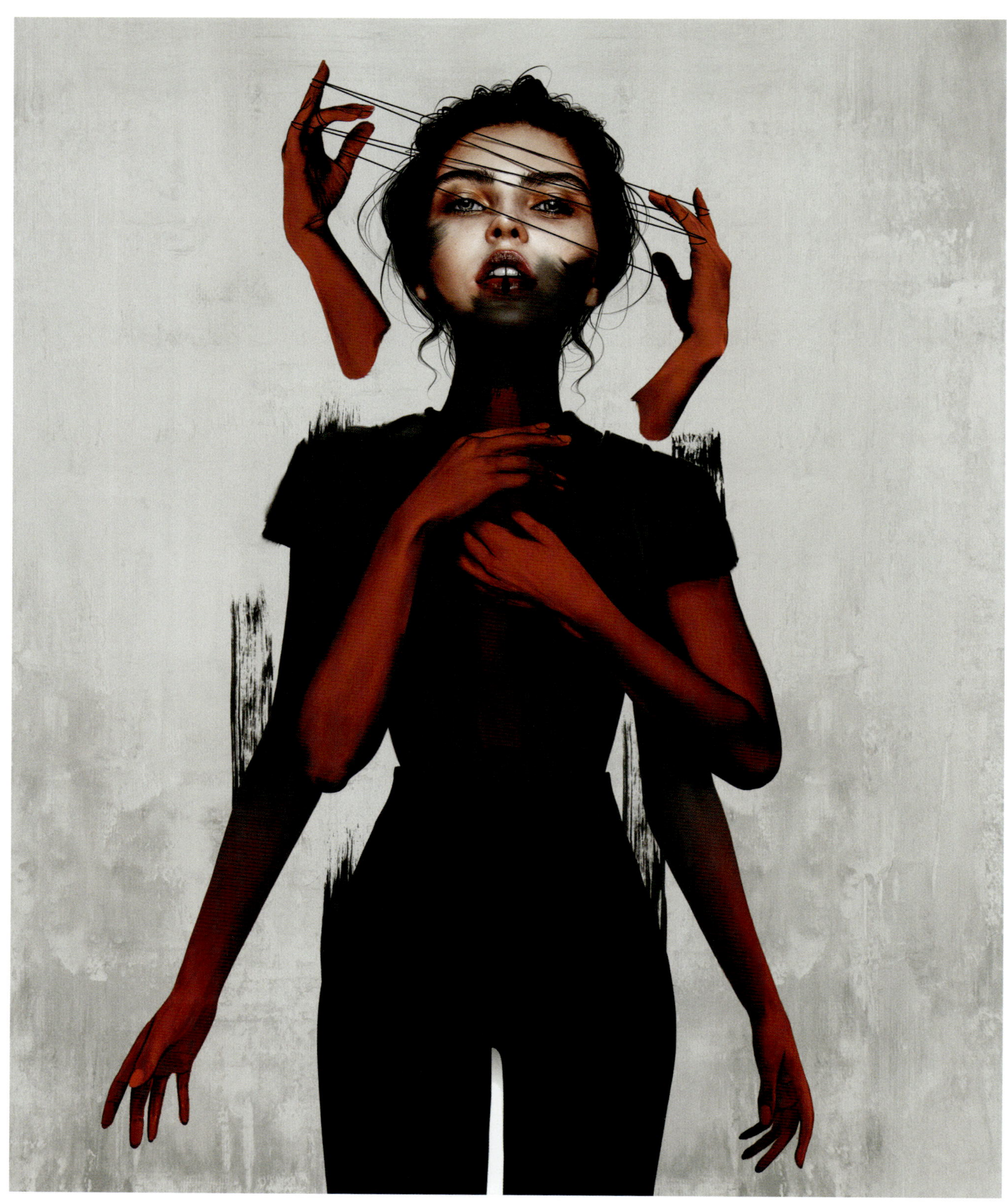

CANCER

Cancer is another part of my zodiac series. Creating a character with a multitude of arms and hands has been a goal of mine for a long time, and that's why this painting is one of my favorites.

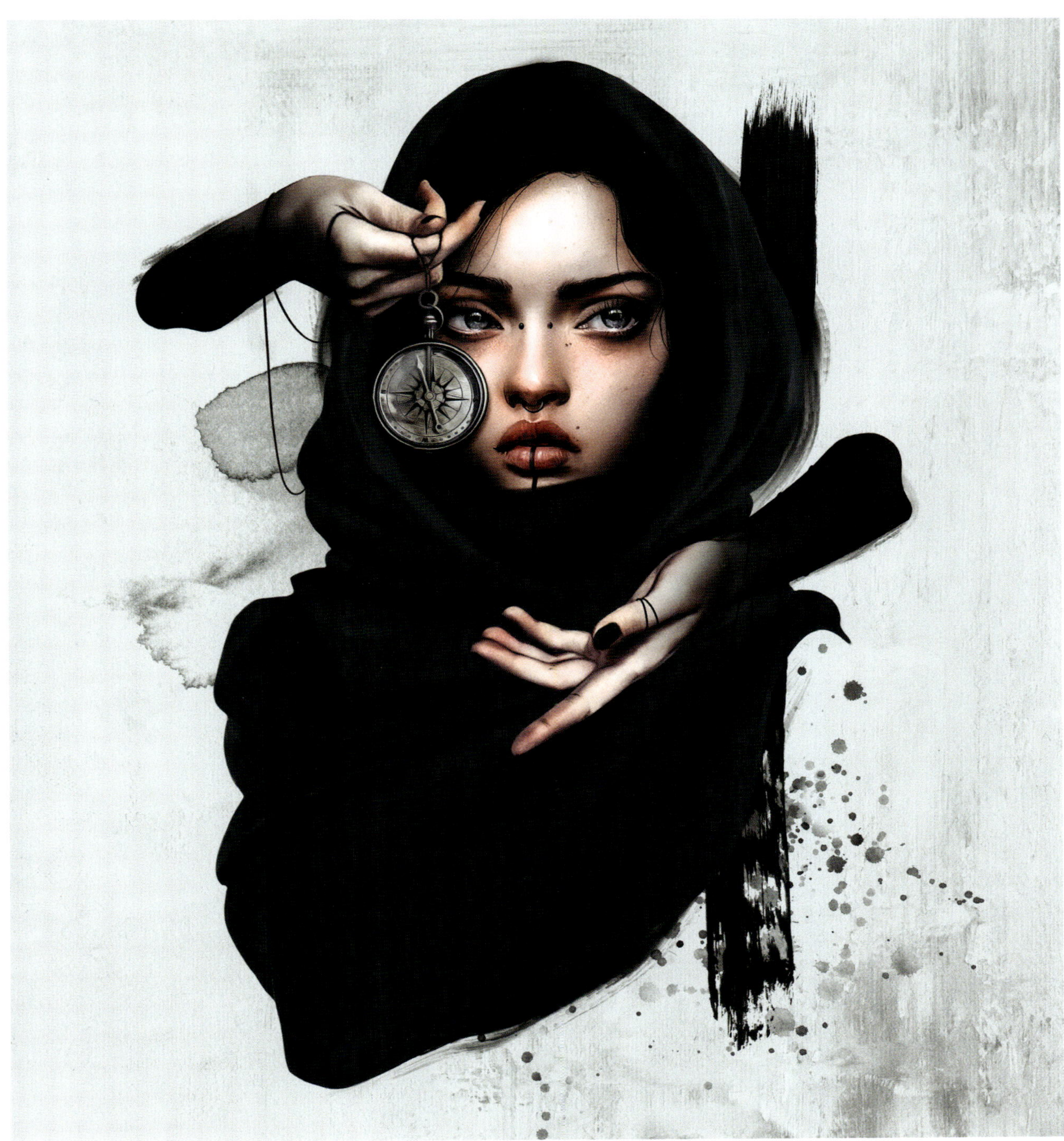

THE ROAD NOT TAKEN

Two roads diverged in a yellow wood,
And sorry I could not travel both
And be one traveler, long I stood
And looked down one as far as I could
To where it bent in the undergrowth;

Then took the other, as just as fair,
And having perhaps the better claim,
Because it was grassy and wanted wear;
Though as for that the passing there
Had worn them really about the same,

And both that morning equally lay
In leaves no step had trodden black.
Oh, I kept the first for another day!
Yet knowing how way leads on to way,
I doubted if I should ever come back.

I shall be telling this with a sigh
Somewhere ages and ages hence:
Two roads diverged in a wood, and I –
I took the one less traveled by,
And that has made all the difference.

– Robert Frost 1916

I love this poem because it's about choices and possibilities in life. It highlights the feeling of regret for all the paths a person doesn't take. I experience this often, and while I don't regret all my decisions, I rue not knowing where other paths would have brought me.

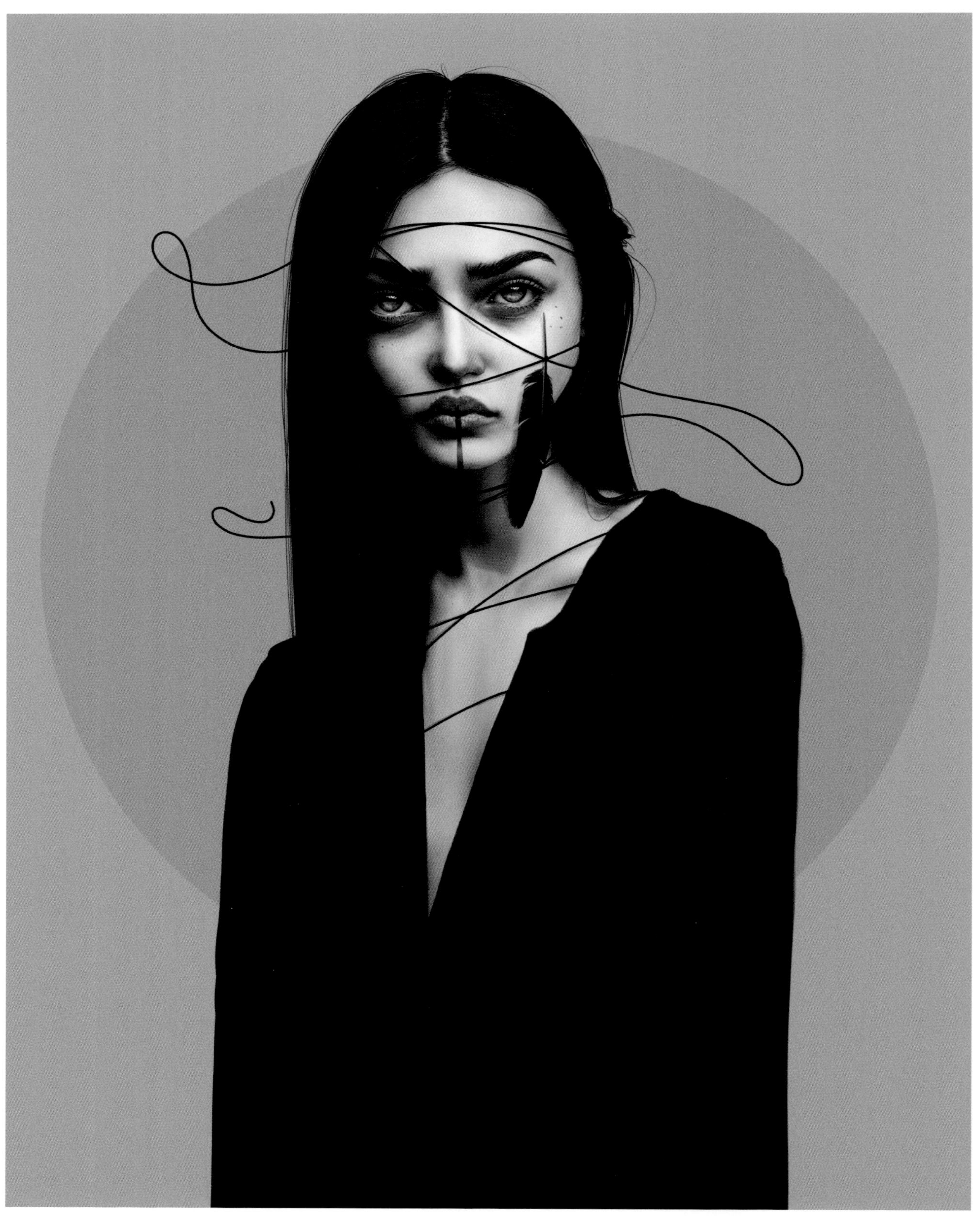

TEARS & FEATHERS

Did you know that crying can actually make you feel better? Tears contain substances that can ease discomfort while promoting emotional positivity, such as the analgesic leu-enkephalin, antibacterial lysozymes, and the hormone prolactin. Next time you feel down in the dumps, try having a good cry!

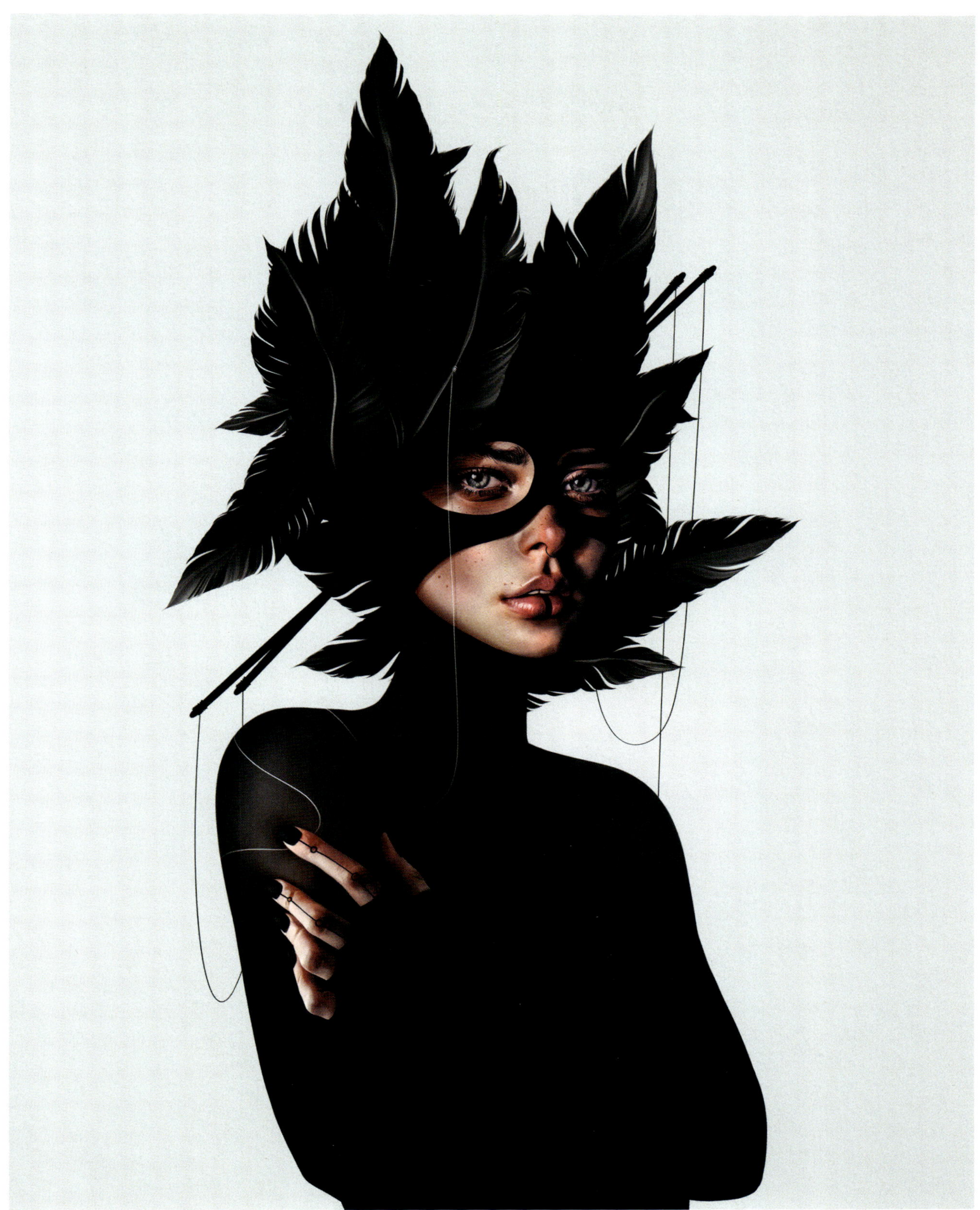

HIDDEN CONNECTIONS

I love uncovering hidden connections in song lyrics, movies, or even books. Maybe I should have become a detective after all! Is there a hidden connection in this painting as well?

CHARACTER DESIGN

"THOSE WHO DO NOT WANT TO IMITATE ANYTHING PRODUCE NOTHING"

– Salvador Dalí

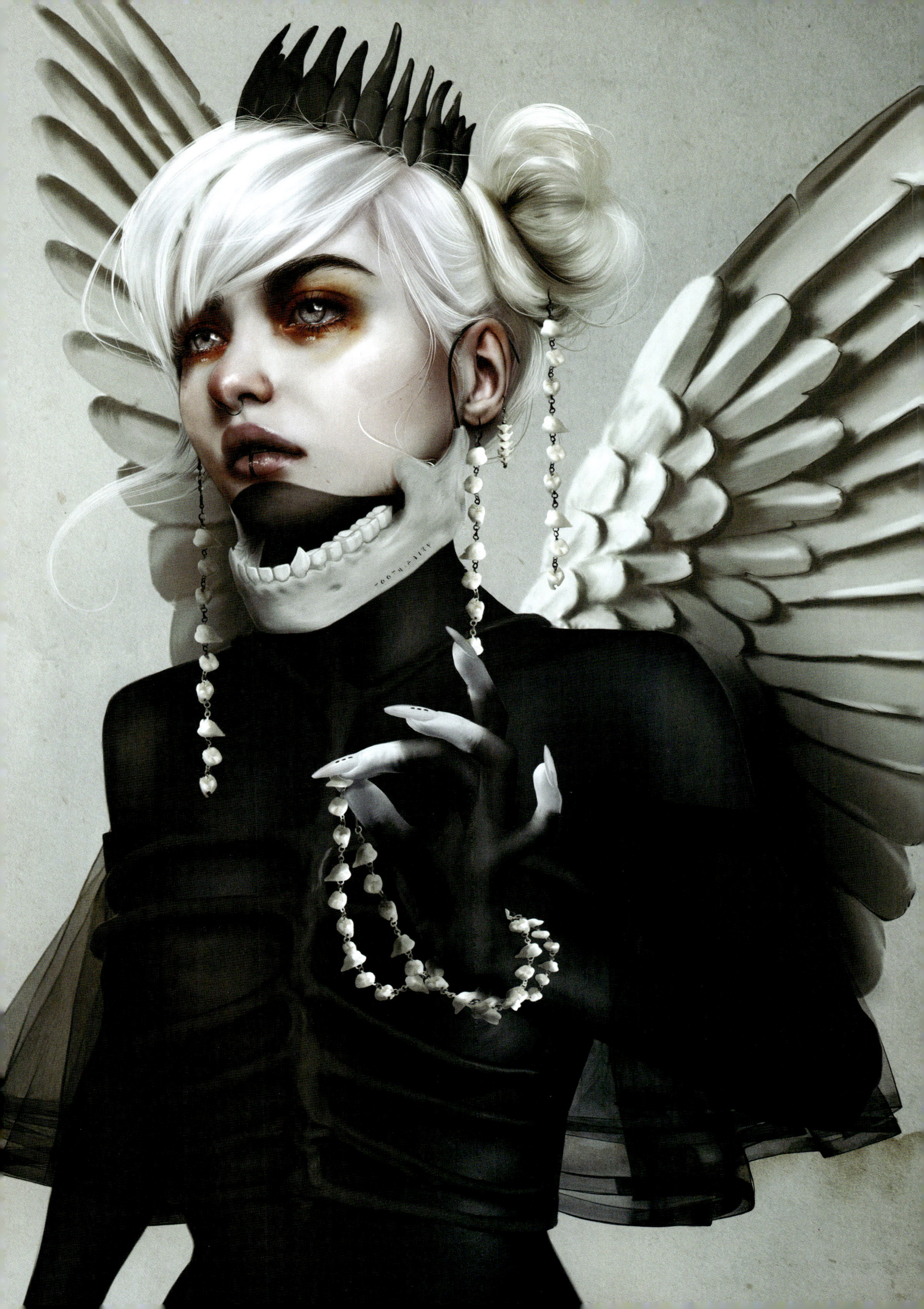

THE VILLAINS

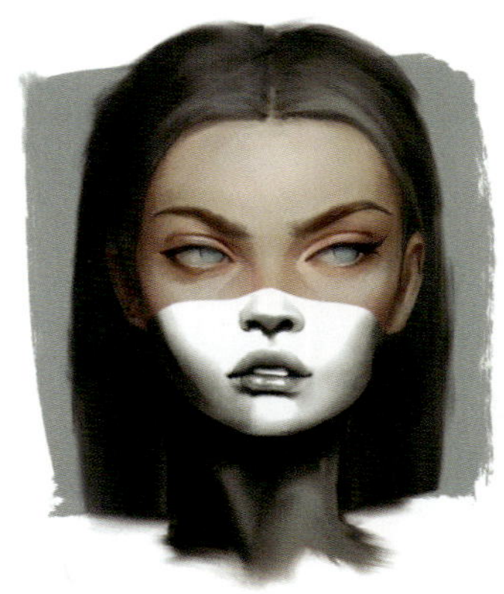

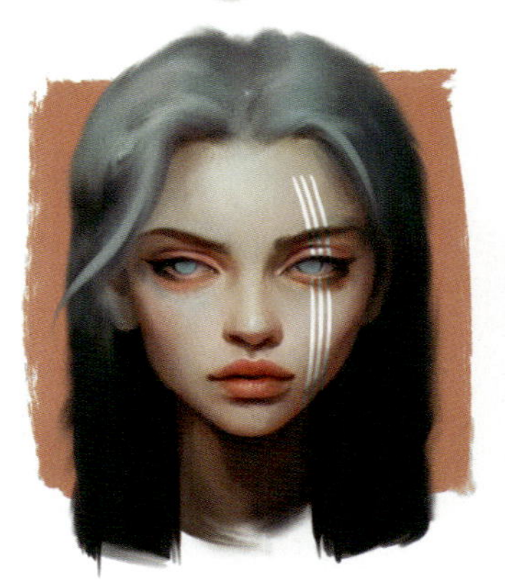

The three characters on the right-hand page were conceptualized during my character design studies and are comprised of *The Warrior*, *The Seer*, and *The Engineer* (left to right).

For all three designs, I created four basic sketches that I shared with my followers, who then picked the best one for me to develop further. I made the decision to let my followers pick because, when left to my own devices, I tend to pick the easiest design. This forced me out of my comfort zone and was a nice change of pace.

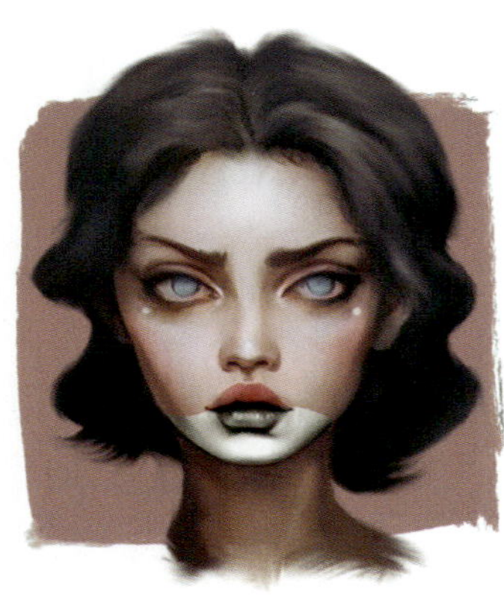

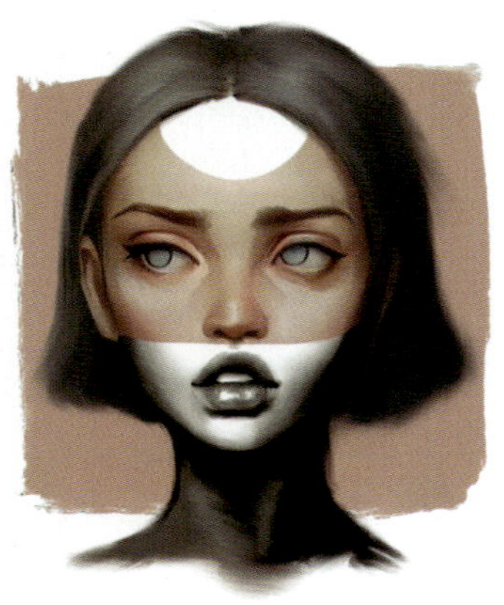

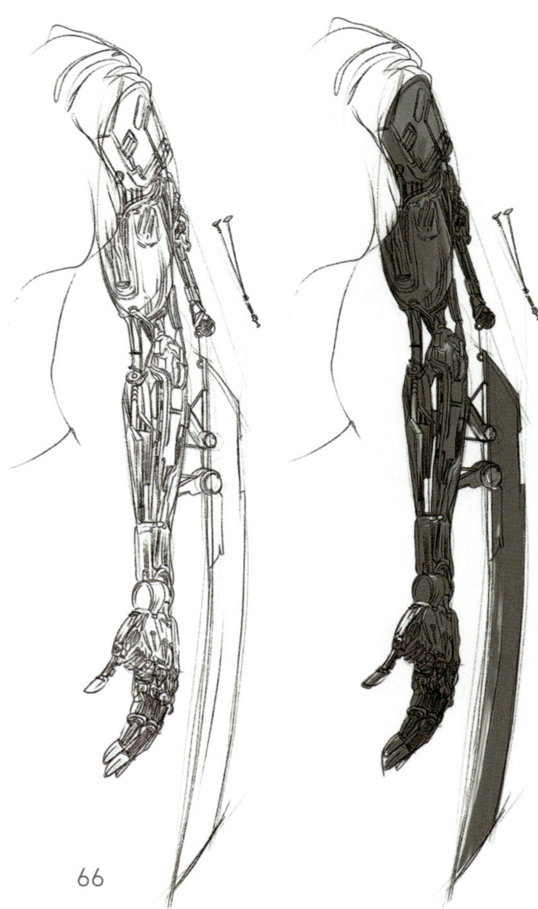

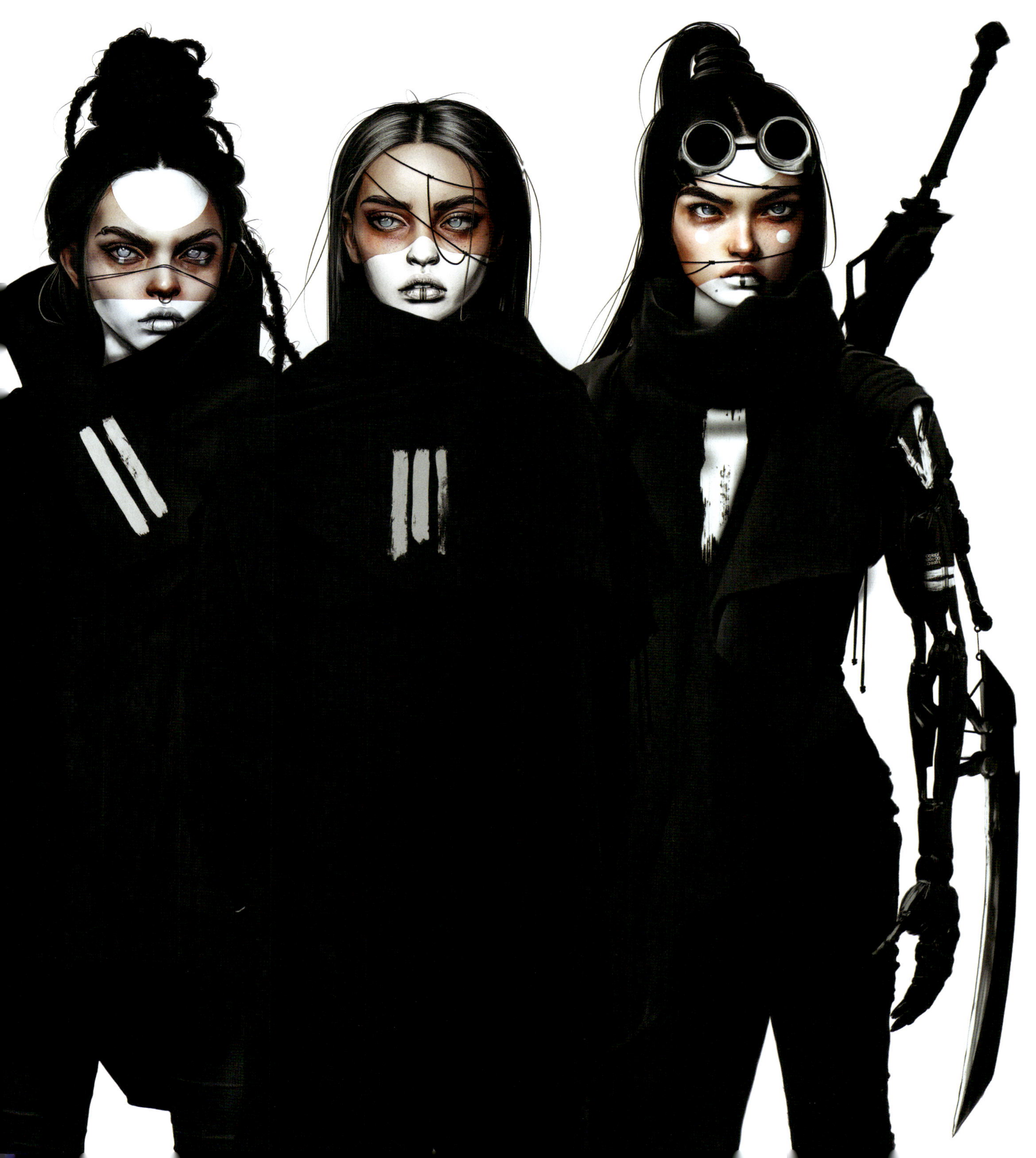

HAWKEYE

Hawkeye is one of my first characters, and also one of my favorites. I like the simple design with the hidden arms and graceful legs. I wanted the character to look petite while also communicating an important message: she's not to be underestimated.

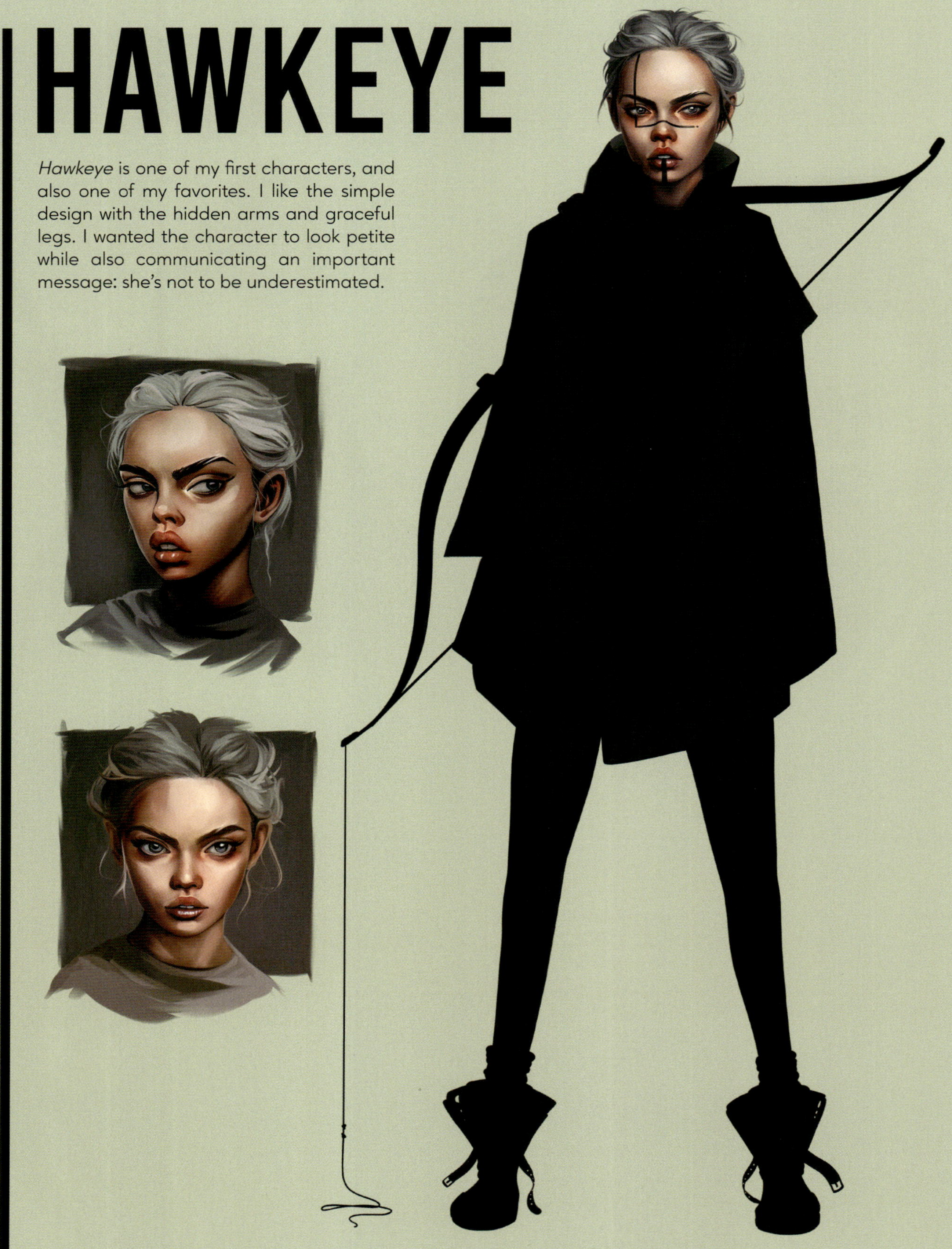

JUSTICE

I originally named this character Riel, but in the end I went with *Justice*. I like to portray strong women and fighters, juxtaposing a petite stature with a determined expression and a confident pose.

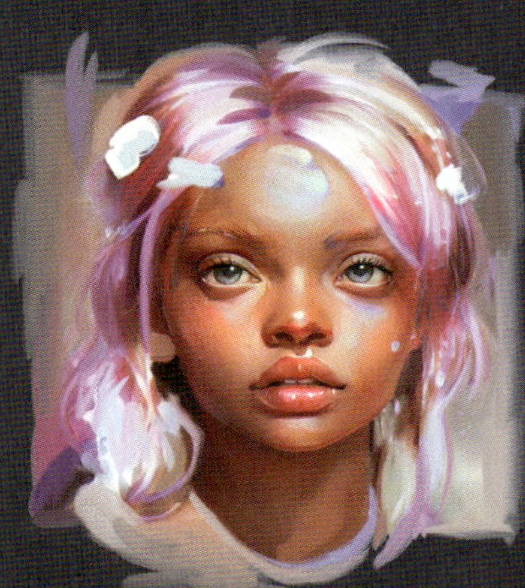

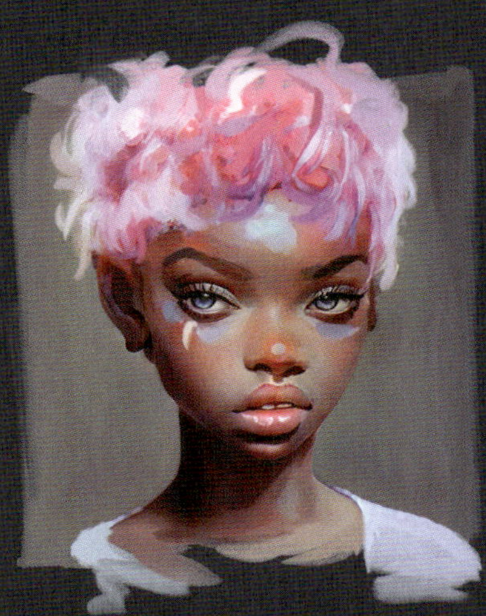

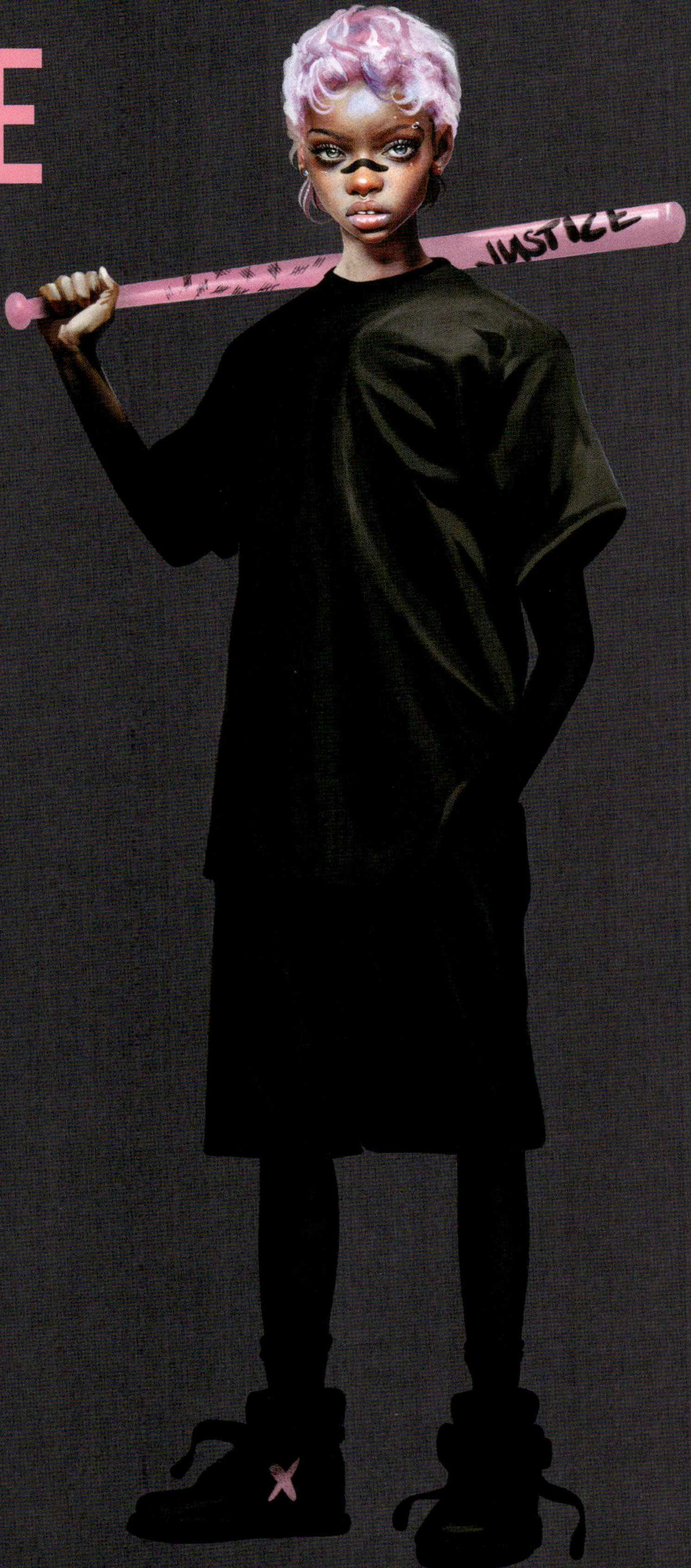

SKYDIVER

Skydiver was also picked by my followers. I love the result, especially how her skin color contrasts with the sky-blue hair and cloud-gray eyes.

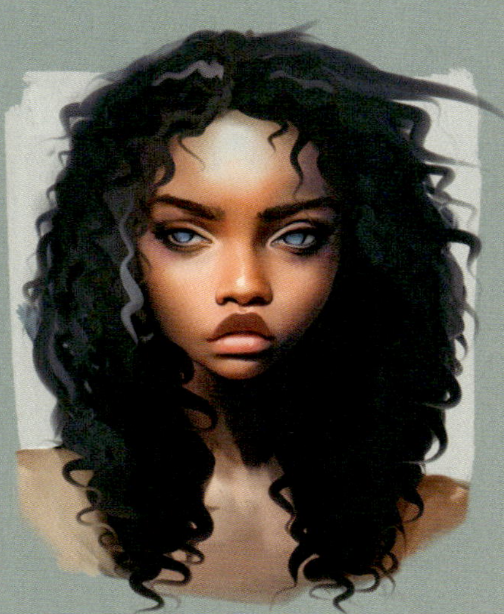

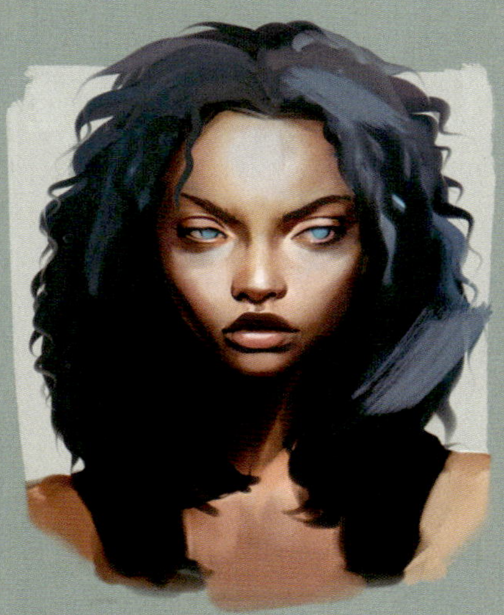

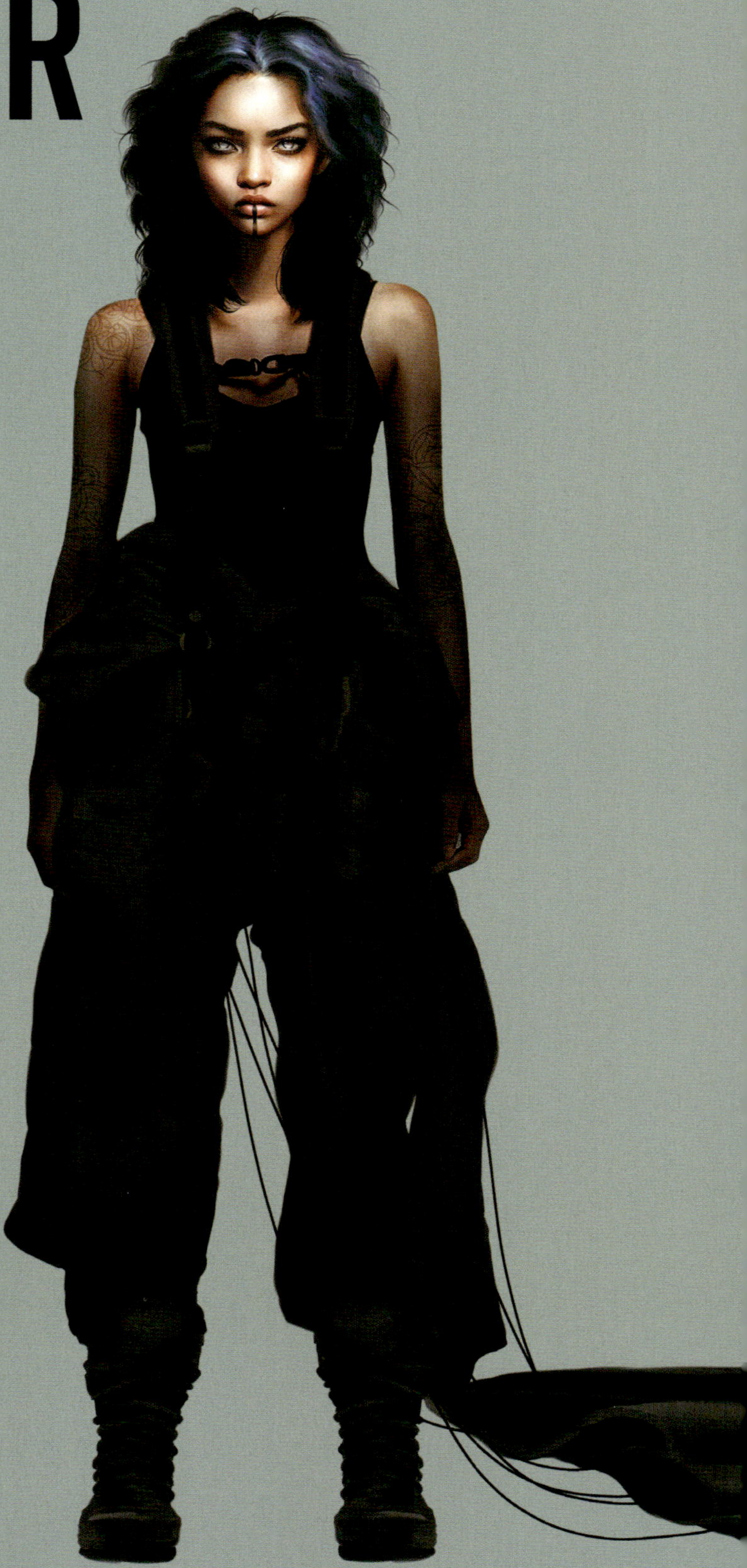

GUMGUN WARRIOR

In my opinion, this is the only type of firearm that should be legal. I mean, have you ever had to remove gum from your hair? That's enough punishment right there.

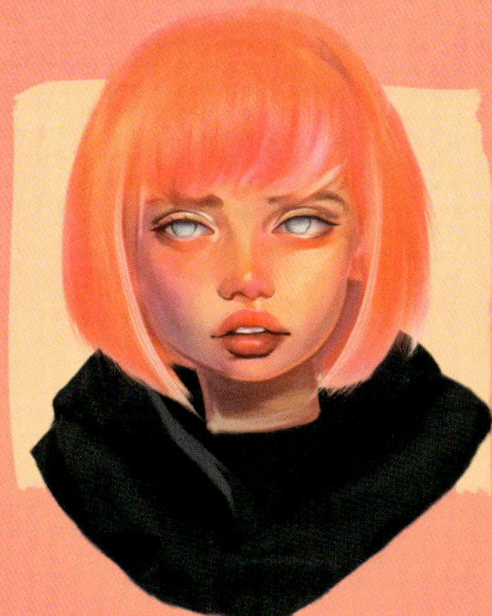

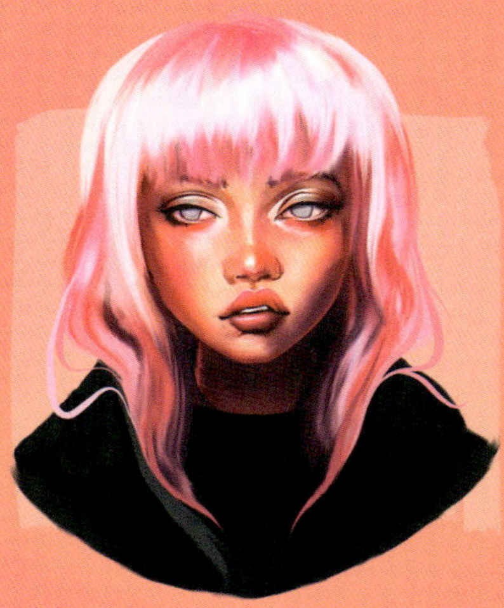

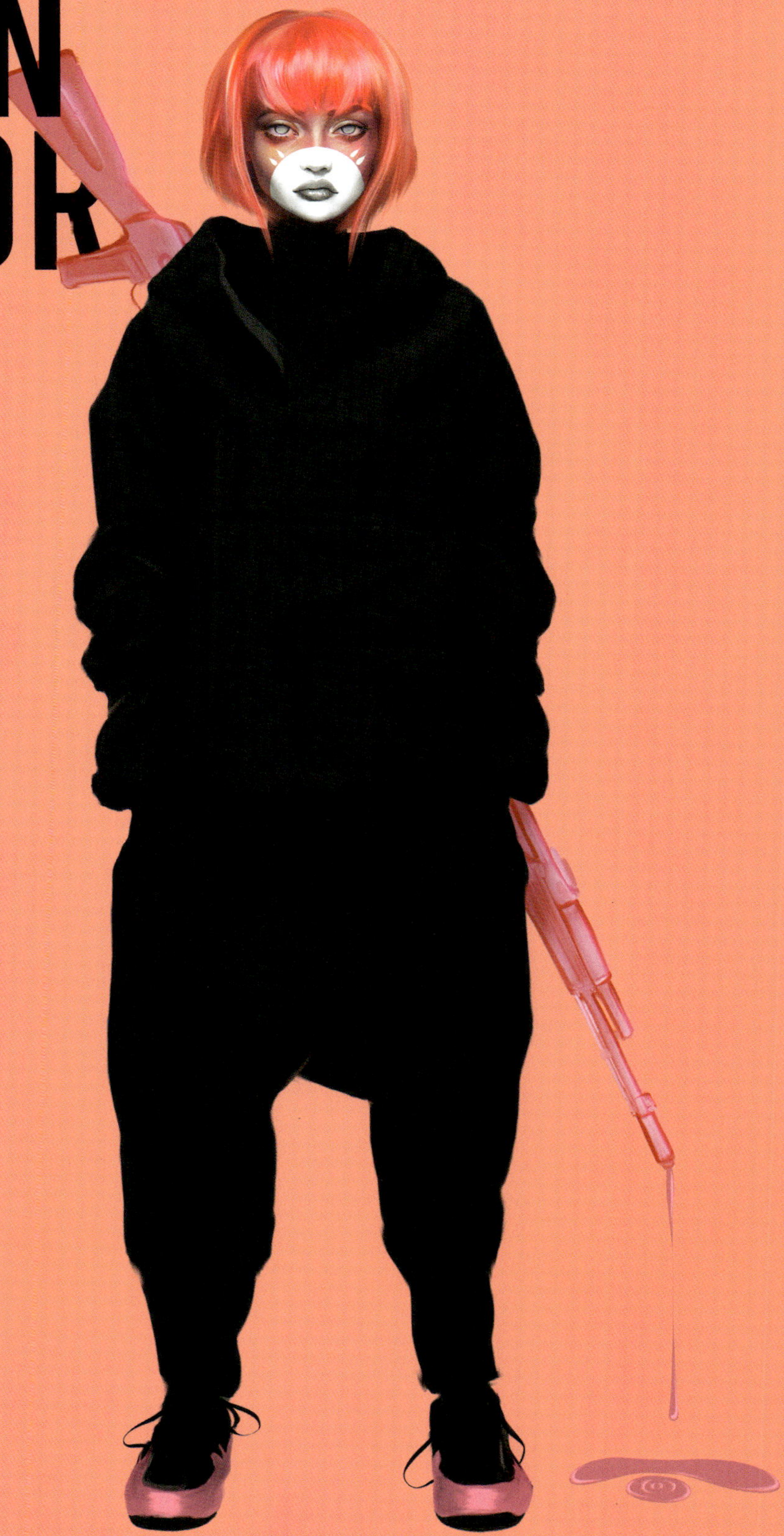

TOOLS

"YOU CAN LOOK AT A PICTURE FOR A WEEK AND NEVER THINK OF IT AGAIN. YOU CAN ALSO LOOK AT THE PICTURE FOR A SECOND AND THINK OF IT ALL YOUR LIFE"

– Joan Miro

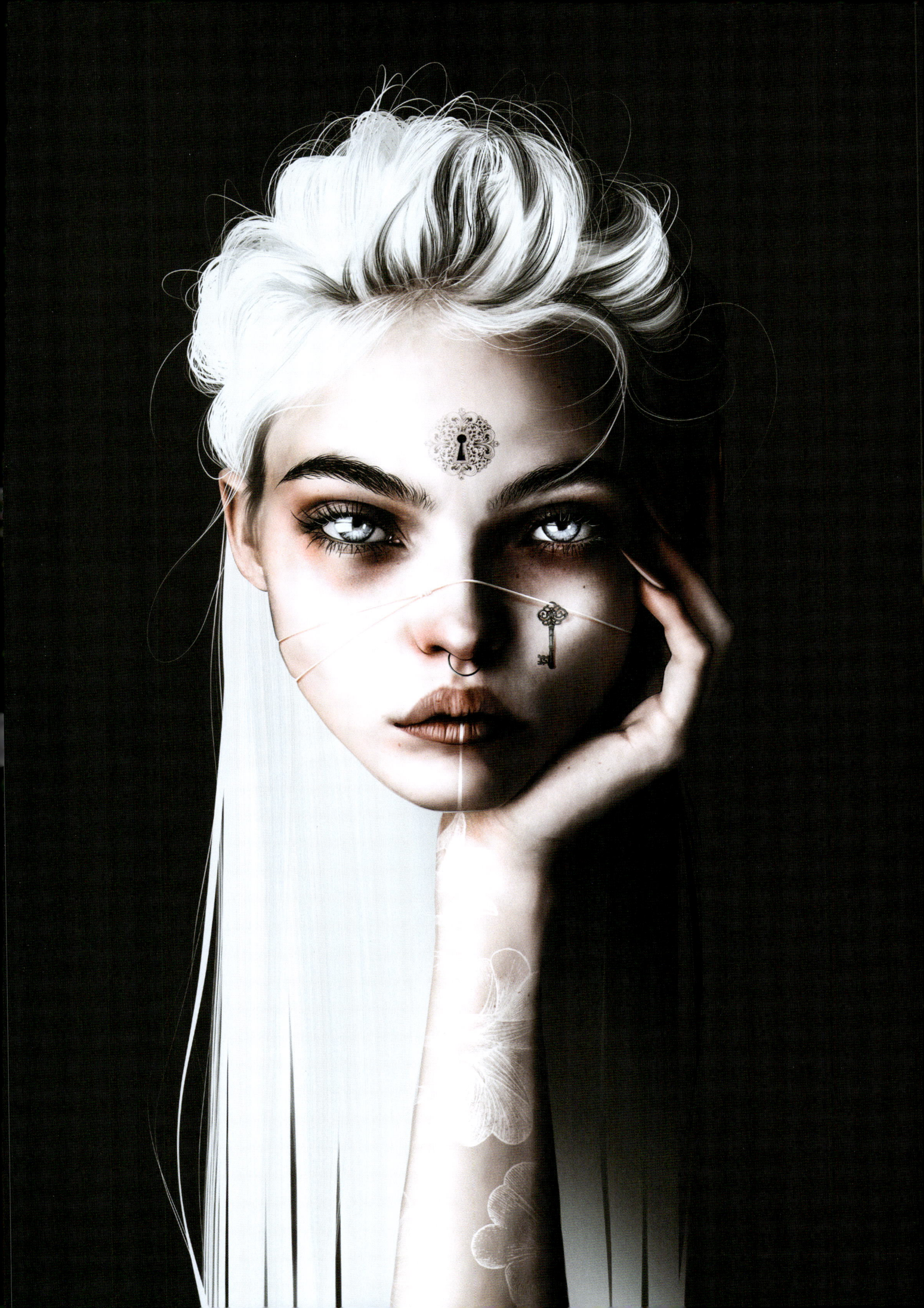

TOOLS

I COULDN'T WORK WITHOUT

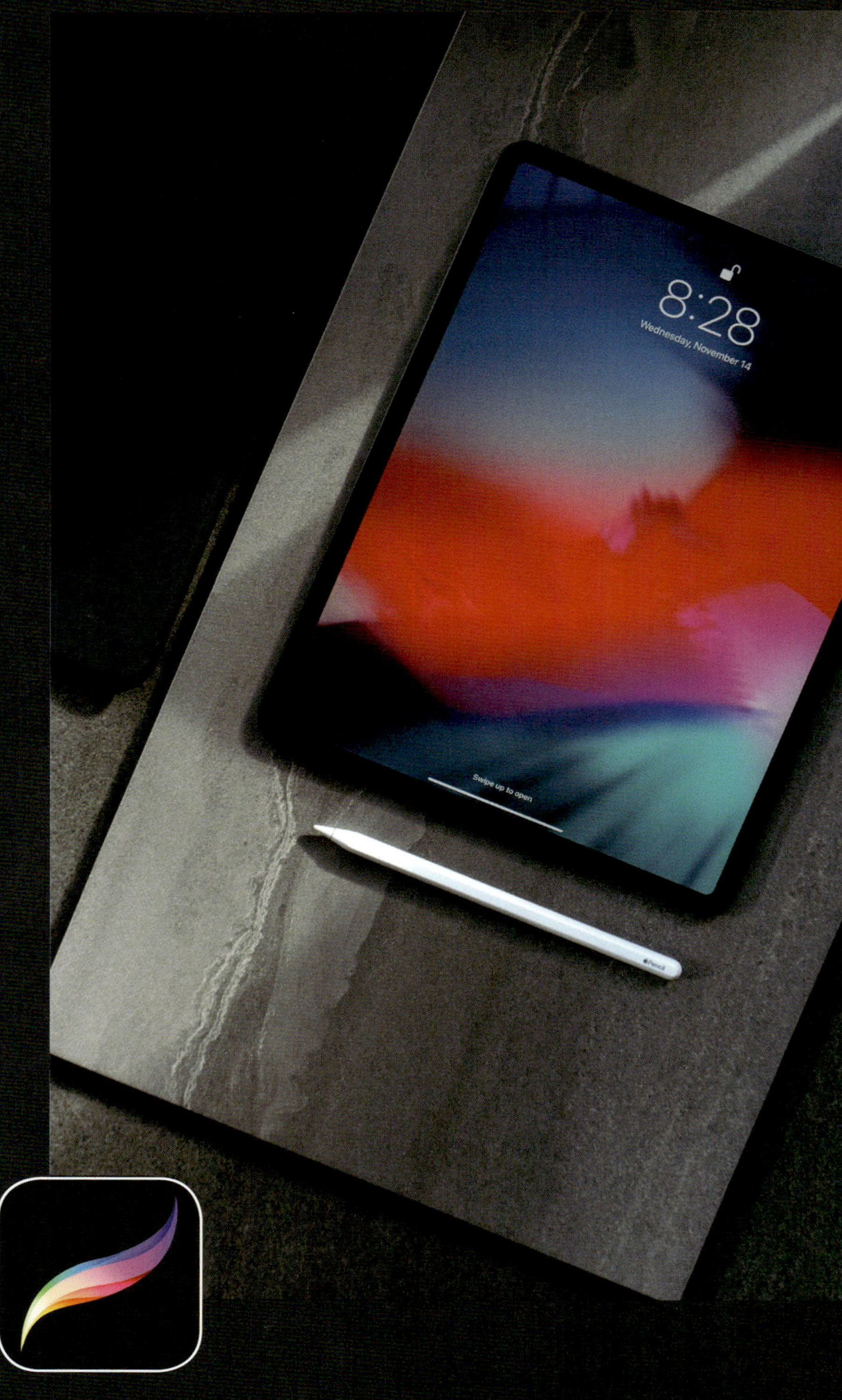

APPLE IPAD PRO

12.9 inch | 5th generation | 1 TB

I usually work with newer models, as the superior hardware allows for more layers in Procreate. I work with files that have dimensions up to 15,000 pixels, so every layer counts. That said, if you're not working with huge prints, you can get good results with dimensions around 4000 pixels, for which a cheaper iPad works just fine.

APPLE PENCIL

2nd generation

There are other styli that work with the iPad, but in my opinion, the Apple Pencil is the best stylus available.

PROCREATE APP

The Procreate app is the most popular app for drawing, painting, and animating that's currently available on the App Store. That said, Procreate is only available for the iPad, and Procreate Pocket is only available for the iPhone.

TOOLS

THAT MAKE WORK EASIER

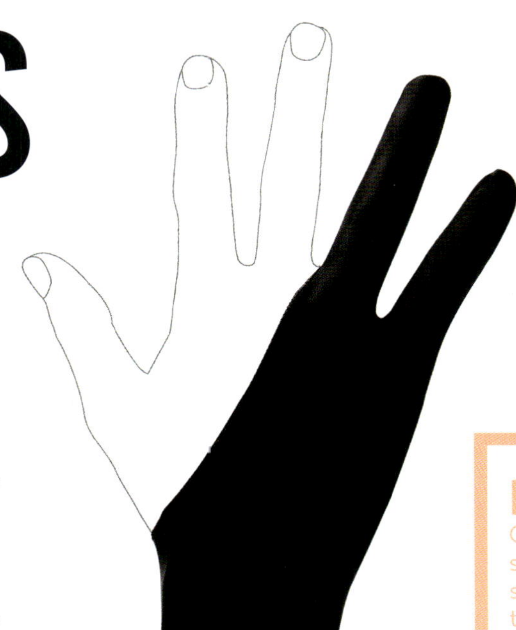

DRAWING GLOVE

A drawing glove is useful – if not necessary – to reduce friction between your hand and the glass screen.

By the way, the brand doesn't seem to matter – all the drawing gloves I've tested so far have been equally good.

PRO TIP:
Order the glove in a smaller size so it fits like a second skin, then cut off the fingertips. The glove will then fit perfectly.

PAPER-LIKE SCREEN PROTECTOR

This type of screen protector doesn't actually protect your screen, but instead adds some friction to your drawing surface, to make it feel more like you're drawing on paper. If you have one of these fitted, you don't need a drawing glove.

TABLET STAND

A tablet stand is useful to change the angle you're drawing at, which can improve your posture and prevent neck issues. I would only suggest this if you are starting to have noticeable discomfort.

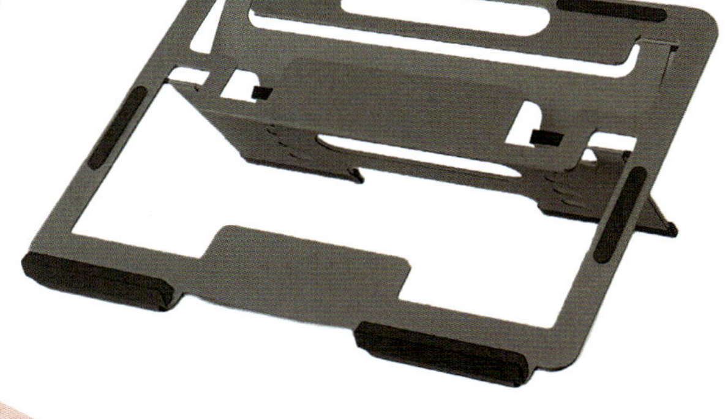

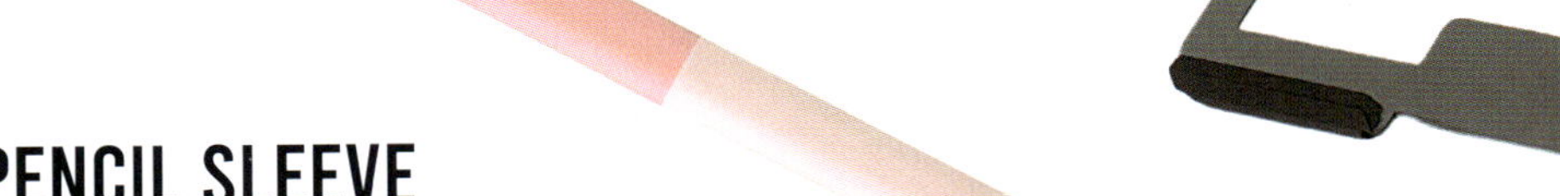

PENCIL SLEEVE

A pencil sleeve helps the stylus feel softer, which, in turn, is more comfortable on your hands and prevents the development of calluses. However, that should only be an issue to worry about if you spend many hours drawing each day.

THE PERFECT PORTRAIT

"LEARN THE RULES LIKE A PRO, SO YOU CAN BREAK THEM LIKE AN ARTIST"

– Pablo Picasso

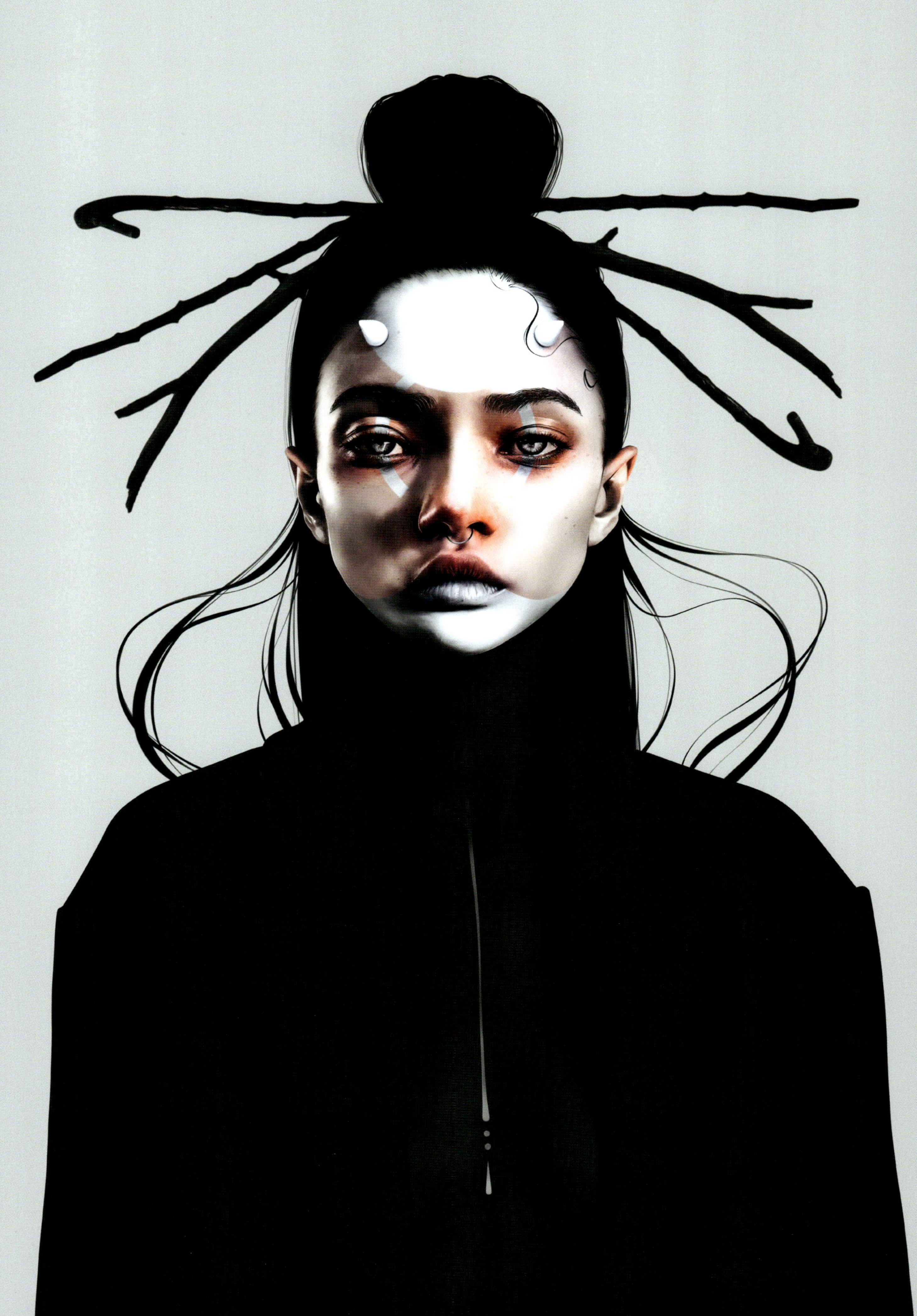

FRAMING

Before starting a new portrait, you must ask yourself two questions: what do you want the character to convey? Are the face and facial expressions enough, or should the posture also be recognized? Even though there's nothing you can't do in art, there are guidelines to help you make decisions. Here's an overview of common crops for portraying characters.

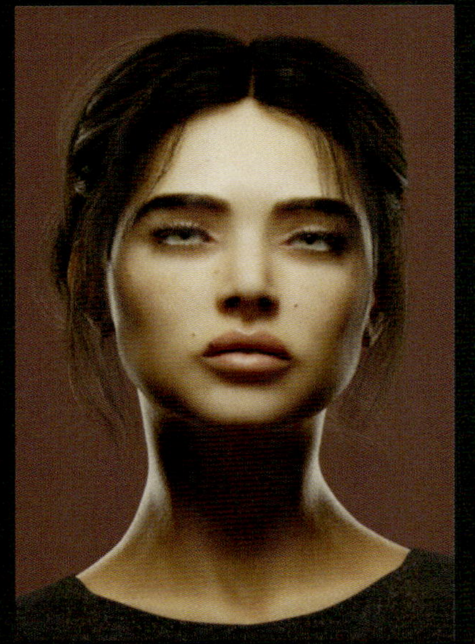

CLOSE-UP

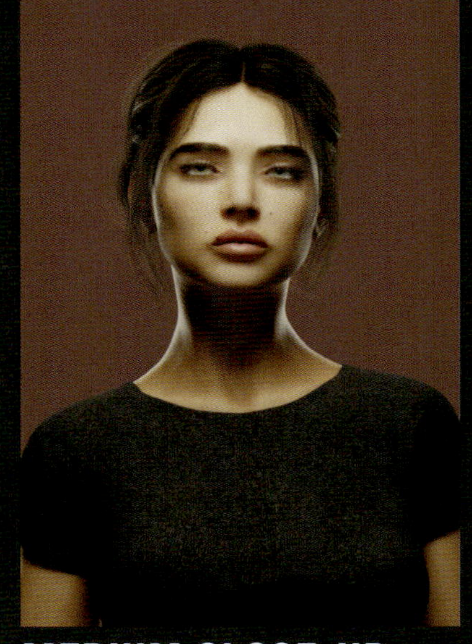

MEDIUM CLOSE-UP

UNCANNY VALLEY

This is Jane, and she's a Daz3D Genesis 8.1 3D Model. The feeling you probably get when looking at Jane is called "Uncanny Valley." This refers to a paradoxical effect we experience when a visual simulation closely resembles a human in many respects, but isn't quite convincingly realistic.

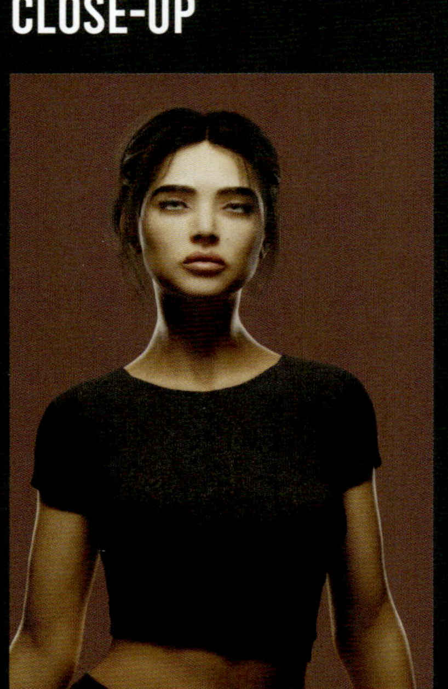

MEDIUM SHOT

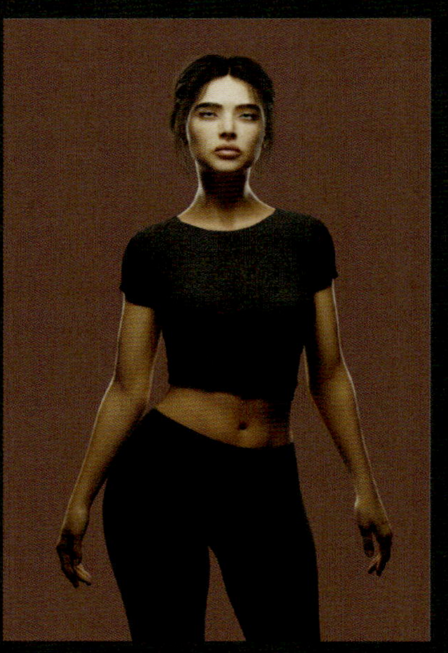

AMERICAN SHOT

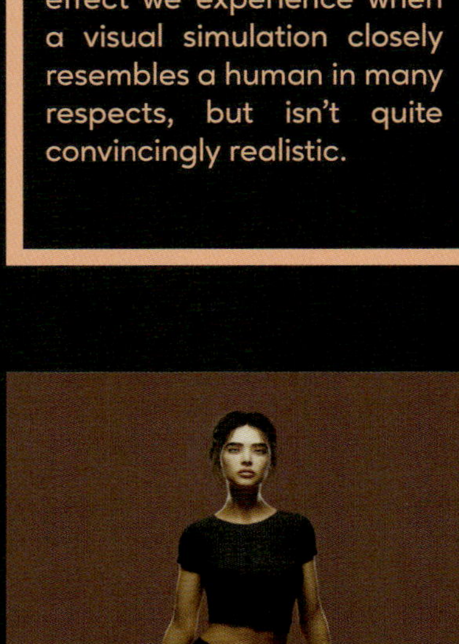

WIDE SHOT

"EVEN THOUGH THERE'S NOTHING YOU CAN'T DO IN ART, THERE ARE GUIDELINES TO HELP YOU MAKE DECISIONS."

The medium close-up and medium-shot formats are the most commonly used frames for portrait paintings. Even though the focus is clearly on the face, there's enough room to incorporate an interesting hand or body pose. Some good examples are Van Gogh's *Self-Portrait* in the medium close-up format (left) or Leonardo da Vinci's *Mona Lisa* in the medium-shot format (right).

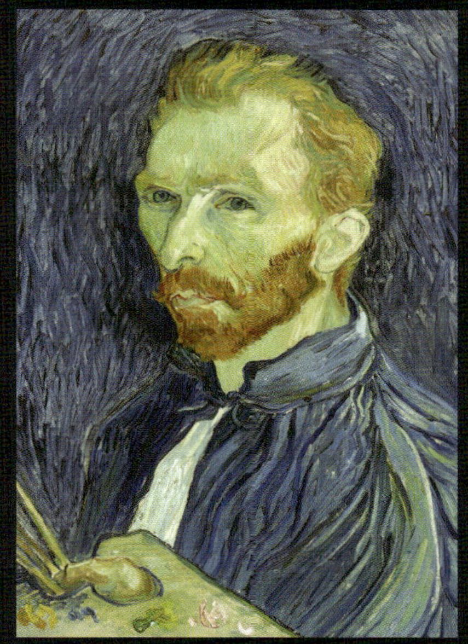

Everett Collection/Shutterstock.com

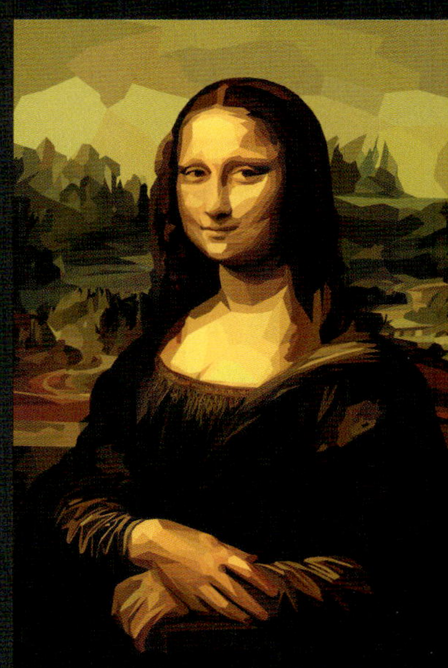

AdobeStock 506062986

The most important rule when cropping is to refrain from cutting off the image at a character's joints – this includes their knees, elbows, neck, and fingers – otherwise your image section will appear jarring and strange.

While creating your initial sketch, be aware of your canvas size and how much room you have to work with. Here are some examples of what to avoid:

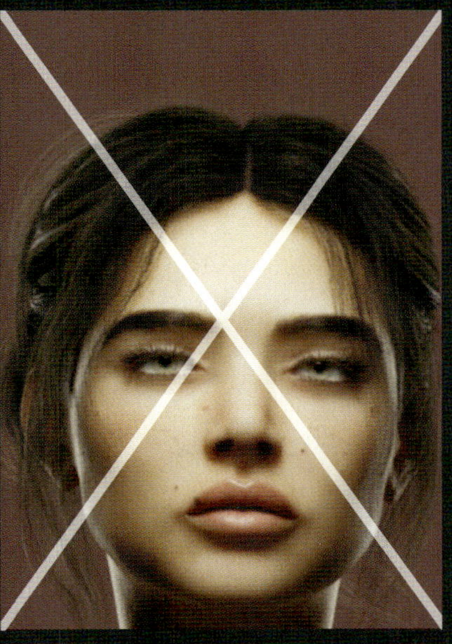

NECK

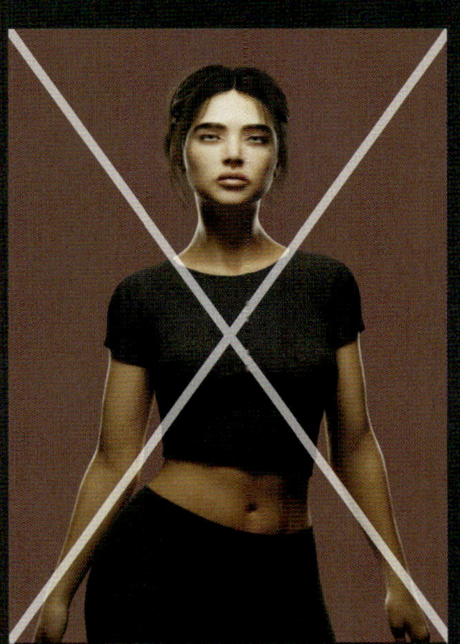

FINGERS

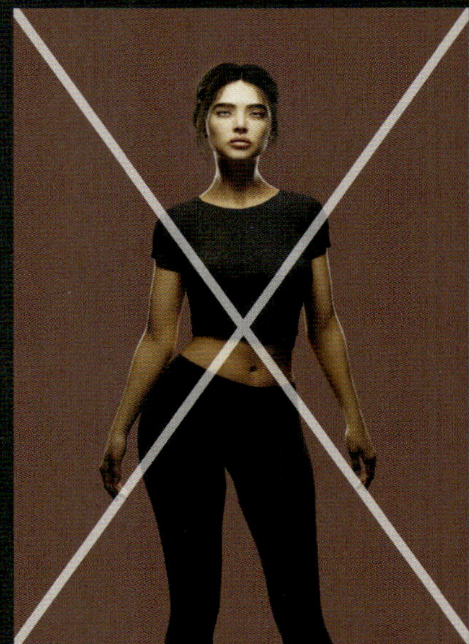

KNEES

COMPOSITION

The composition of your painting can leave a lasting impression on your viewers. Although portraits are often centered (which is pleasing to the eye), an asymmetrically positioned subject could elevate your painting, making it feel more intriguing and dynamic. This is especially true when working with multiple, correlated subjects.

GOLDEN RATIO & THE RULE OF THIRDS

To assess the harmony in your compositions, try applying the rule of thirds and the golden ratio. A branch of the latter, called the golden spiral, can be found all throughout nature, from seashells to sunflowers, and even fingerprints. It's also present in famous artworks and architecture, such as *The Great Wave* by Katsushika Hokusai and the Parthenon in Greece.

The golden ratio, also known as the golden section and often denoted by the Greek letter ϕ (phi), is a ratio approximately equal to 1:1.618. This ratio is intricately linked to the Fibonacci sequence, from which we can derive another way to divide an image: the phi grid.

The rule of thirds is a similar grid that will help you to develop good composition in your artwork. It's a simplified version of the golden ratio, which makes it easier to calculate and use. For this method, you simply divide both the width and the length of your image into thirds to create nine equal parts.

If you incorporate one of these rules into your work, you'll achieve an organic, dynamic, and aesthetically pleasing composition. Of course, it's not absolutely necessary to use these rules, but they can be very helpful when you're unsure how to start.

THE GOLDEN RATIO

The image on the right is an example of the golden ratio deciding the image composition. There are many different ways to align your character along the spiral, and you can find plenty of great examples online if you search for "The golden ratio composition."

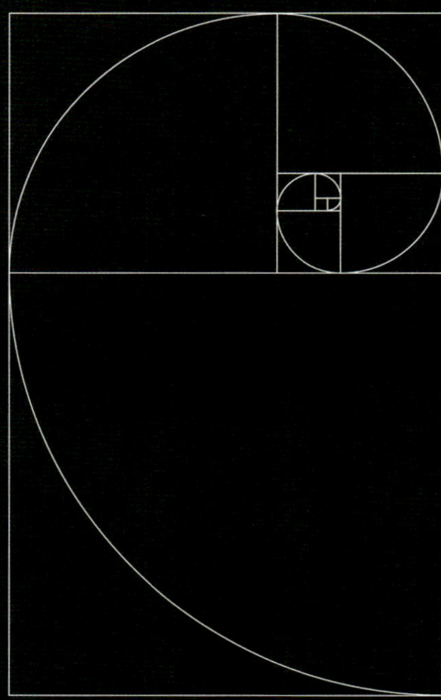

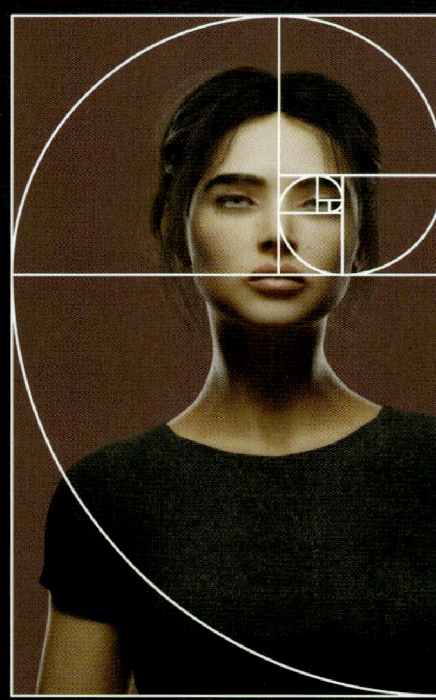

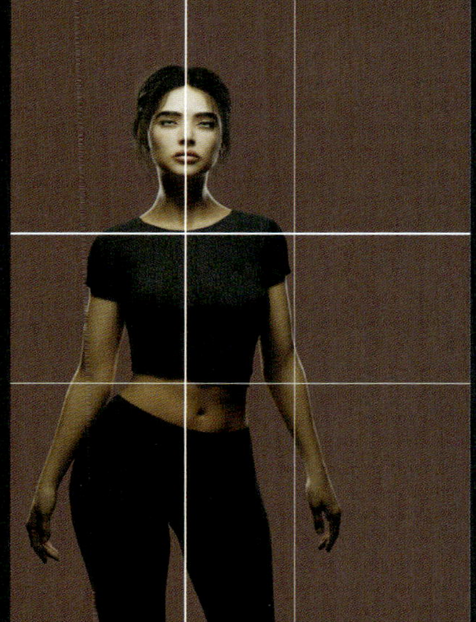

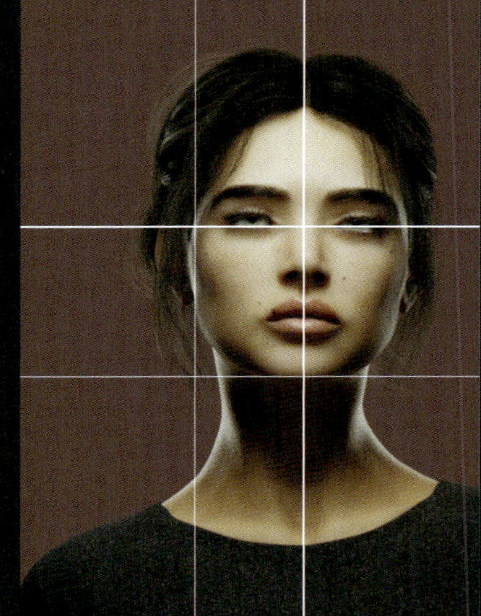

THE PHI GRID

(based on the golden ratio)
This grid consists of a 1:1.618 ratio. You can align your character (and/or their scale) along one or more of the resulting intersections, lines, or sections.

CREATIVE CROPPING

(based on the phi grid)
Of course, it's possible to find some more abstract and creative ways to compose your image.

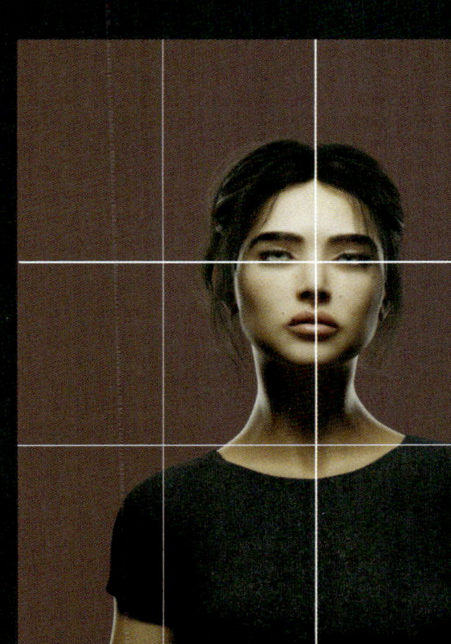

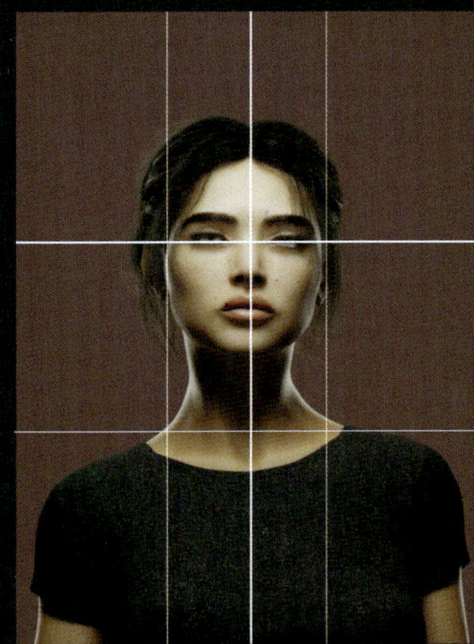

THE RULE OF THIRDS

The image is divided into thirds along both axes. Now the character (and/or their scale) can be aligned along one or more of the resulting intersections, lines, or sections.

THE RULE OF THIRDS + SYMMETRY

The rule of thirds can be combined with symmetry. In this example, the character is aligned with an axis, while she's centered horizontally.

POSING

We've arrived at the fun part! Your character's pose is extremely important and a great indicator of their personality. While anything you imagine can be realized in art, below is a small overview of aesthetic poses that I often use in my paintings.

Firstly, my personal rule of thumb: I like to position my character's eyes slightly above the viewer's eye level. This makes the character seem like she's looking down on the viewer, providing her a sense of strength and authority.

I also pay extreme attention to my character's shoulders. To signal confidence, I always make sure they're slightly drawn back, making her posture straight and self-assured. Since my characters usually have fragile expressions, the juxtaposition of posture and perspective is very important. My aim is for them to appear vulnerable while radiating strength.

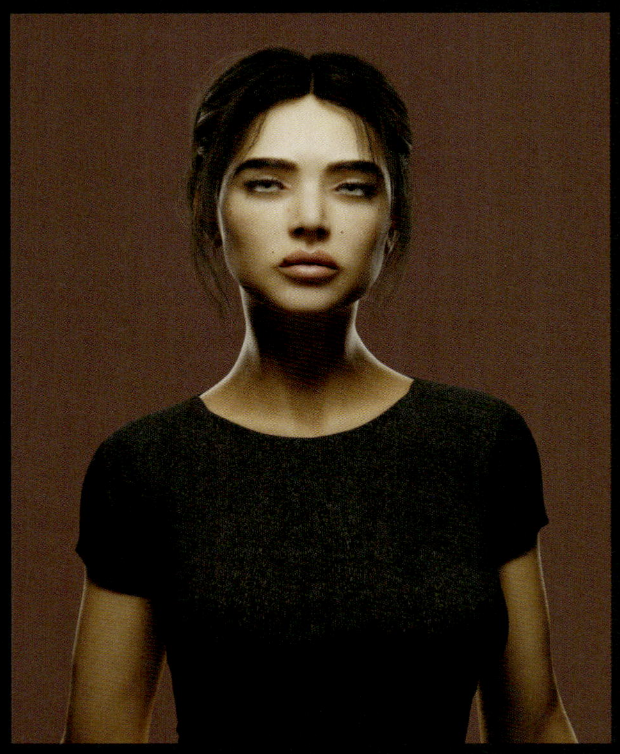

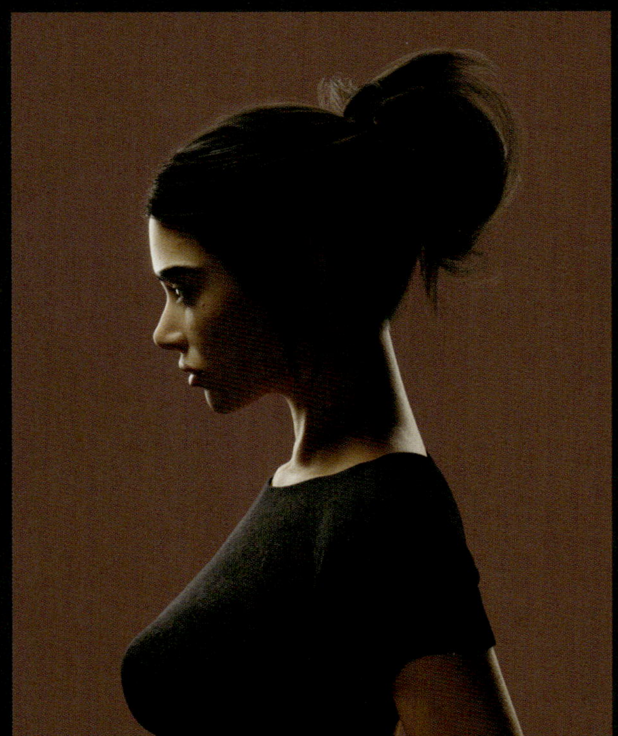

FRONTAL

This forward-facing view is the most frequently used pose for portraiture because it creates an excellent stage for the face. Notice the shoulders aren't perfectly symmetrical; this prevents the pose from looking too stiff, and, in turn, makes it appear more dynamic.

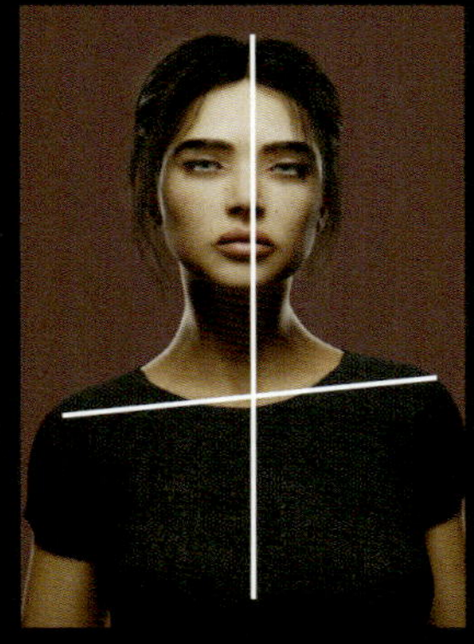

PROFILE

A profile pose can be very elegant and aesthetic. Notice how the diagonal line stretching from her chin to her hair is almost parallel to the line extending from her collarbone to her chest.

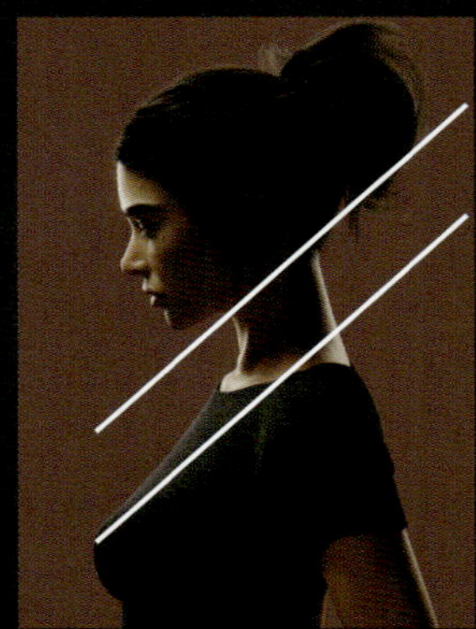

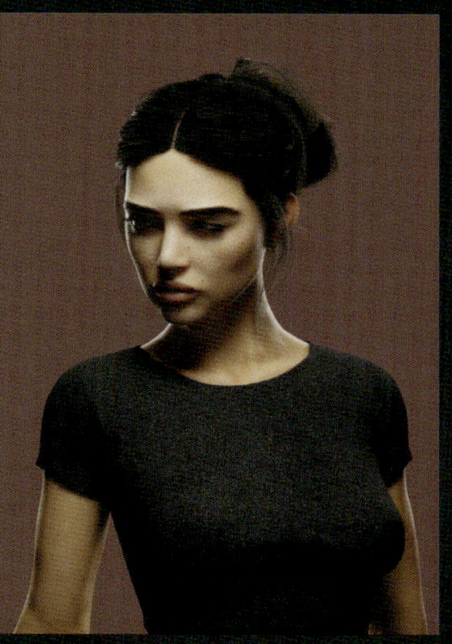

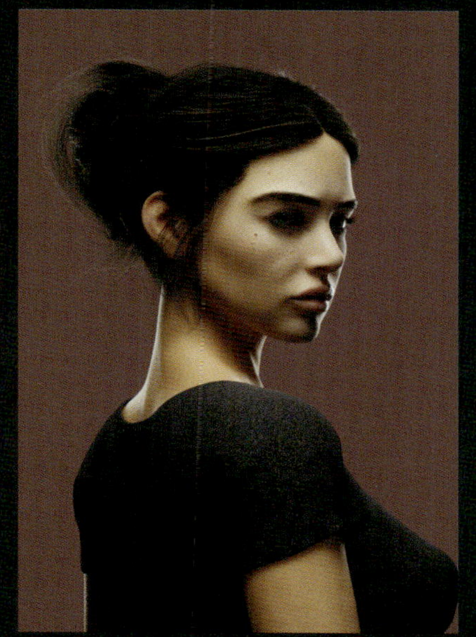

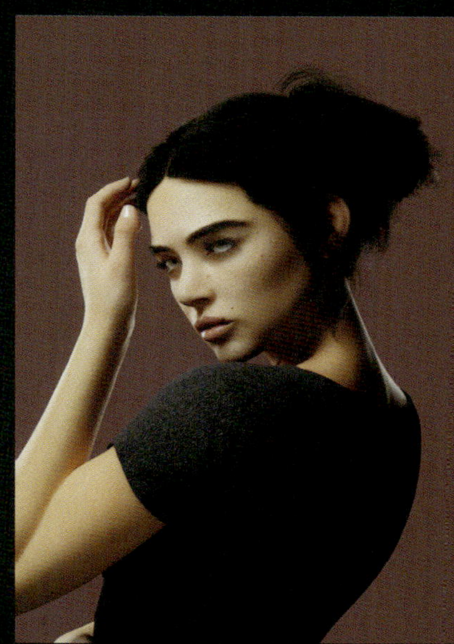

FRONTAL WITH 3/4 VIEW OF FACE

Although this pose is similar to the frontal pose, a face leaning away from the viewer may add some tension and mystery.

OVER THE SHOULDER

This pose is frequently used in movie posters, as the shoulder posture makes the subject appear confident and strong. Since she's not facing the viewer directly, it also adds a sense of mystery.

DYNAMIC

The bent back in this pose may seem unnatural, but it's also fresh and modern, which makes it fit in well with recent posing trends. This is also a good reminder that hands and their posture can add a lot to an image.

LIGHT & SHADOW

Light and shadow are extremely important when considering the mood of a piece. For example: a character standing in the light with a shadowed face could represent internal conflict.

PAST OR FUTURE

Body angles are also an effective way to convey a character's mood. If the subject is facing right, it may mean they're looking toward the future, while if they're looking left, it could mean they're reminiscing. If the character's body is facing right, but their gaze is directed left, it could indicate a preoccupation with the past. These rules of thumb are especially important in film and animation.

PHOTOGRAPHIC LIGHTING PATTERNS

Understanding the effects of lighting is imperative for portrait painting. In this section you'll find an overview of the most commonly used lighting setups for portrait photography.

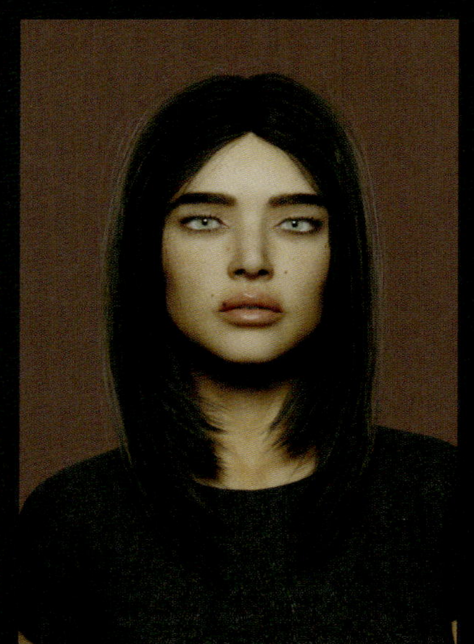

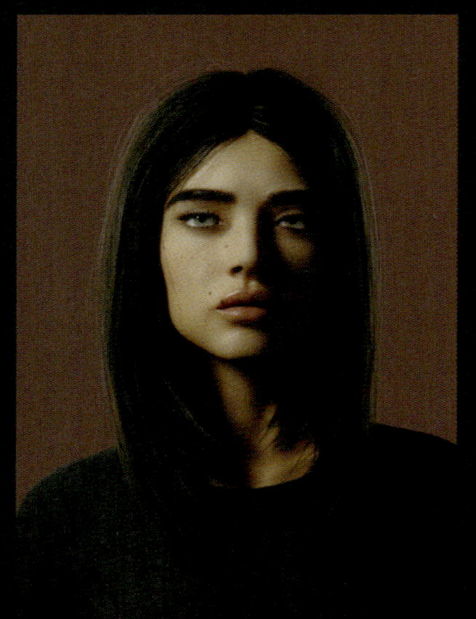

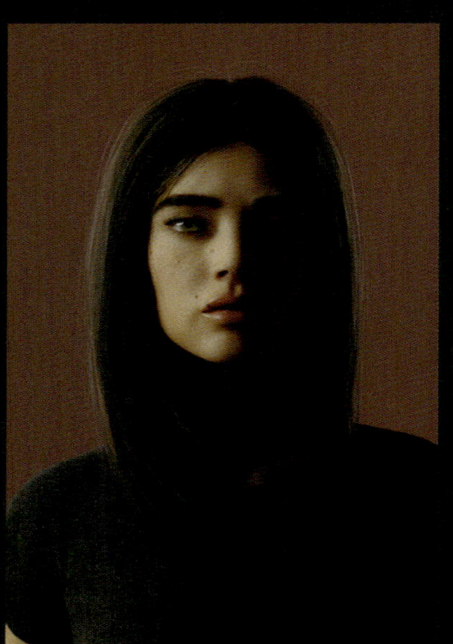

FLAT LIGHTING

Flat lighting eliminates any shadows on your subject's face. This is a type of beauty lighting; the lack of shadows can smooth skin tone and hide imperfections like under-eye bags and blemishes. Many artists use this lighting in their work because it's easy to master and difficult to make mistakes. I use it frequently because placing shadows on the face is something I find difficult. But, I also think it's a little boring compared to other lighting setups.

REMBRANDT LIGHTING

This is an example of compelling portrait lighting. Famous Dutch artist Rembrandt van Rijn often used the shadows cast by the nose and the cheek to create a triangle of light on the subject's face.

SPLIT LIGHTING

Although similar to Rembrandt's technique, split lighting divides the face into two equal halves instead of focusing on the character's cheek.

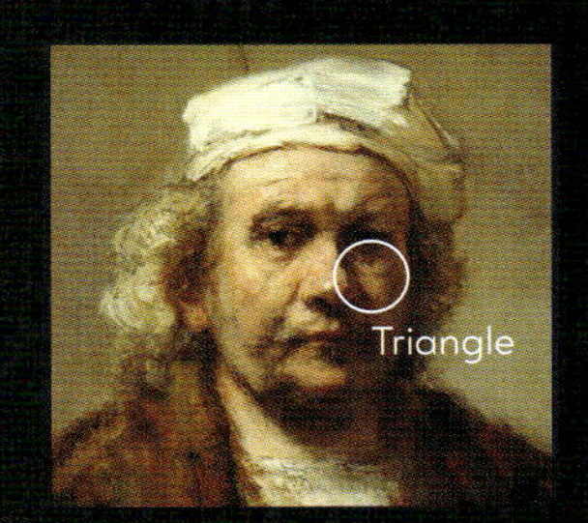

WHO WAS REMBRANDT?

Known simply by his first name, Rembrandt van Rijn is a well-known Dutch Baroque painter and considered one of the greatest visual artists in history.

Rembrandt, *Self-Portrait with Two Circles*, Detail (c. 1665-1669)

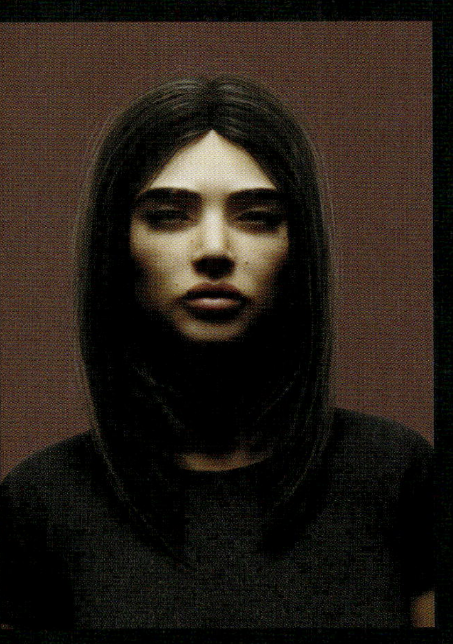

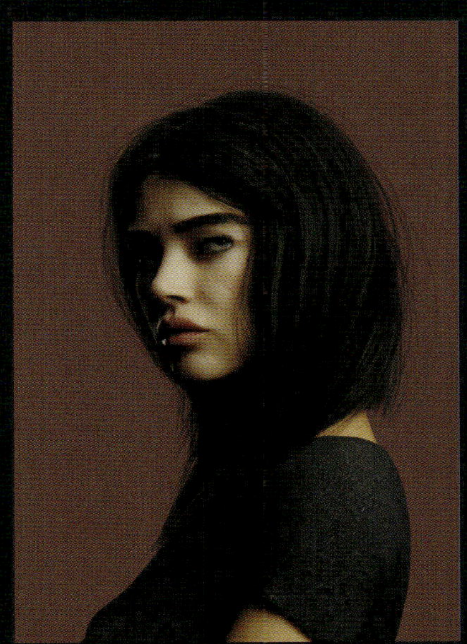

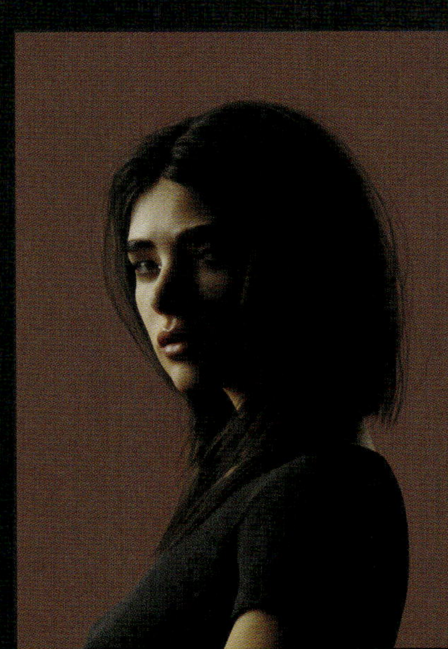

BUTTERFLY LIGHTING

This dramatic use of light emphasizes the cheekbones, resulting in an epic, high-contrast look. Using a slightly downward angle, a strong key light is placed directly in front of the subject to illuminate them evenly, resulting in a butterfly-like shadow beneath the nose. This setup is also referred to as Paramount lighting, which originated in Hollywood glamour shots in the 1920s.

BROAD LIGHTING

This technique is used to brighten the areas of the face that are in direct line of the camera. This makes the face appear wider.

SHORT LIGHTING

Short lighting is essentially the opposite of broad lighting. Here, the side of the face turned away from the viewer is illuminated, whereas the closer side remains shadowed, making the face appear thinner. This is the hardest setup for me to realize, but I think it contains the highest emotional impact.

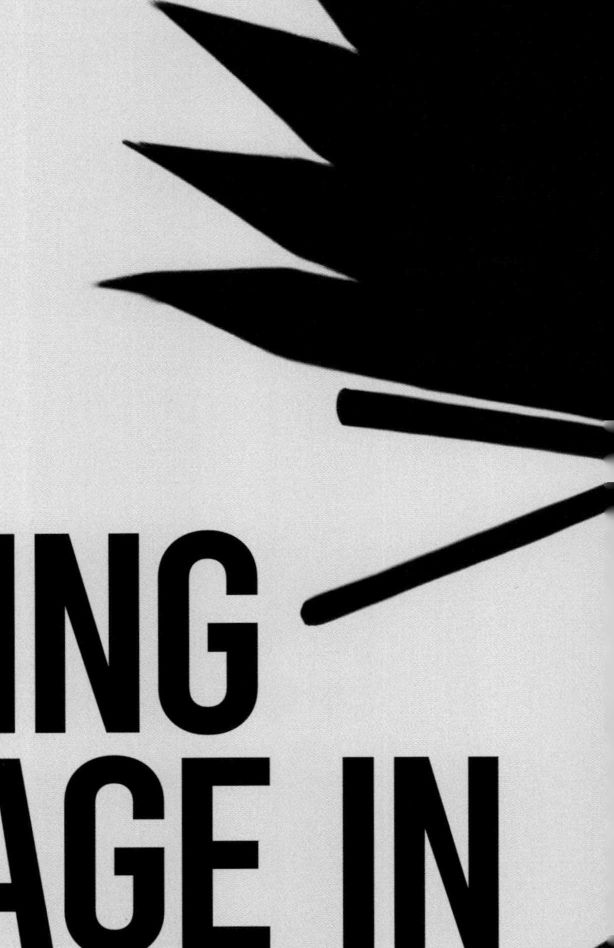

CREATING AN IMAGE IN PROCREATE

"CREATIVITY IS INTELLIGENCE HAVING FUN"

– Albert Einstein

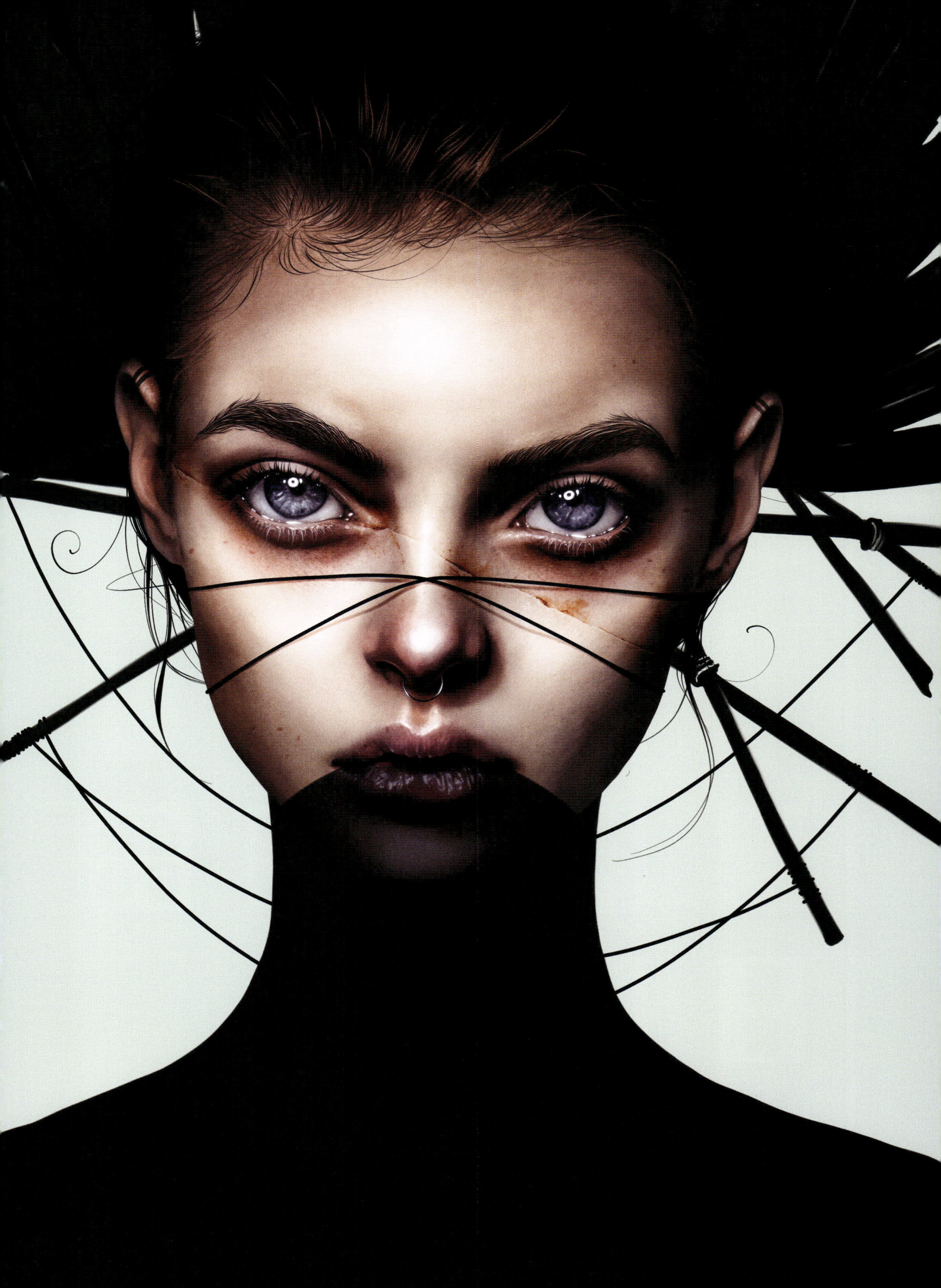

GETTING STARTED

PROCREATE GALLERY

To prepare, I'll guide you through the basics in Procreate, including an overview of the user interface, how to create a new canvas, and how to navigate the gallery.

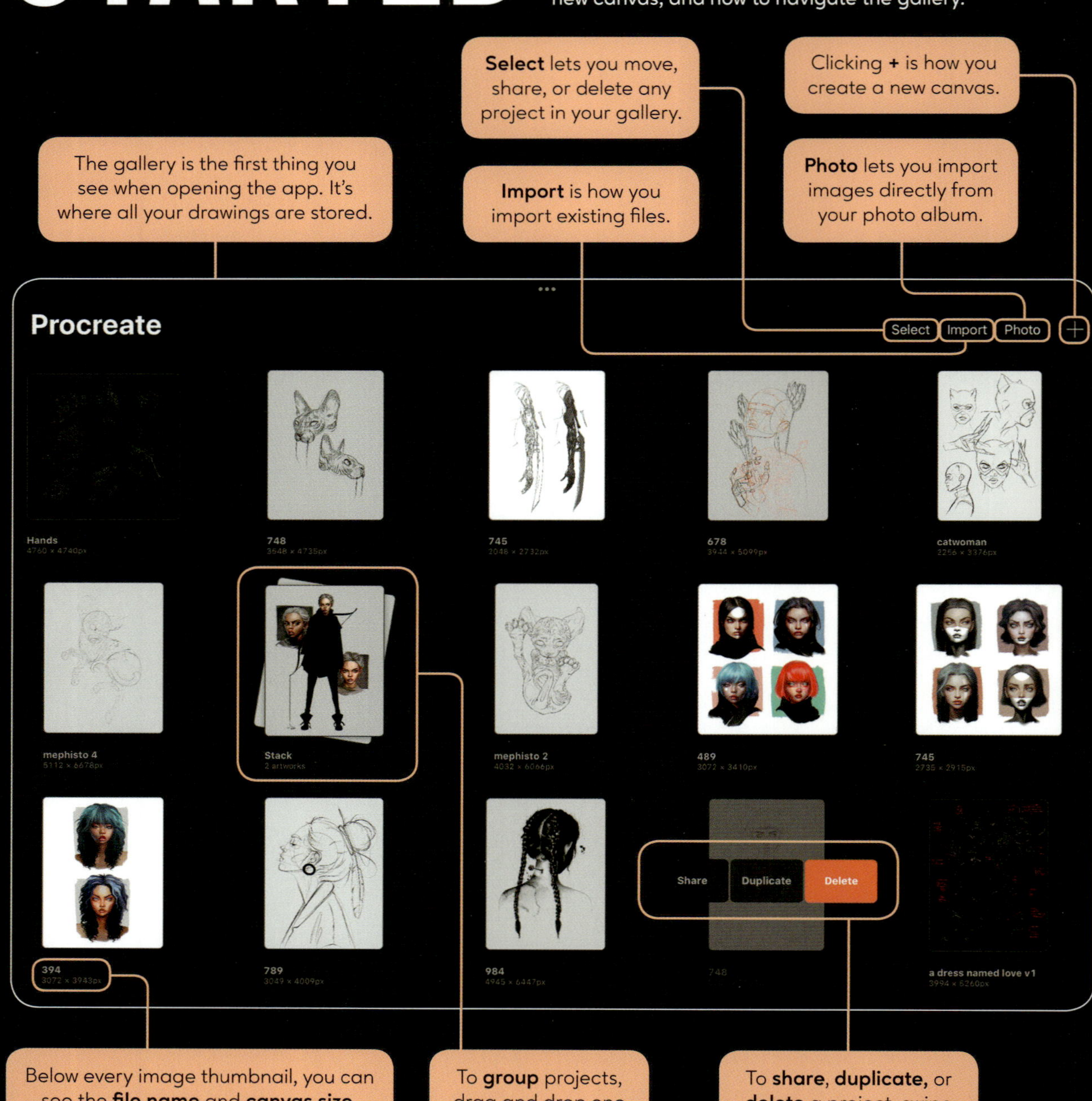

Below every image thumbnail, you can see the **file name** and **canvas size**.

To rename a file, just tap on the existing file name.

To **group** projects, drag and drop one on top of the other.

To **share**, **duplicate**, or **delete** a project, swipe left on a thumbnail.

STEP1

CREATE A NEW CANVAS

Now that we're familiar with the gallery, let's make a new canvas. Tap on the + icon in the top right corner to get started. Instead of choosing a preset dimension, we'll create a new one by tapping on the rectangular symbol to the right of **New Canvas**.

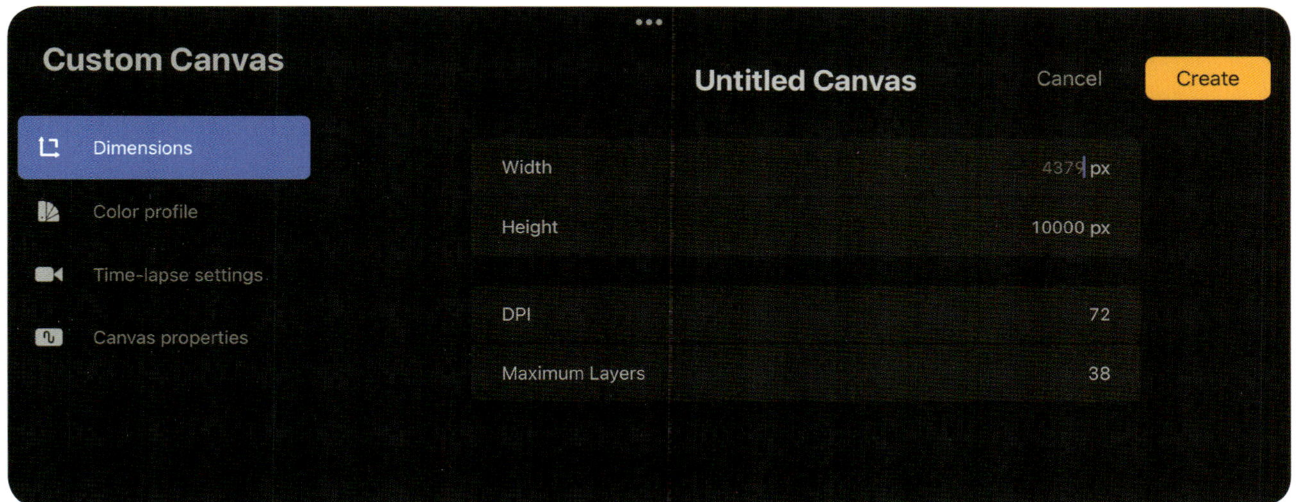

DIMENSIONS

Tap on **Untitled Canvas** to rename your project, then set your new dimensions by clicking on the **Width** and **Height** options below. I tend to use 3000 pixels for sketches and anywhere between 5000 pixels and 12,000 pixels for realistic portraits designed for print.

RULE OF THUMB FOR CANVAS SIZE

Never go smaller than 3000 pixels. Aim for around 4000×5200 pixels to allow at least 20 layers.

I know what you're thinking: why don't we just start with 12,000 pixels? It's because the higher the pixel count, the fewer the layers.

The Maximum Layers count will change proportionally as you modify the canvas size, with newer iPad models allowing for more. To start, it's best to work with a size that provides at least 20 layers.

Dots per inch (dpi) has nothing to do with the level of detail in your work. In fact, it only really matters for printing. For example, a 3000×3000 pixel canvas at 300dpi would print at 10×10 inches, while a 3000×3000 pixel canvas at 100dpi would print at 30×30 inches. Though the 30×30-inch print has the same degree of precision, it would appear blurrier up close when distributed over a larger space. In short, if you don't want to print your project, use 72dpi. If you do, then use 300dpi. All the other numbers are irrelevant when you're just starting out.

Don't panic if you accidentally try to print a 72dpi painting – the printers will usually inform you.

RULE OF THUMB FOR DPI SETTINGS

Use 72dpi for digital use and 300dpi for a project designed for print.

It's also possible to change the dpi settings when creating print data, but it only works if your canvas is a decent size. Find more information about preparing your artwork for print at the end of the tutorial.

COLOR SPACE & PROFILE

Next up: picking a color profile. You'll have a choice between several **RGB** and **CMYK** profiles.

The RGB (Red, Green, Blue) spectrum is an additive color space that all screens can display. The CMYK (Cyan, Magenta, Yellow, Black) spectrum is a subtractive color space that simulates analog/printed colors. We use the former when planning to keep artwork digital, and CMYK when looking to print. The main visual difference is that RGB provides the entire color spectrum, including colors that don't exist in a subtractive color space (think neon colors, which require light to achieve intensity). CMYK has a smaller color range, and emulates how colors are shown in print: less saturated and bright.

I always work in RGB color spaces because my artwork is shown both digitally and in print. When submitting projects for print, I change the color space to CMYK.

RULE OF THUMB FOR RGB/CMYK

Start working in an RGB color space, and only change over to CMYK when you submit your work for printing.

If I started with CMYK, I wouldn't be able to share it online because some internet browsers display CMYK incorrectly.

When you've chosen your color space, it's time to select your color profile. I always use Display P3 – the color profile recommended by Procreate – as the other available options are device/printer specific. If you decide on the CMYK color space, I recommend the Generic CMYK Profile.

TIME-LAPSE SETTINGS & CANVAS PROPERTIES

As these settings don't relate to the canvas itself, feel free to disregard. You can always change them later.

Tap on **Create** in the top right corner, and your new canvas is ready!

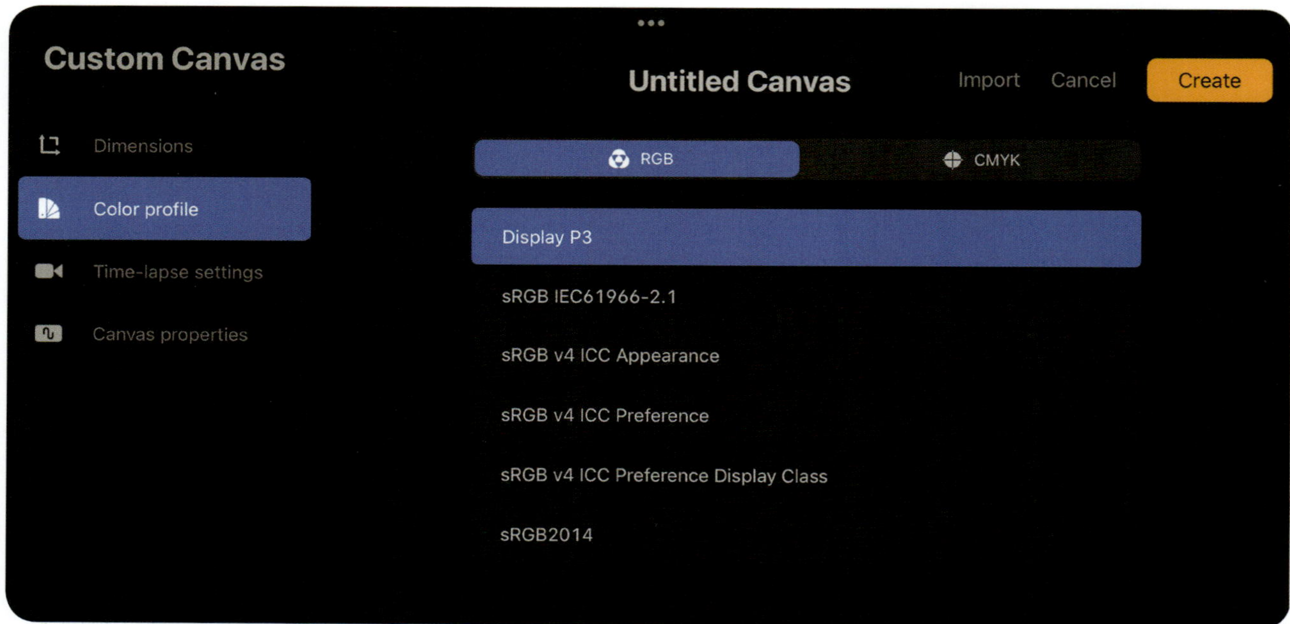

PROCREATE INTERFACE

Once you've created a new file, you'll start out with a blank canvas. Below is an overview of your new workspace:

The Procreate interface is fairly simple to understand and navigate. Before you dive in headfirst, take some time to explore and familiarize yourself with the buttons – you'll get the hang of it quickly! **Procreate also saves your work automatically,** so you can close your project and come back to it anytime without fear of losing progress.

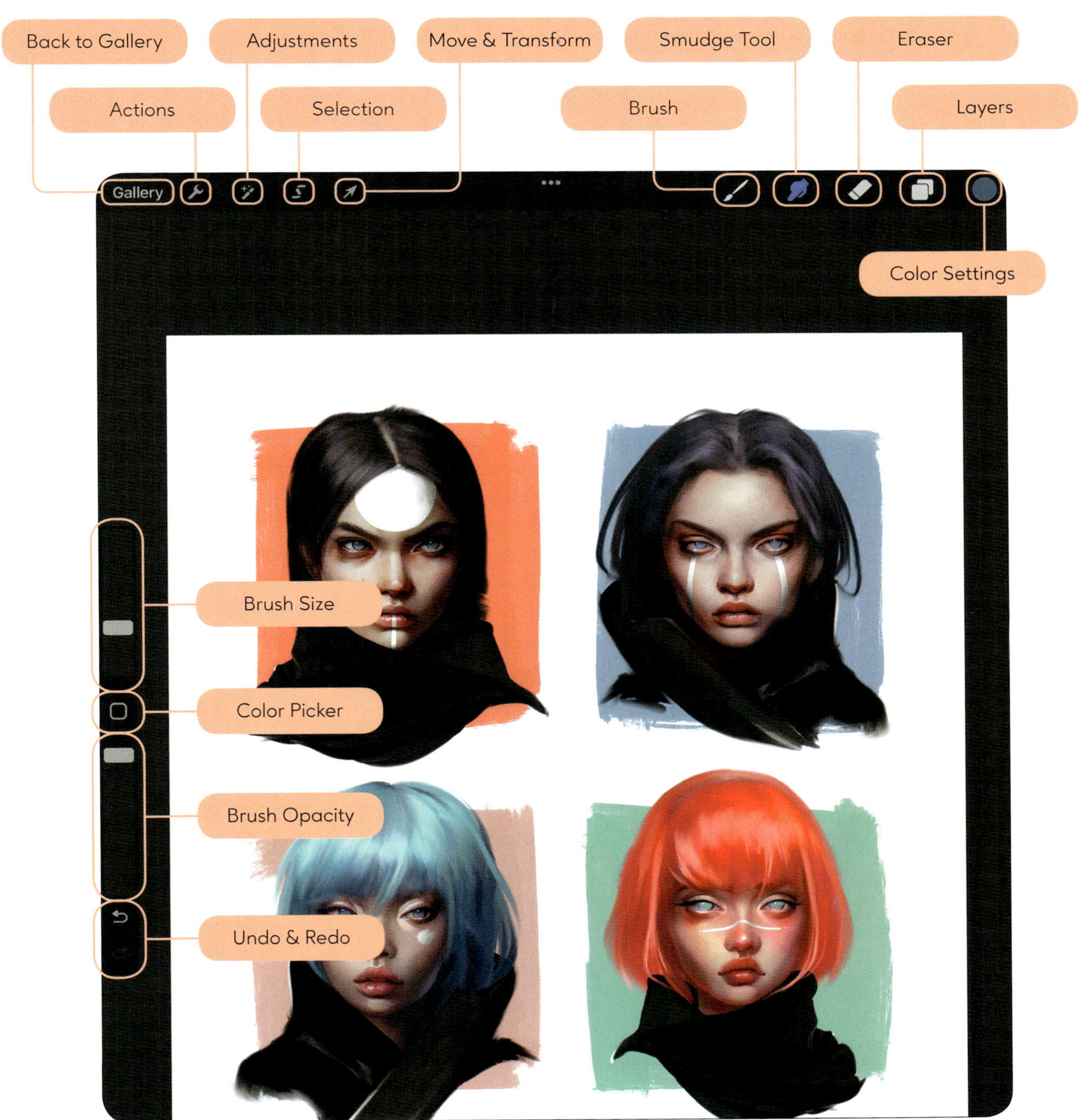

STEP2

FIND INSPIRATION & CREATE A MOOD BOARD

Before we start sketching, we need to know what to draw! Let's find some inspiration to help us get started. When I don't know where to begin, I collect images of people or objects that I find interesting, then arrange them on a mood board.

You can even create a mood board directly in Procreate. To do so, download all the images you'd like to add (keeping color schemes in mind) and import them into the app using the wrench icon. Then, under **Actions**, select the **Add** button, followed by **Insert a photo**. Once the image has been uploaded onto your canvas, move and resize it to your liking.

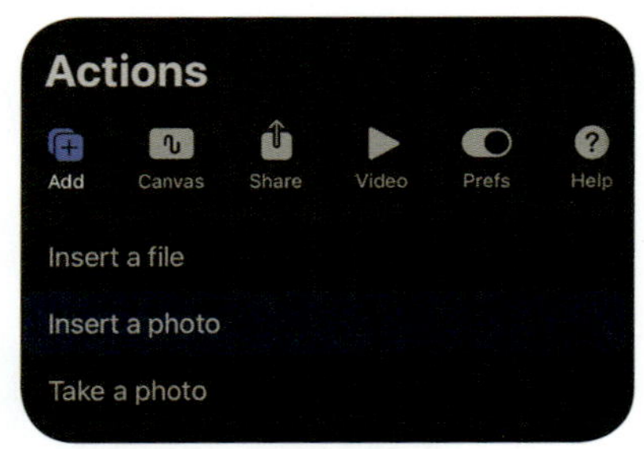

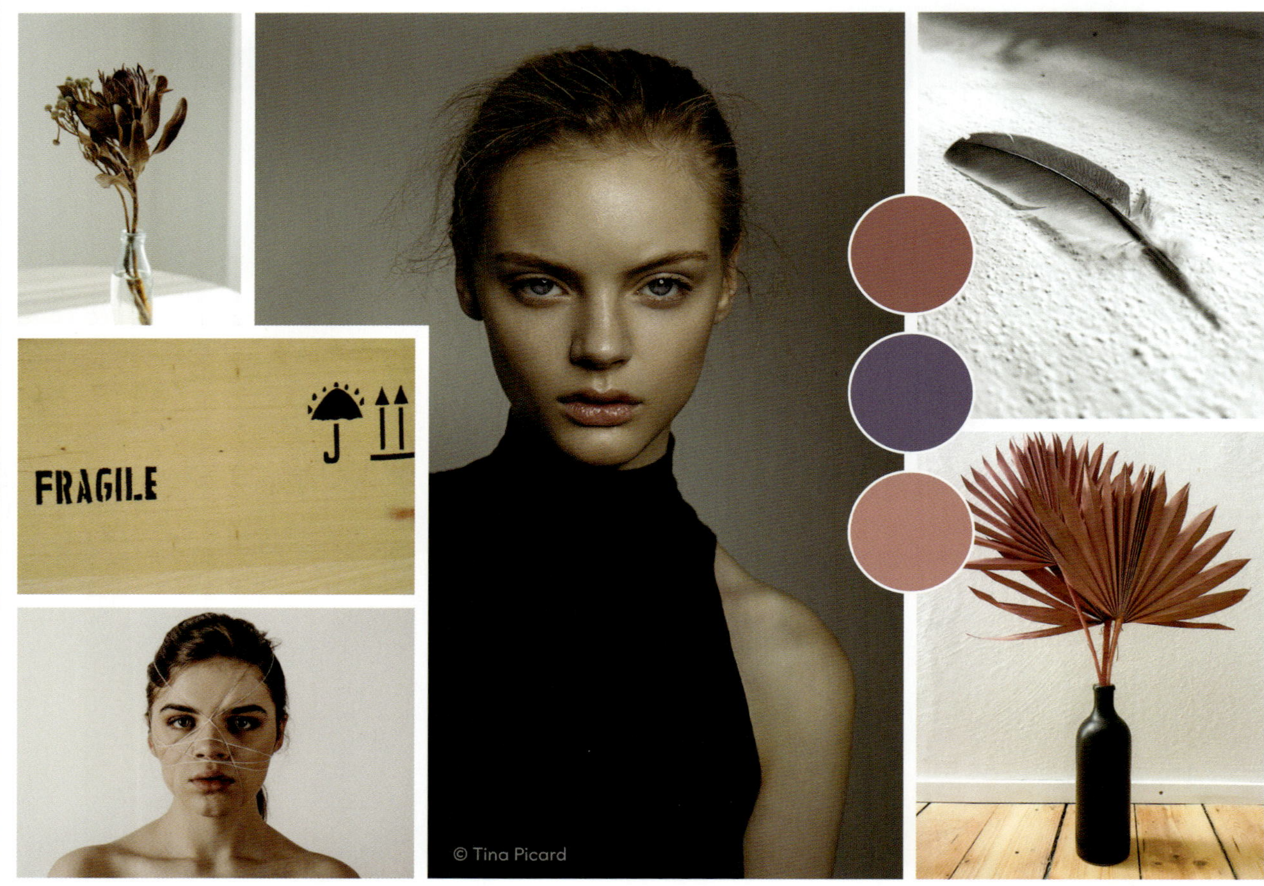

© Tina Picard

STEP3

REFERENCE IMAGES

Good luck trying to create realistic portraits without references! While it's certainly possible, you might end up drafting characters who look too similar. That's why I recommend sourcing legal reference images.

A COPYING AN IMAGE 1:1

There's no issue copying an image directly, but you must have permission from the copyright holder to sell your version. Without their consent, it's illegal. However, most people don't mind, if you credit them accordingly, so do yourself a favor and ask the copyright holder for permission or risk forfeiting your future sales.

B DRAW FROM IMAGINATION OR USE YOURSELF AS A REFERENCE

From a legal standpoint, drawing from the imagination is the easiest option. Creatively? It's the hardest. Very few artists can design realistic, detailed portraits out of thin air. To avoid any legal complications that may come with using reference photos, try taking a photo of yourself and using it for your drafting!

C PURCHASING RIGHTS TO YOUR REFERENCE IMAGE

Another option is to buy the image rights. For instance, you could contact a photographer to ask about licensing fees, or you could peruse stock websites that display their pricing outright. The main disadvantage is that licenses can be very expensive, and stock websites don't always have the types of images you want.

HERE IS A SHORT LIST OF WELL-KNOWN STOCK ARCHIVES:

Paid: Shutterstock | Adobe Stock | 123RF
Free: Pixabay | Unsplash | Pexels

D CREATING A NEW SUBJECT FROM SEVERAL REFERENCE IMAGES

Why not channel your inner Frankenstein and create your own model! You'll be pleased to learn that it's legal to use parts of faces for character inspiration. However, I'd err on the side of caution as boundaries are blurred when it comes to deciding how much of a copyrighted image is used. Your reference image should not be recognizable in your final image.

FOR THIS TUTORIAL, LET'S GO WITH OPTION NUMBER FOUR AS IT CAN BE INTIMIDATING TO PULL FROM VARIOUS SOURCES. I CAN'T WAIT TO GET STARTED!

THE MODEL

For this tutorial, I chose one of my absolute favorite models, shot by the incredibly talented Tina Picard. I love everything about this image: the pose, composition, light, expression… everything! I'm beyond thrilled that Tina gave me permission to use her work as a reference in my tutorial.

By no coincidence, I've used many of Tina's photos as references in the past. I'd often browse online and save images I liked, only realizing later they belonged to her. I just love the authentic way in which she captures the models.

If you have a favorite photographer, it's absolutely worth trying to get in contact with them. They might be open to a collaboration!

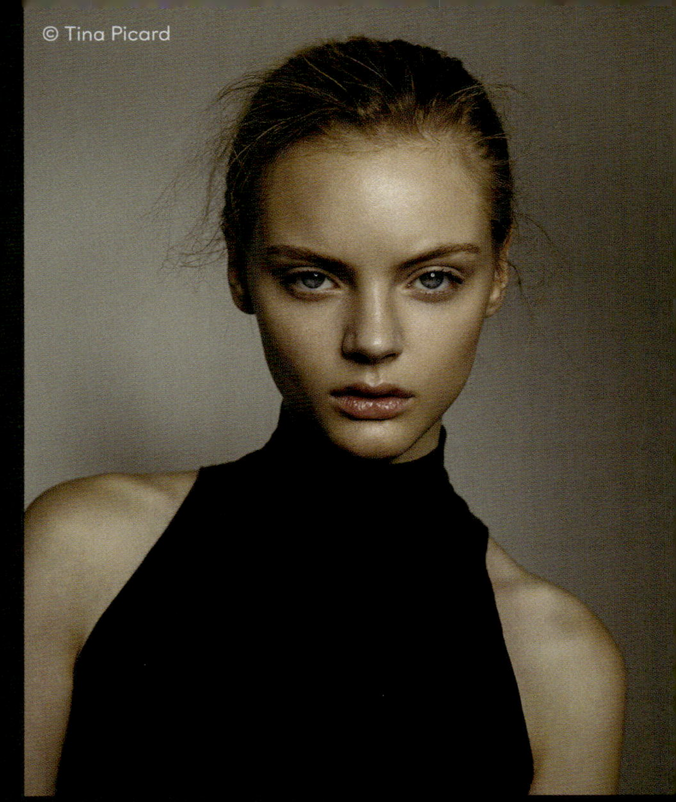

INTRODUCING TINA PICARD:

"Tina's passion for art and photography translates in her work as she captures clean and simple, yet strong, vibrant, and dynamic images. With over 10 years of experience as a portrait, fashion, and beauty photographer, and as a creative director, she has created a remarkable body of work that reflects each niche. Her uniqueness and ability to compose diverse images allow her to capture and direct the perspective of the viewers. Tina's talents spread internationally as she is now established in Toronto, Montreal, and New York City."

tinapicard.com | @tinapicardphoto

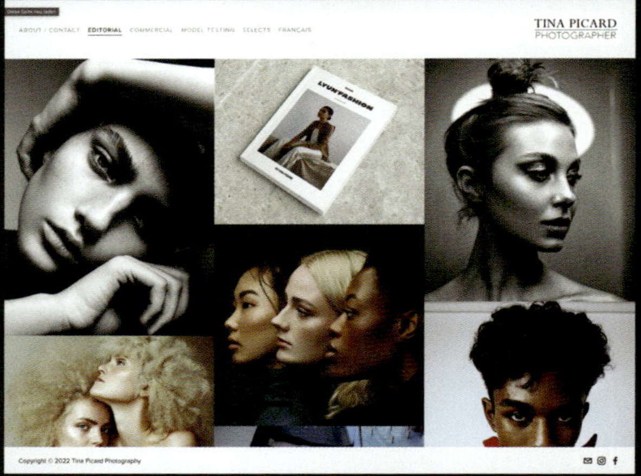

COMPOSE REFERENCE

As we chose option D earlier, we'll only be taking parts of the image instead of copying the whole thing directly. I'll be using Procreate to cobble our reference images together.

I'm working with three different images: Tina's photo, a photo of myself, and a 3D model I created using the app ArtPose to give my character a new, more unrealistic body.

I love the cowlick in her hair, but I'd prefer it to be on the left side.

I increase the eye size, elongate the neck, and narrow the shoulders. This new uncanny look should capture the viewer's attention; her frame doesn't look natural but it's still aesthetically pleasing.

Later in the tutorial, I'll redraw her eyes so they look a little bigger and further apart.

I've taken her nose and eyebrows from my own reference image. The nose angle isn't quite right, but that will be an easy fix when I start painting.

I lower the corners of her mouth a little more.

To create her upper body, I use the 3D model and position it symmetrically.

YOU SHOULD REALLY ONLY USE ONE PART OF THE FACE PER REFERENCE IMAGE. TO MAKE THE TUTORIAL UNCOMPLICATED, I MADE AN EXCEPTION HERE.

PICTURE-IN-PICTURE REFERENCE

I take a screenshot of my little collage and re-import it as a reference by opening the **Actions** menu, followed by **Canvas**, before sliding the **Reference** button on. Feel free to move your reference as you draw, adjusting the size and zoom as you see fit.

If you still need some practice drawing realistic facial proportions, you can use your reference image as a stencil and trace over it on a new layer. I prefer not to stencil because drawing freehand makes it easier to adjust the proportions as I go.

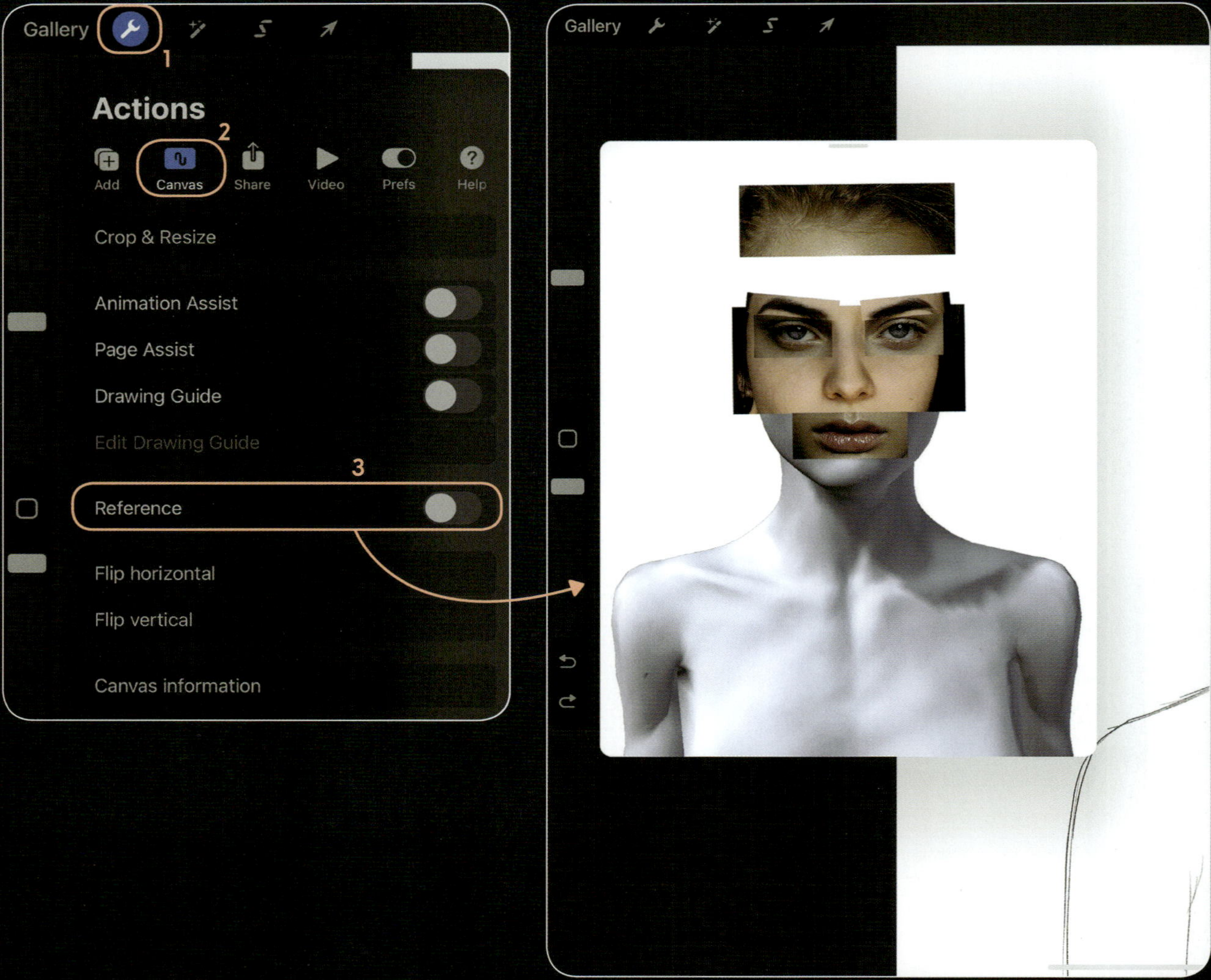

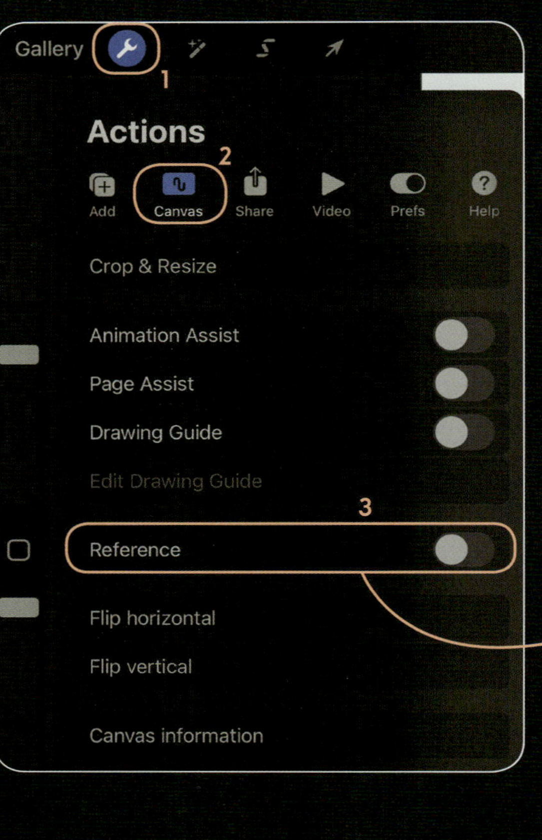

Gallery

STEP4

CREATING THE SKETCH

For the basic head grid, use the Loomis head construction method. Here's a quick example from a ¾ perspective:

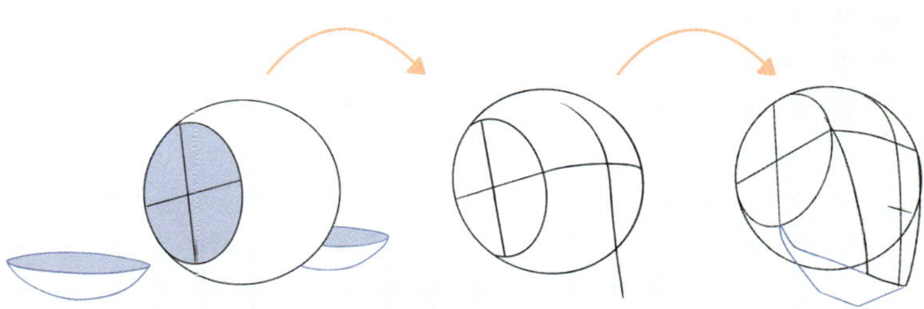

4.1 BASIC HEAD GRID

For the basic grid, only sketch the head and upper body, and leave her facial features for later. The parallel lines shown will help you place her eyes, nose, and mouth. Copy line layouts straight from the reference image.

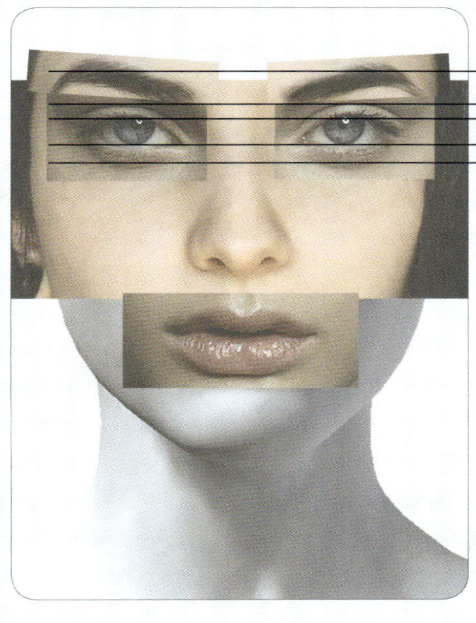

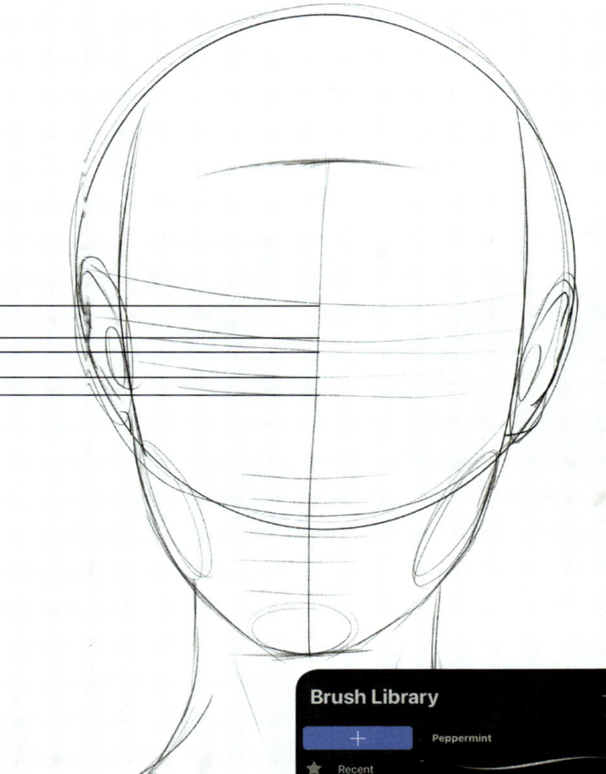

BRUSHES

For sketching, you can use brush presets like the **HB Pencil** from Procreate's **Sketching** category. To help develop your character throughout this tutorial, I recommend using brushes specifically made for realistic portraits. They'll save you a lot of work!

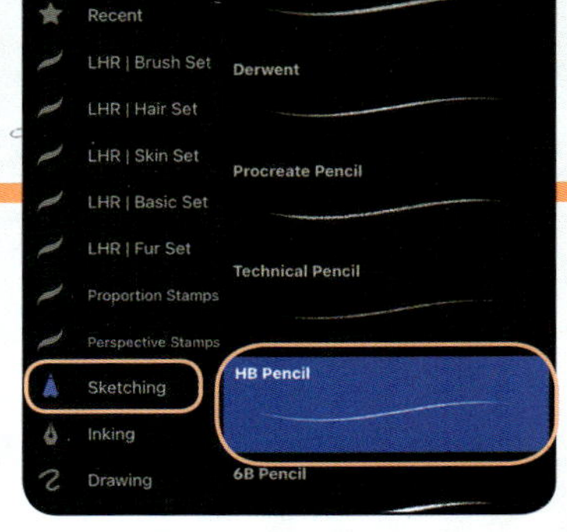

4.2 BASIC FACE GRID

Here, you will only draft very simple shapes to mark the eyes, nose, and mouth.

First, create a new layer. This way, if you mess up while drawing, you can easily erase mistakes without disturbing the rest of the sketch.

Generate a new layer by tapping the **+** button in your layer menu. I recommend renaming the layer to better organize your file.

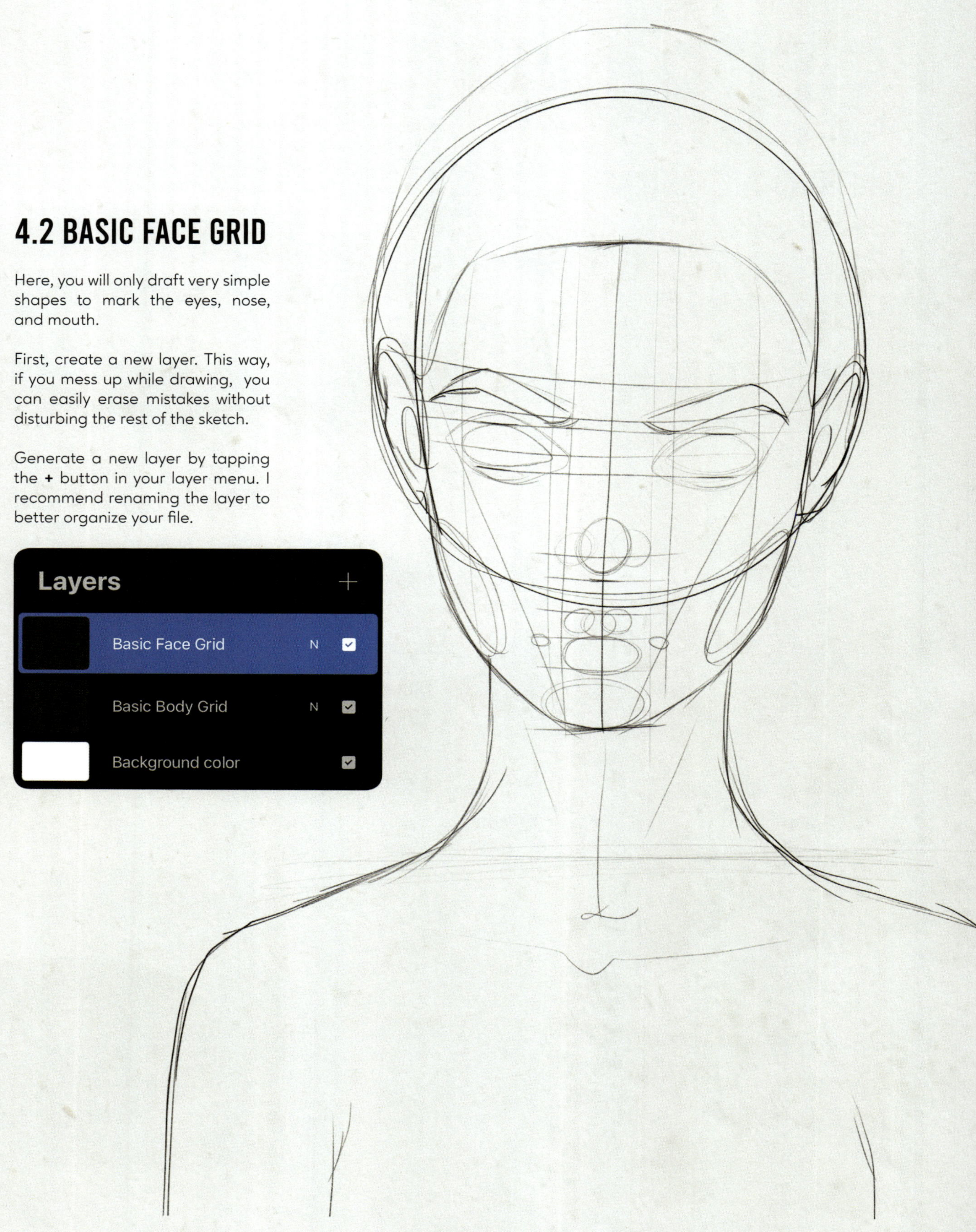

4.3 CLEAN FACE OUTLINES

It's time to draw the outlines of the eyes, nose, and mouth. You're also indicating the placement of the ears and hair, so I suggest creating a new layer. You can even sketch with a different color to avoid any confusion.

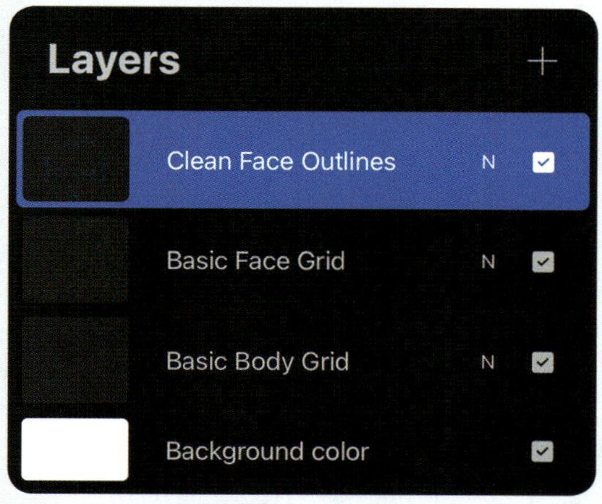

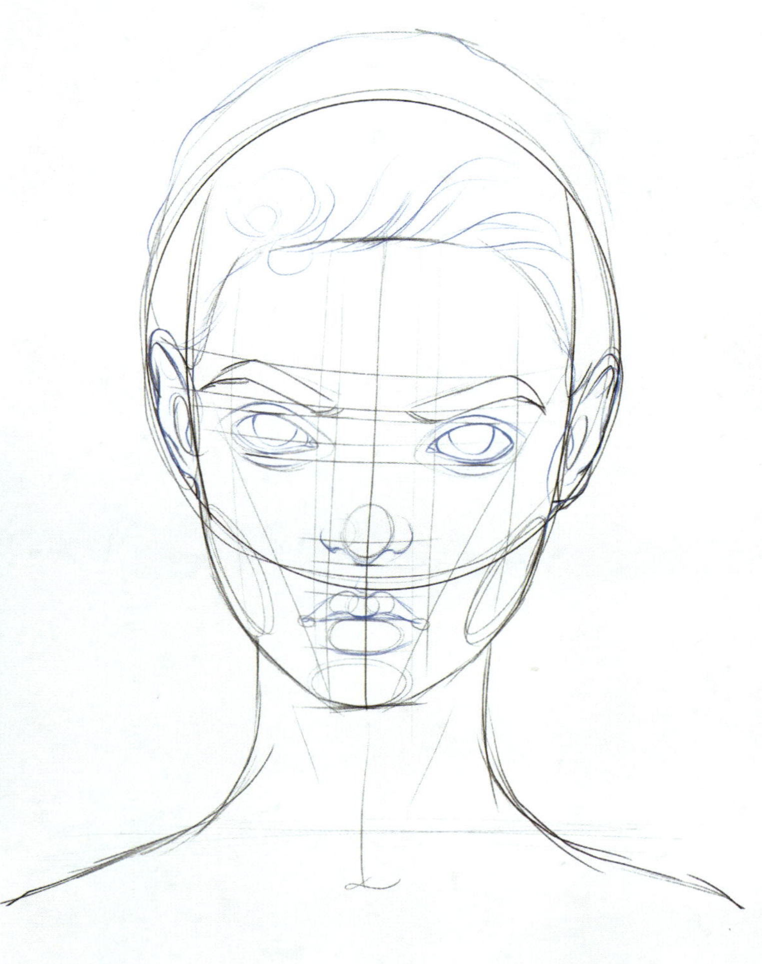

4.4 SHADOW AREAS

On a new layer, use red to mark the areas that will be shadowed. You could use hatching to show the exact shadow placements, but it's better not to crowd your sketch with too many lines. At this stage, the simpler, the better.

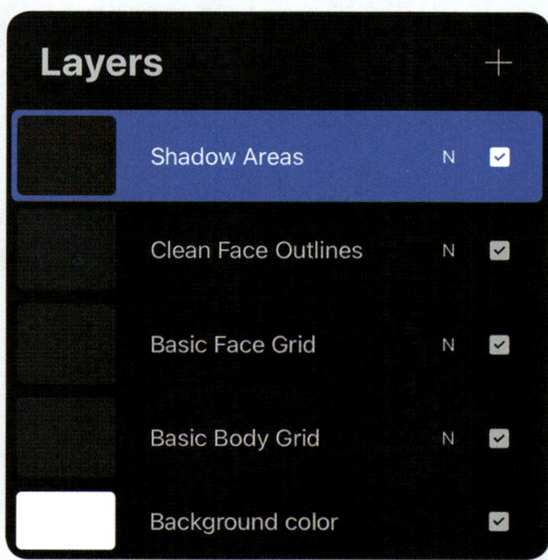

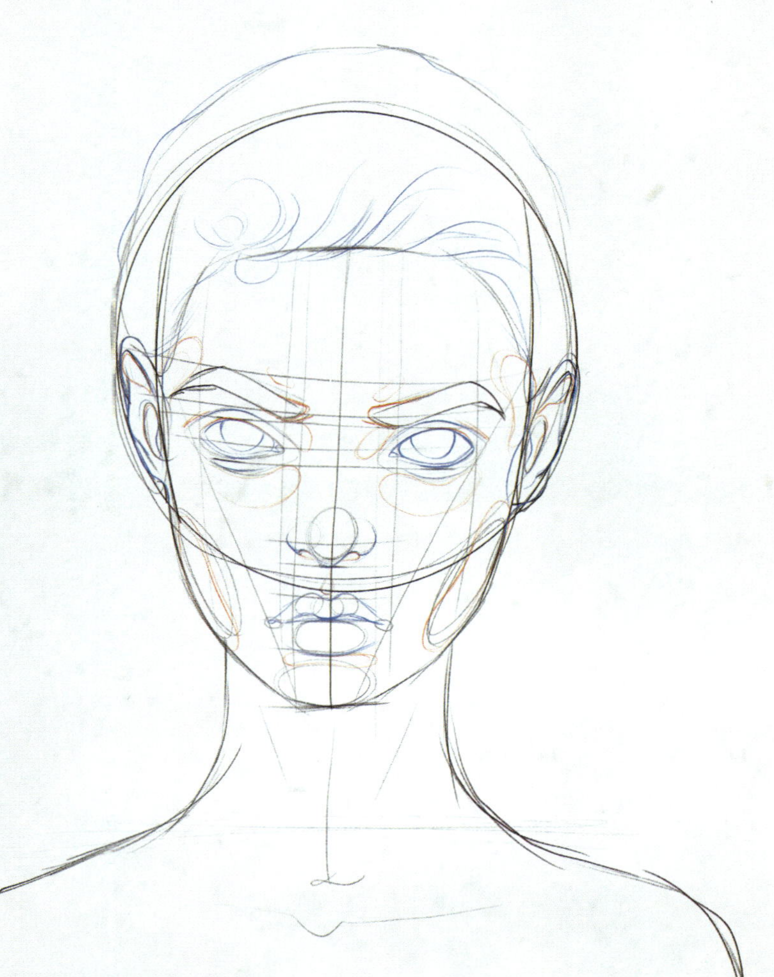

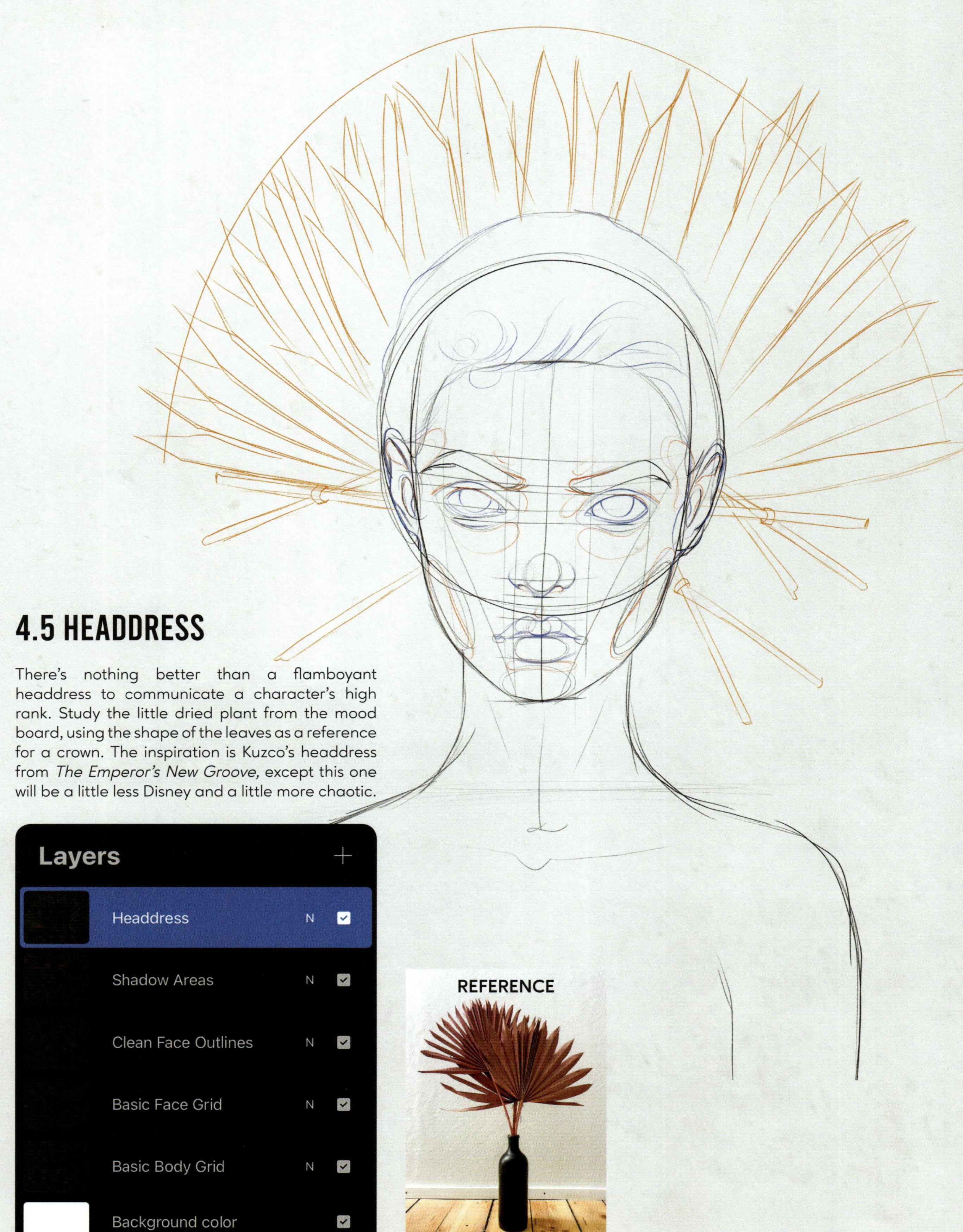

4.5 HEADDRESS

There's nothing better than a flamboyant headdress to communicate a character's high rank. Study the little dried plant from the mood board, using the shape of the leaves as a reference for a crown. The inspiration is Kuzco's headdress from *The Emperor's New Groove,* except this one will be a little less Disney and a little more chaotic.

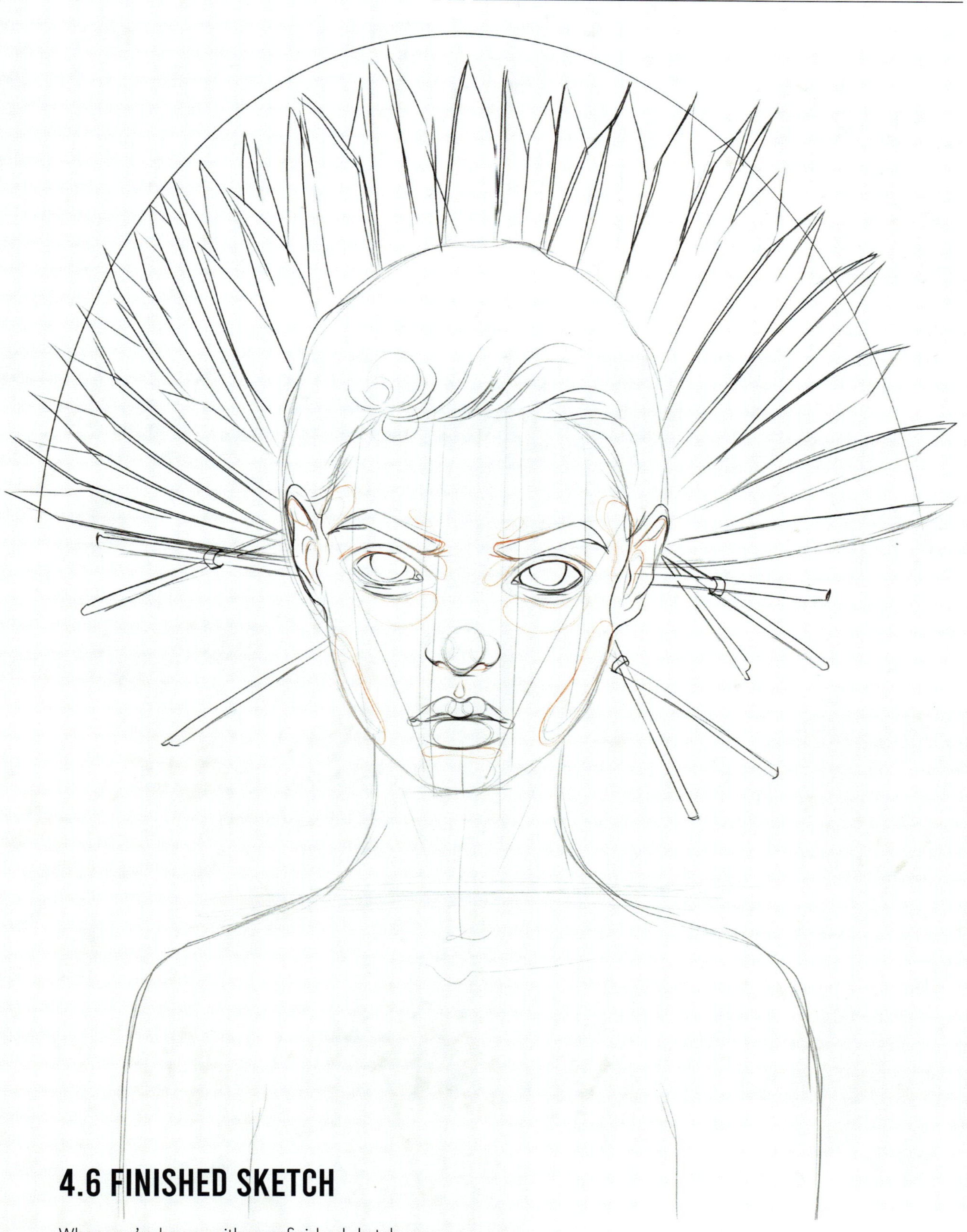

4.6 FINISHED SKETCH

When you're happy with your finished sketch, you can merge some of the layers together to free up some room – either tap twice on the top layer and select **Merge Down**, or pinch the layers together using your fingers. You can also erase some of your construction lines to clean up the sketch.

LAYERS & MASKS

As you no doubt noticed, I use a lot of layers to form a sketch. But why are layers so important? And what are layer masks?

LAYERS

Think of layers as new, transparent canvases that sit above your original canvas. They are like chockstones that climbers use as a safety measure to quickly arrest a life-threatening mishap.

MASKS

If you use the erase tool on a layer, whatever you remove is gone forever. Layer masks are a non-destructive alternative – they are able to render parts of a layer invisible. Since nothing has been erased, it's easily reversible. You can apply a mask to any layer.

Layers are listed in order from bottom to top. When you create a new layer, it's placed on top of the stack. Read the diagram from the bottom up, starting at number one.

4 **LAYER MASK**
A mask can be applied to any layer, making parts of it invisible.

3 **NEW LAYER**
If you're experimenting and unsure whether you want to keep any changes, create a new layer. If you end up erasing it, you'll only lose progress on that layer instead of the whole image.

LAYER EFFECTS
Effects can also be applied to any layer. They are very versatile and can produce useful results, such as adding a glow or applying colors to the existing layers below.

2 **CANVAS**
The second layer is your canvas. You always start with two layers in Procreate.

1 **BACKGROUND COLOR**
The first layer is always the background color of your project.

If you're learning about all this for the first time, it may feel a bit confusing. But don't worry! It will all make sense later. We're just covering all of our bases before we continue with the tutorial.

BRUSHES

Unlike traditional artists, you have the advantage of having access to thousands of brushes at any given time. There's a large variety of default Procreate brushes that come with the app, but if you aren't satisfied with those, there are endless options available to download online. If you want to get a little fancy, you can even create your own brushes in Procreate!

CREATE YOUR OWN BRUSHES

The Procreate **Brush Studio** allows you to adjust brushes to your liking, or even create new brushes from scratch. To edit a brush, open the **Brush Library** and tap twice on the one you want to edit. To design a new one, open the brush library and tap the **+** button.

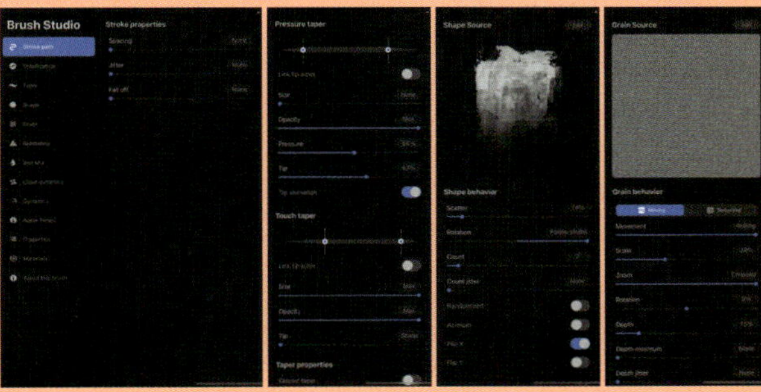

Procreate has tutorials available online that explain all the various brush settings. However, I'll explain one that everyone needs sooner or later: **Brush Stabilization.**

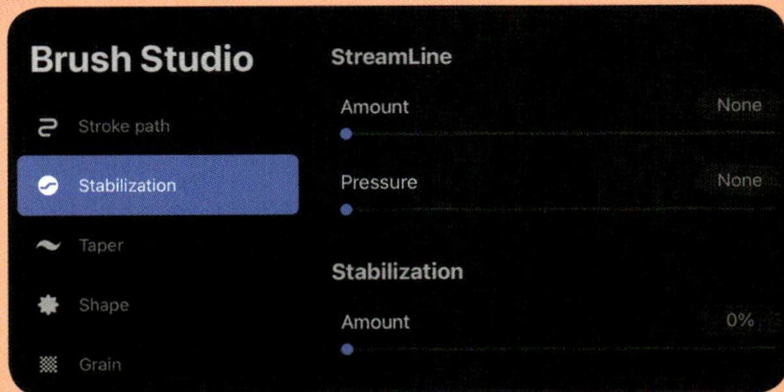

Just as it sounds, this setting serves to eliminate jitter as you draw. Here's an example:

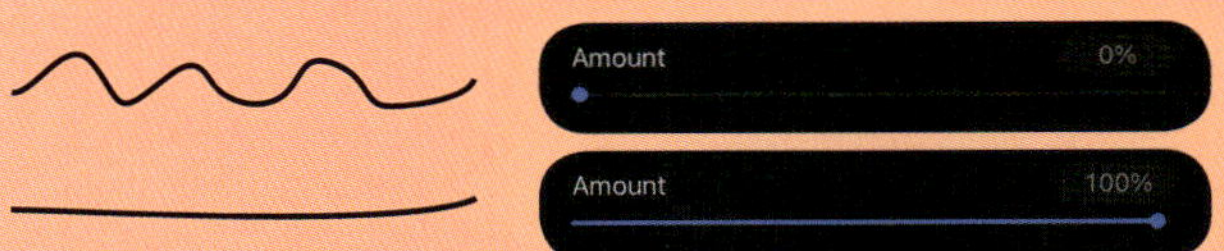

MY BRUSHES

A few years ago, I noticed the brushes I'd downloaded online weren't really optimized for my workflow, so I decided to create my own set.

Every brush foundation consists of the **Shape Source** and the **Grain Source**:

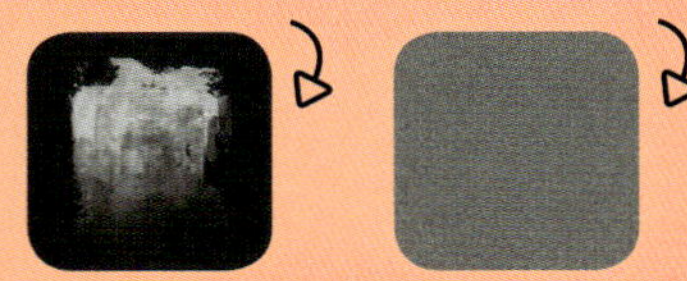

That means I needed a lot of photos containing different textures. Over many months, I learned everything there was to know about skin types and the textures of wood, sand, and stone.

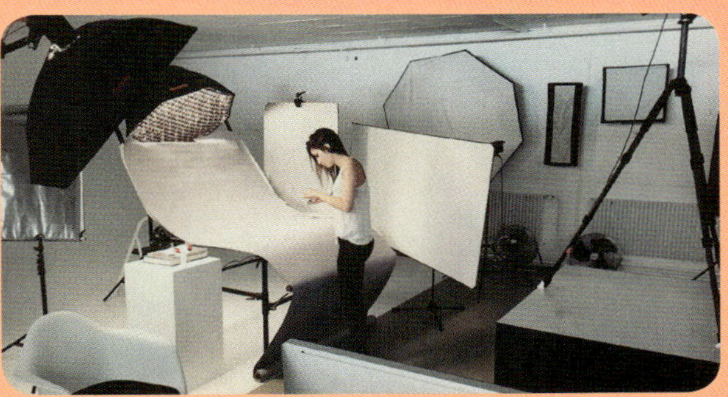

I used these photos to create hyperrealistic hair and skin brushes. Three years and 9000 pictures later, my personal brush collection is now in the hundreds, and 102 of them are featured in my favorite brush set. They are my secret weapon, which I will use throughout the tutorial.

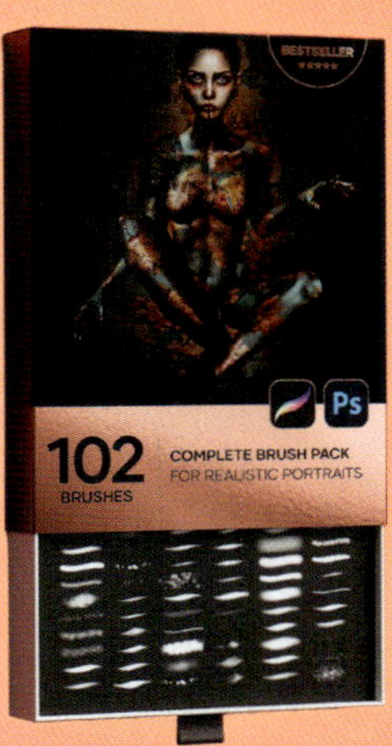

STEP5

CREATING A COLOR PALETTE

Before we begin coloring our sketch, we need to create a color palette. This important guide will encourage you to use more than just beiges and browns.

5.1 To start, I look for a reference image that has pleasant colors. For now, everything else is irrelevant.

5.2 Next up, I import the image into Procreate and adjust the contrast and saturation to achieve a more vibrant color palette.

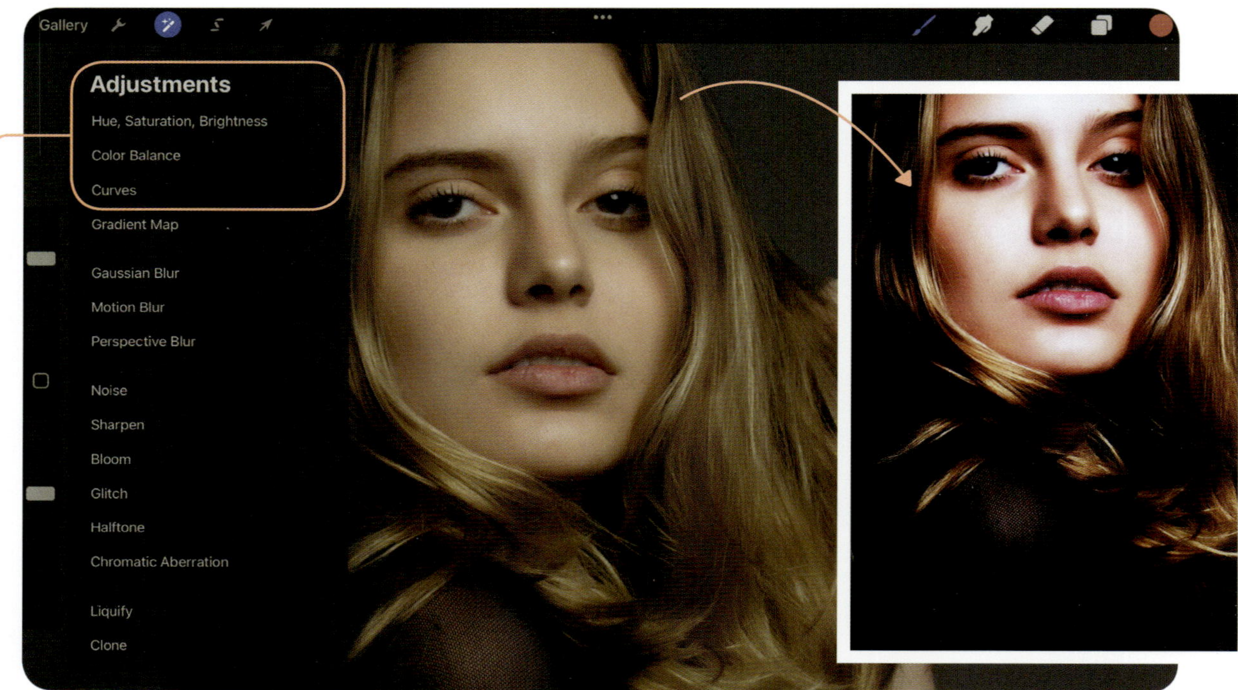

With the **Hue, Saturation, Brightness, Color Balance,** and **Curves** settings, you can make the necessary edits. Each setting has sliders you can mess with until you're happy with the result. Try not to focus on the content of the image; we're only interested in the colors.

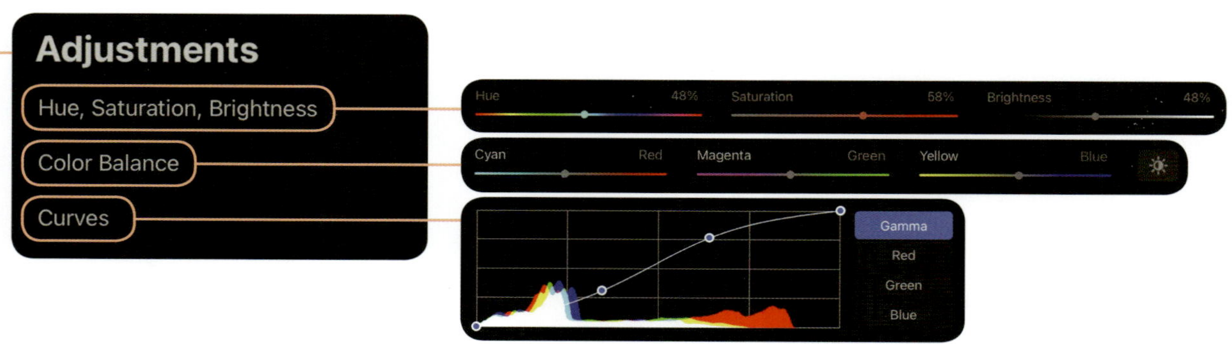

5.3 Either take a screenshot of the image, or export it as a JPG. However, the latter usually takes up more space and time.

5.4 Tap **Color Selector** in the top right corner, then **Palettes** in the bottom right. Here, you can find a collection of your saved color palettes. Tap on the **+** in the top right, and then on **New from photos**.

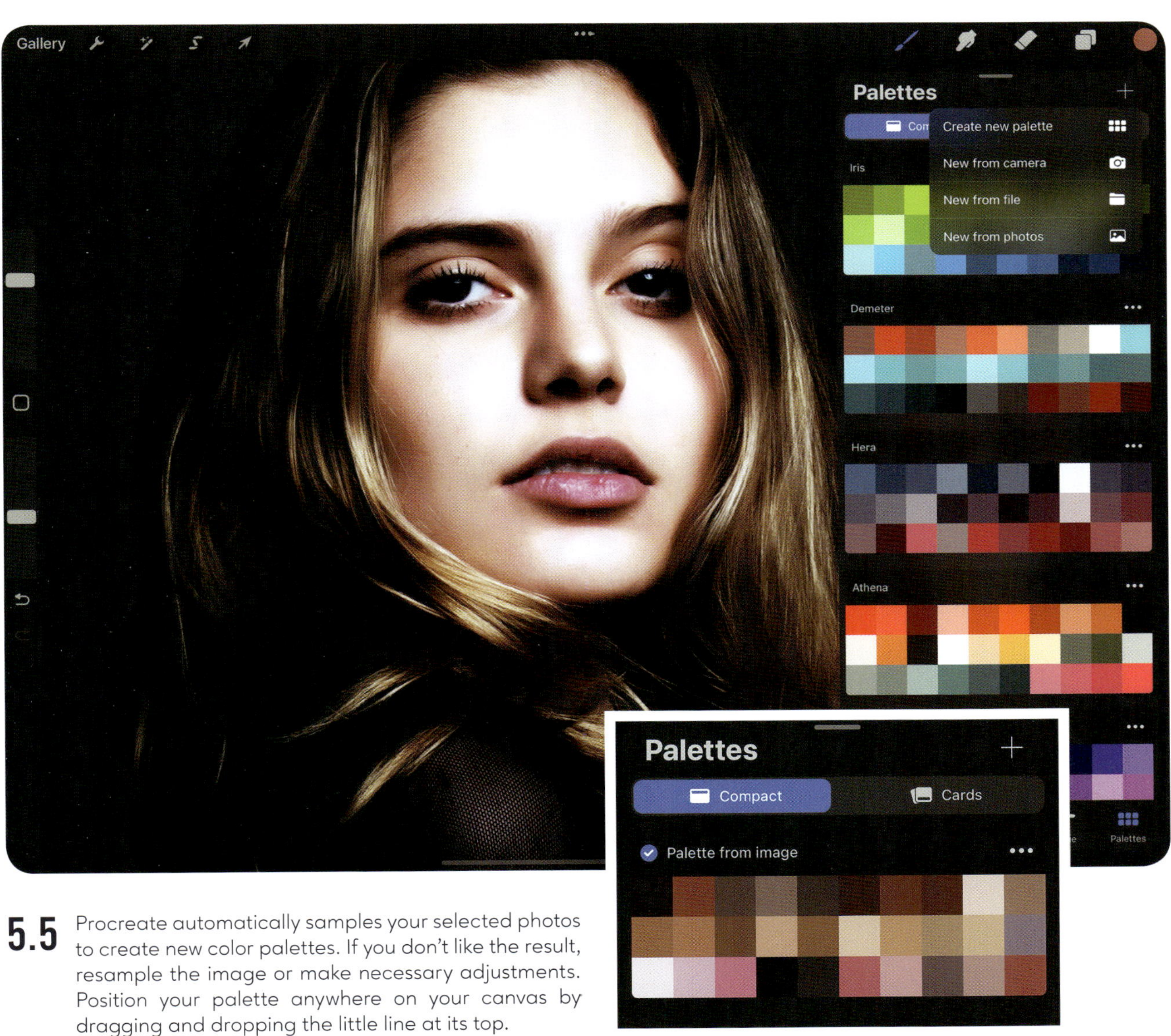

5.5 Procreate automatically samples your selected photos to create new color palettes. If you don't like the result, resample the image or make necessary adjustments. Position your palette anywhere on your canvas by dragging and dropping the little line at its top.

STEP6

6.1 BASIC COLORS

Now you can finally start coloring your image with your shiny new color palette. Create a new layer and position it below your sketch layers to avoid painting over your line art.

I'm ignoring the headdress for now and won't paint it until the very end.

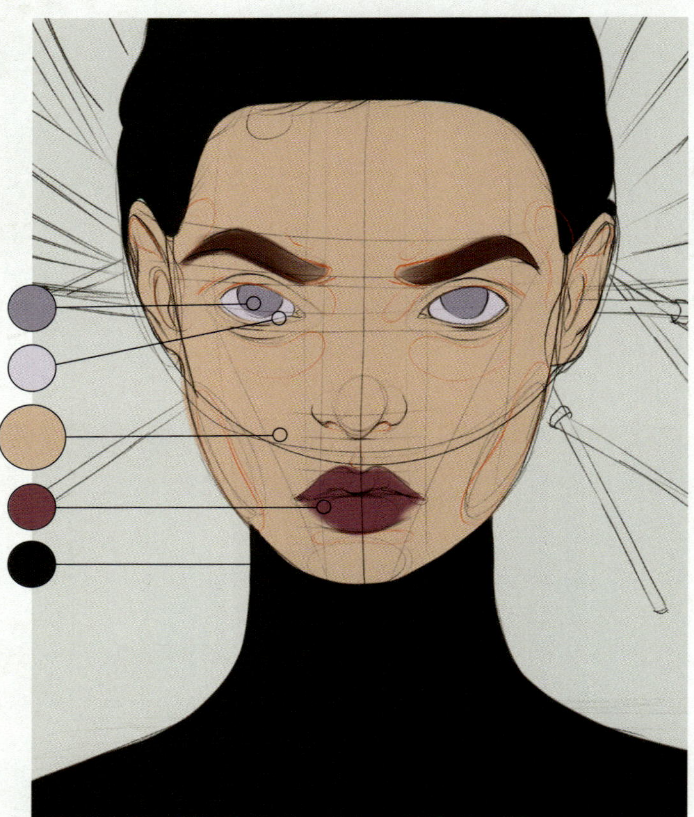

BRUSHES

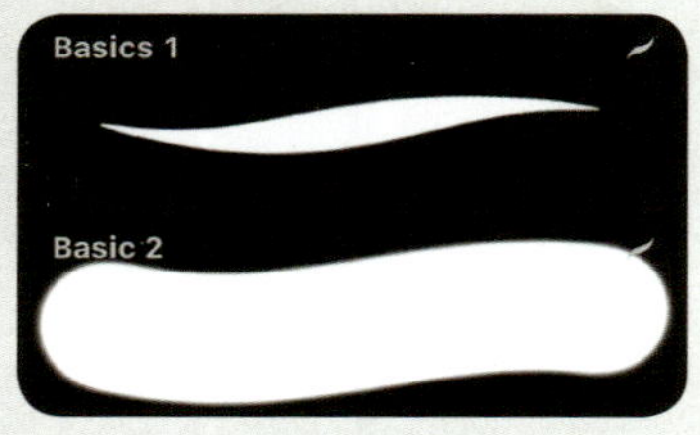

6.2 SECONDARY COLORS

Create a new layer and choose at least three more colors to define your highlights and shadows. The highlights are located on the forehead, nose, mouth, chin, and cheekbones. For the shadow areas, you can refer back to your sketch (in my case, they're denoted by the red lines).

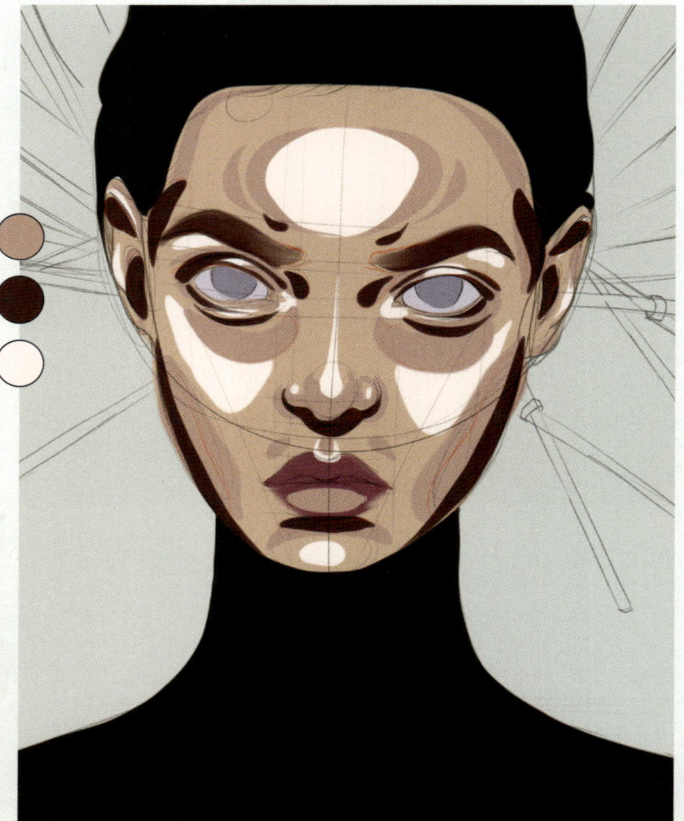

LAYERS

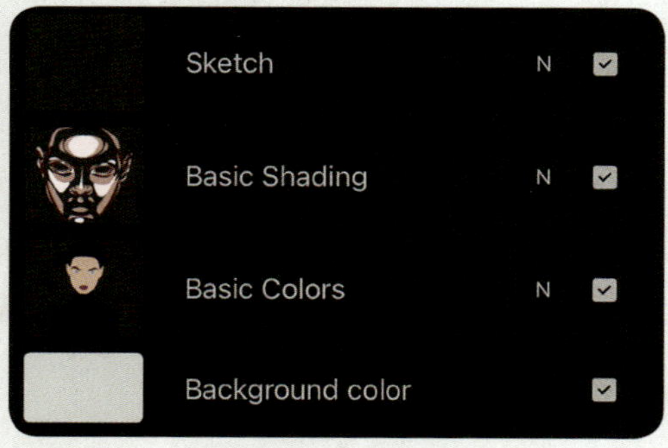

6.3 MIXING COLORS

Switch from the **Brush** to the **Smudge** tool. With the smudge tool you can blend colors together, while simultaneously creating a skin-like texture.

BRUSHES

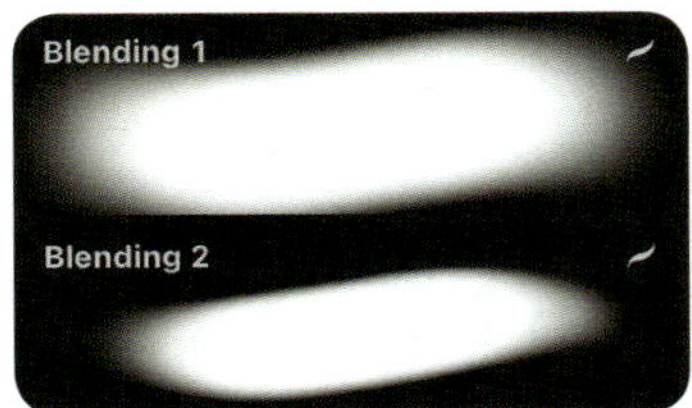

LAYERS

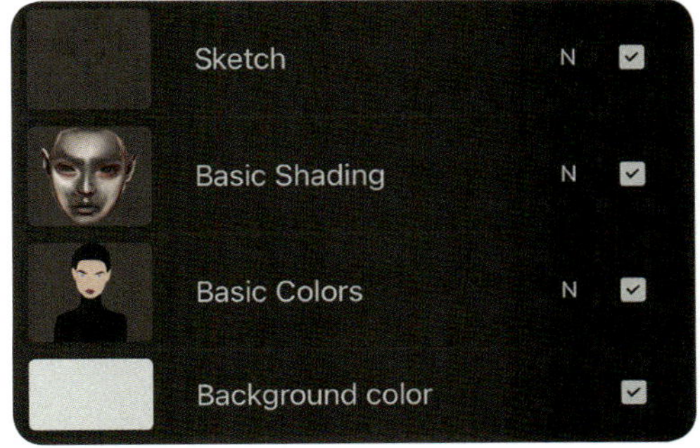

If you duplicate the **Basic Shading** layer and change the **Layer Effect**, you can easily add more depth to your image. To do that, swipe left on your layer and select **Duplicate**. Now tap on the **N** at the right side of your layer and change the layer setting from **Normal** to **Linear Burn**. If the effect is too strong, you can turn down the layer opacity.

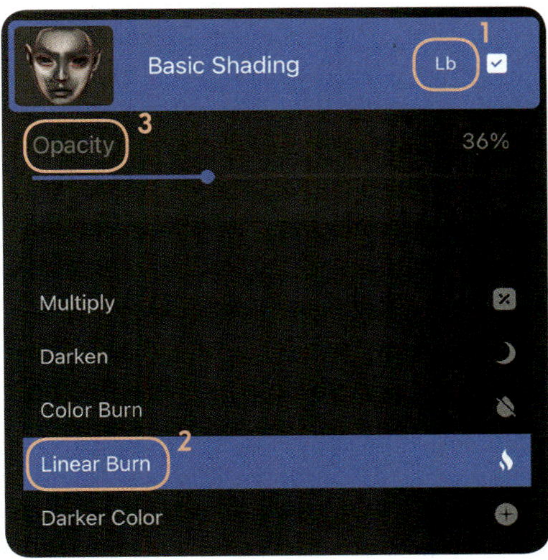

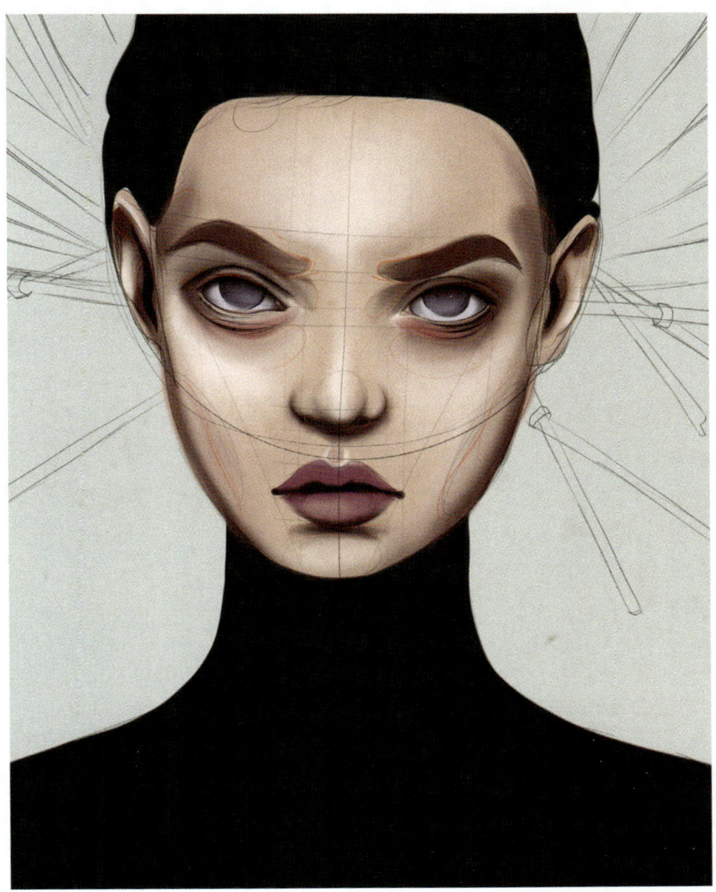

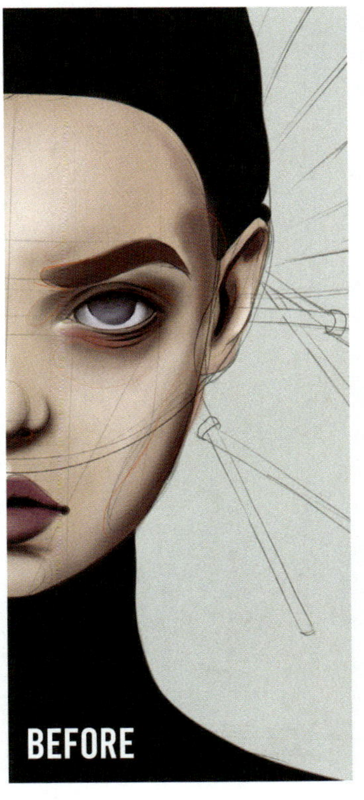

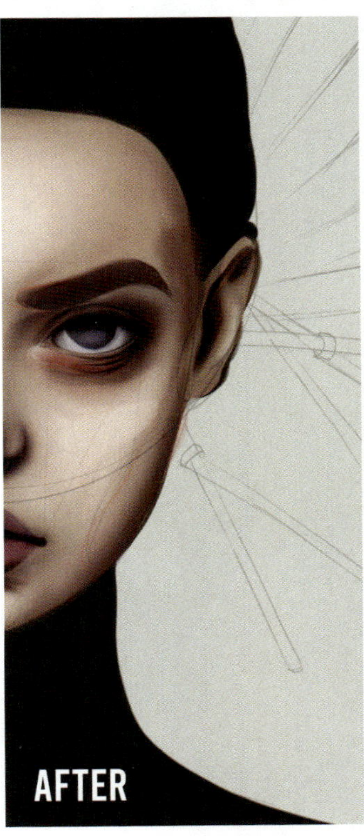

6.4 REPETITION

Repeat the previous two steps with more colors from your palette, or add in new colors that you think might fit. Incorporate soft yellow hues around the bridge of the nose, and blue tones below the eyes.

Remember to create a new layer for every pass. Once you're sure you want to keep your changes, you can merge the layers to save space. If in doubt, it's better to have too many layers than too few. If you reach your maximum layer capacity, Procreate will let you know.

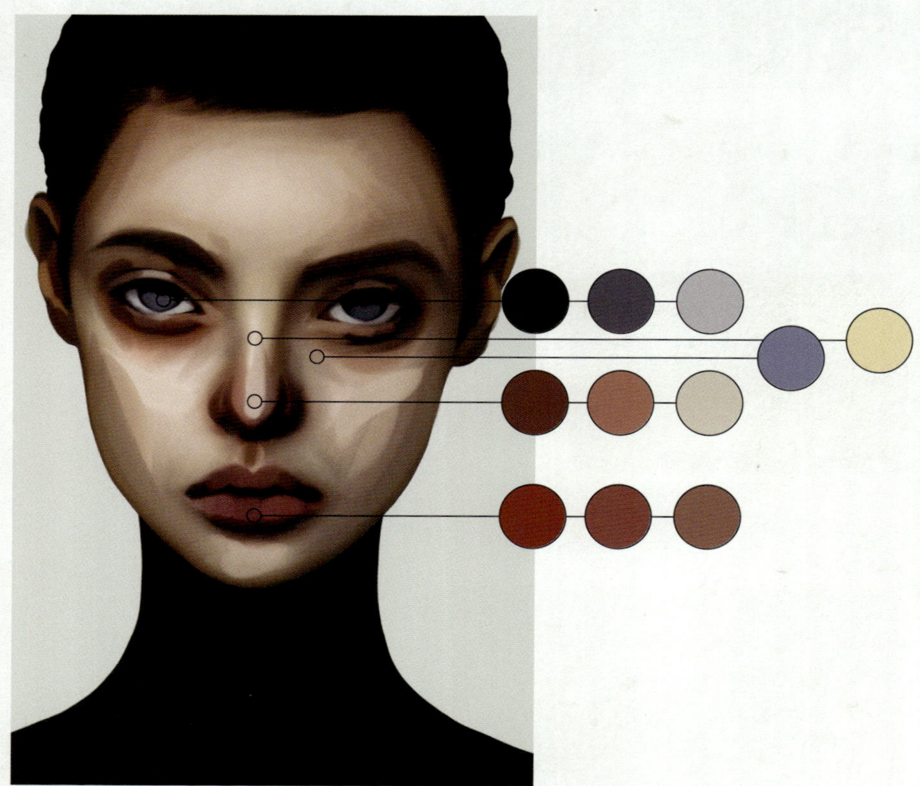

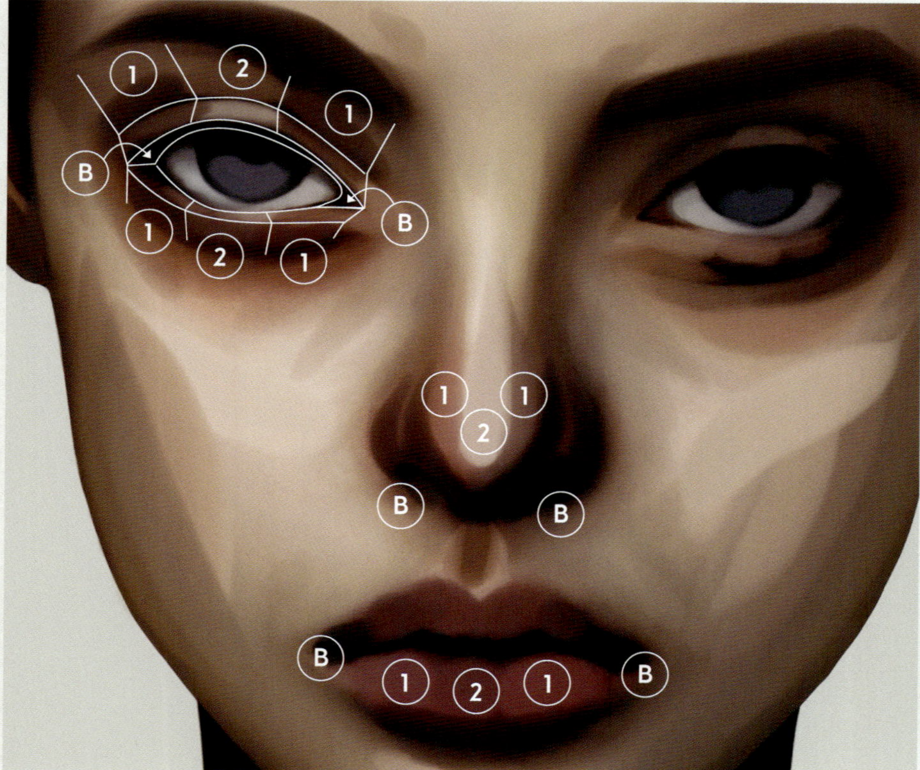

You can add color to your painting systematically or by freehand. If you prefer to have more structure, I'd suggest working in sections of three. To do that, pick two colors (for now), one darker and one lighter.

In the example to the left, areas marked with the number 1 are colored using the darker shade, while areas marked as 2 show the lighter color.

The **B** stands for black, emphasizing the darkest areas of the face. Use it to define the areas of the face that get the least amount of light: the corners of the eyes and mouth, and the nostrils.

6.5 VALUE RANGE

Repeat these steps until you're happy with your basic color scheme. At this point, your character should have even, untextured, doll-like skin. We'll add texture and detail in the next step.

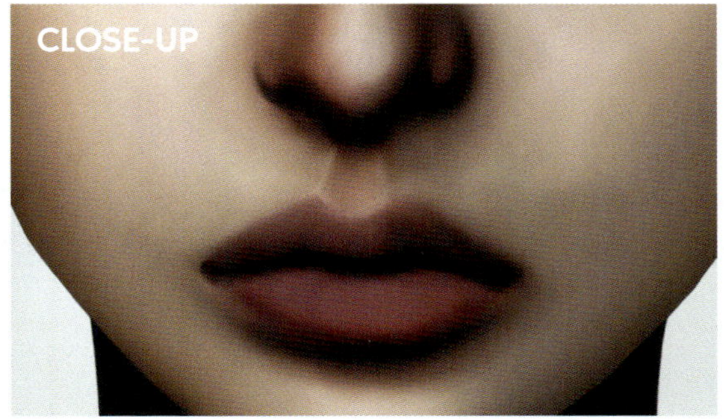

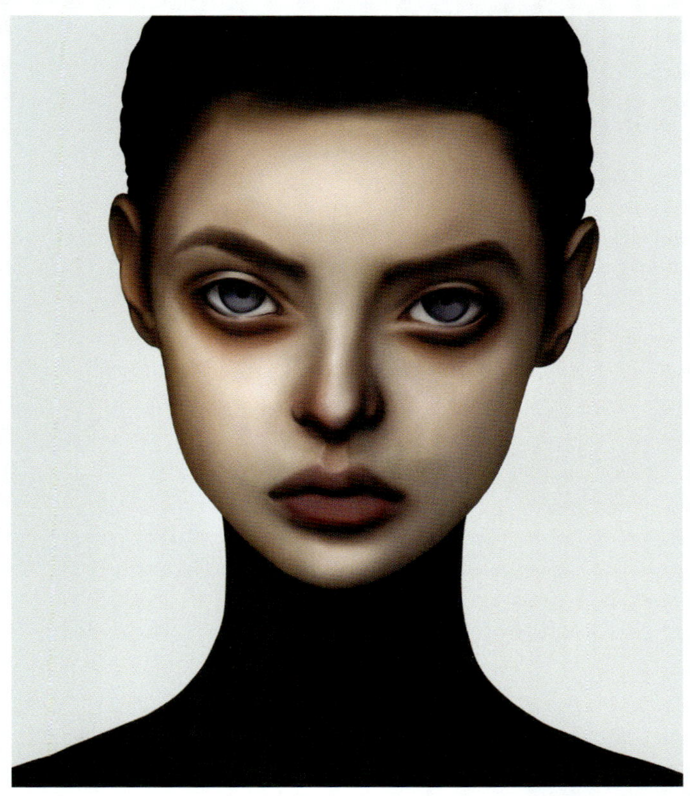

It's important to add enough contrast to your character's face to avoid it looking flat.

To check whether you have a good value range (i.e. contrast), look at your project in grayscale. If it looks drab or flat, try using colors that will deepen your shadows or lighten your highlights.

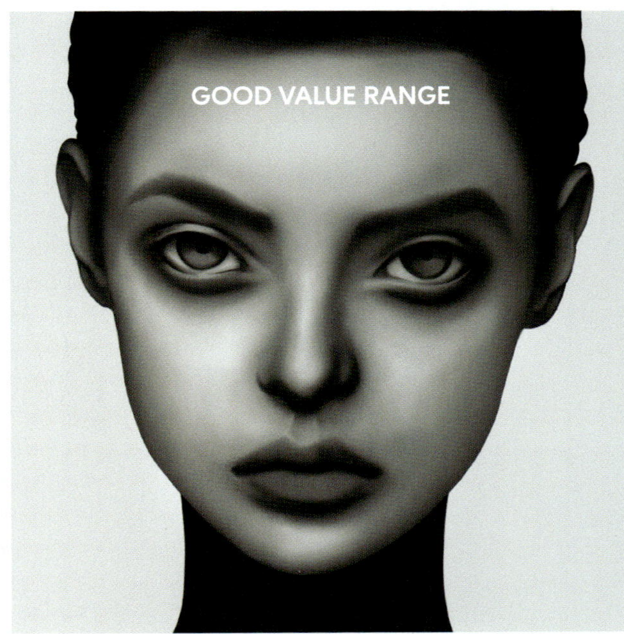

This is an example of a balanced value range. There is a clear separation between light and shadow. The range will improve even more once we add highlights at the end.

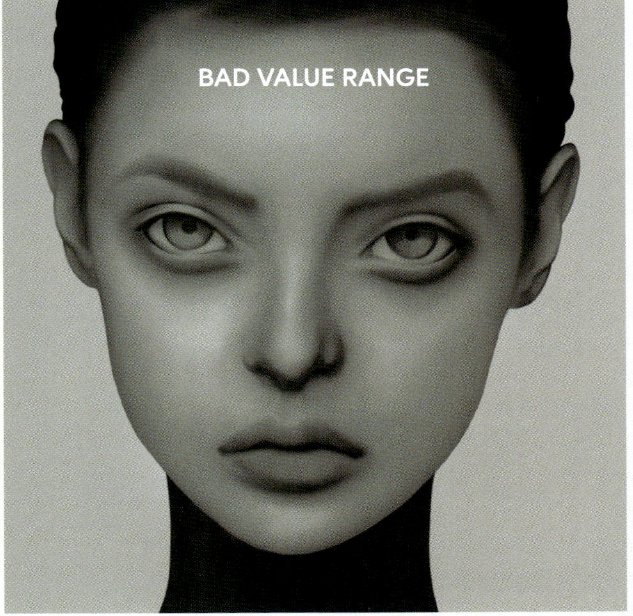

This is an example of a bad value range. No area of the face is distinctly in light or in shadow.

6.6 SIMPLE DETAILS

Use the smudge tool on the lip area to paint in some bumps and roughness. You don't have to use any additional colors for this. Instead, just smudge what's already there.

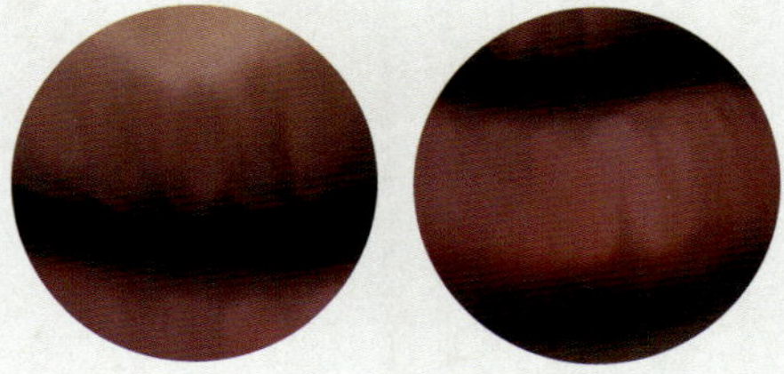

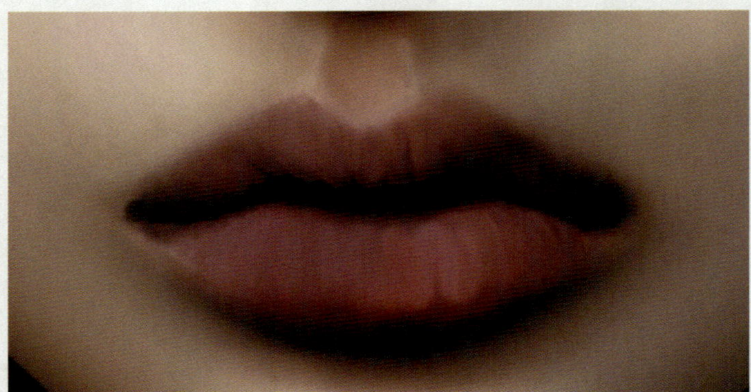

Now we'll do the same to the iris. As with the lips, there's no need for additional color. All you have to do is smudge some of the lines. Start near the pupil and stroke outward, as if the smudges are sunbeams.

Smudge the eyebrows to indicate stray hairs.

You can mark the hairline by smudging the lighter skin color into the darker hair. This way, you get a natural-looking transition.

To add texture to the nose, we'll use the pen tool. Highlight the areas above each nostril, but make sure not to make it too light.

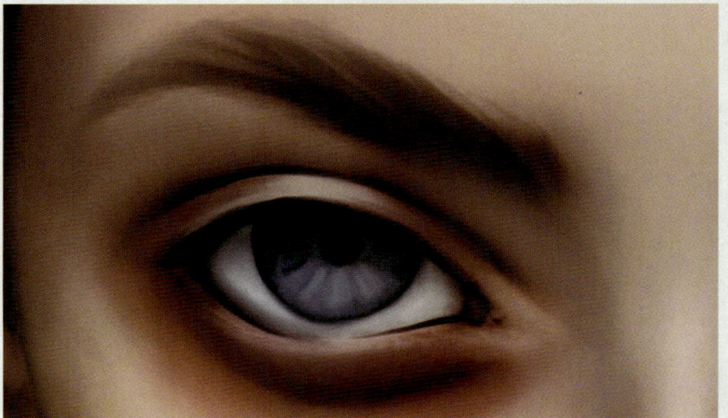

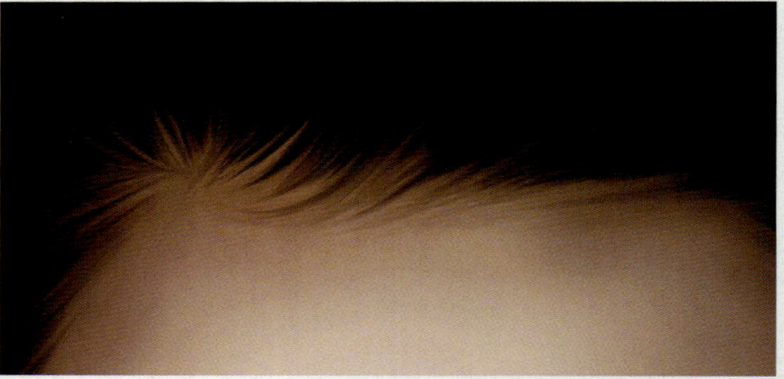

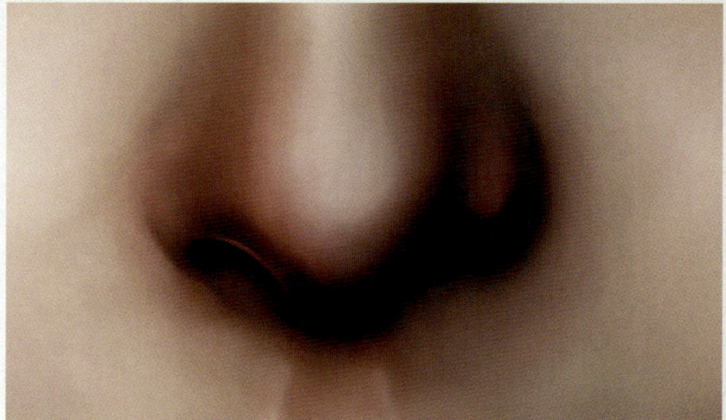

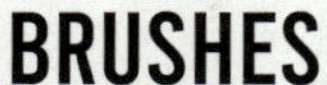

BRUSHES

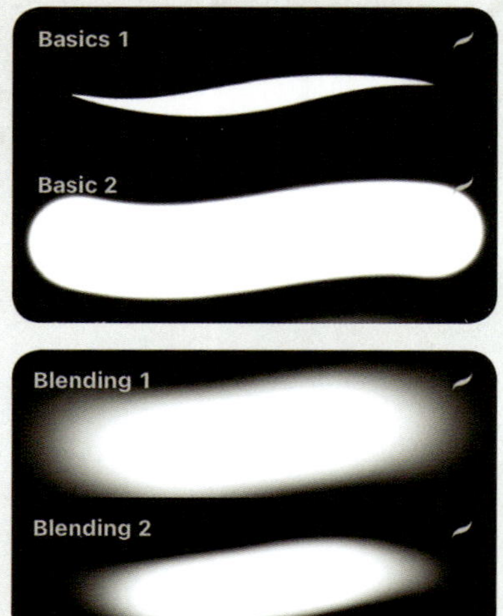

6.7 LIGHT & SHADOW

Next up, we'll properly define light and cast shadows. Since we haven't yet decided where our light is coming from, we don't know where the shadows are located. Thinking back to our lesson on lighting (page 82), I decide to use a dramatic, top-down light similar to **Butterfly lighting.**

There's a simple layer effect that will help with painting realistic shadows. Create a new layer and change the layer effect from **Normal** to **Soft Light.** This will blend your shadow color with the existing color. To paint the shadows, use a dark brown color instead of black to avoid it looking unnatural.

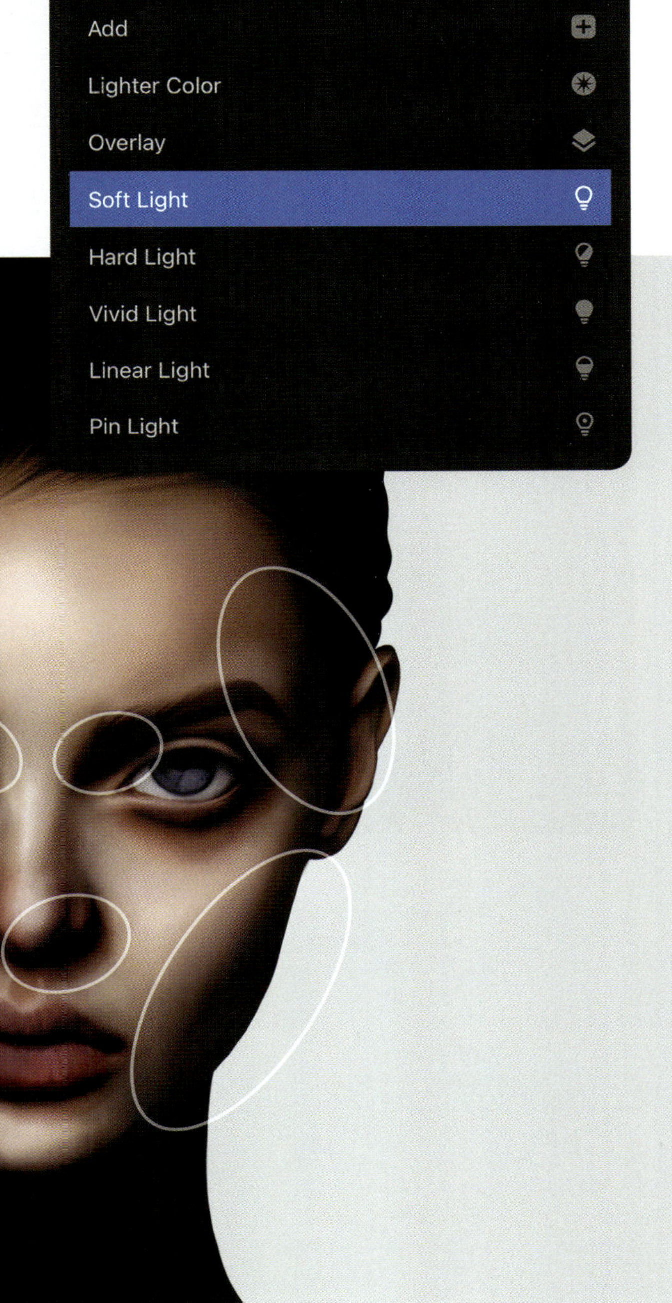

STEP7

REALISM

Now it's time to fix our character's doll-like appearance by adding some realistic skin texturing.

7.1 DARK BASE TEXTURE

Create a new layer and change the layer effect from **Normal** to **Soft Light**, or even **Hard Light**, depending on what looks better for your particular character and lighting situation

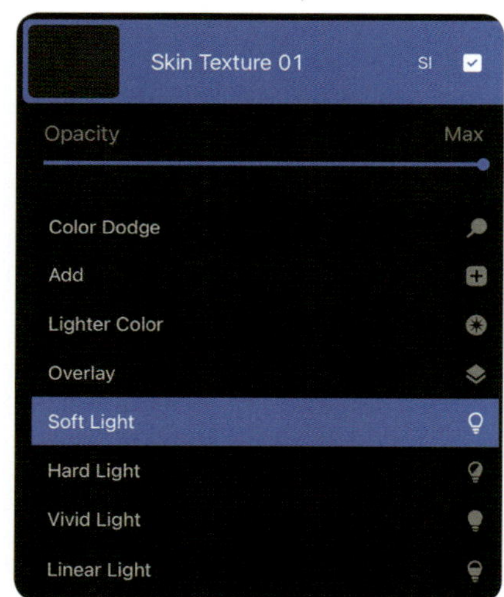

I use the brushes named **Skin 1** and/or **Skin 2** in combination with a darker color (see examples) to create a basic skin texture. These brushes have a soft, gritty texture and are perfect to use on the whole face.

Applying the same layer settings as before, I create a new layer and use slightly grainier brushes (**Skin 3**, **Skin 4** and/or **Skin 7**) to paint over the corners of the eyes, mouth, and nostrils. Here, less is more – reduce the layer opacity to avoid her skin looking too rough.

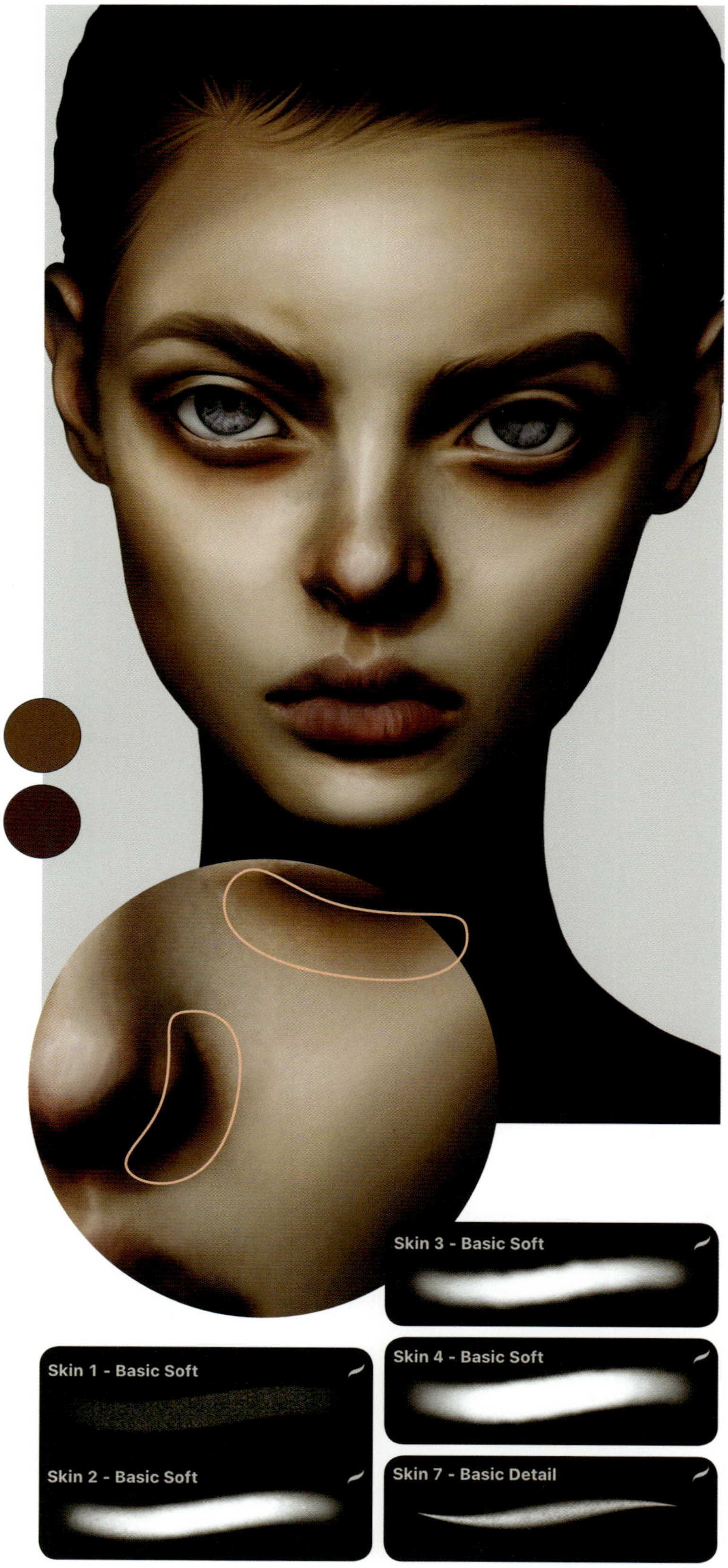

Skin 3 - Basic Soft

Skin 1 - Basic Soft

Skin 4 - Basic Soft

Skin 2 - Basic Soft

Skin 7 - Basic Detail

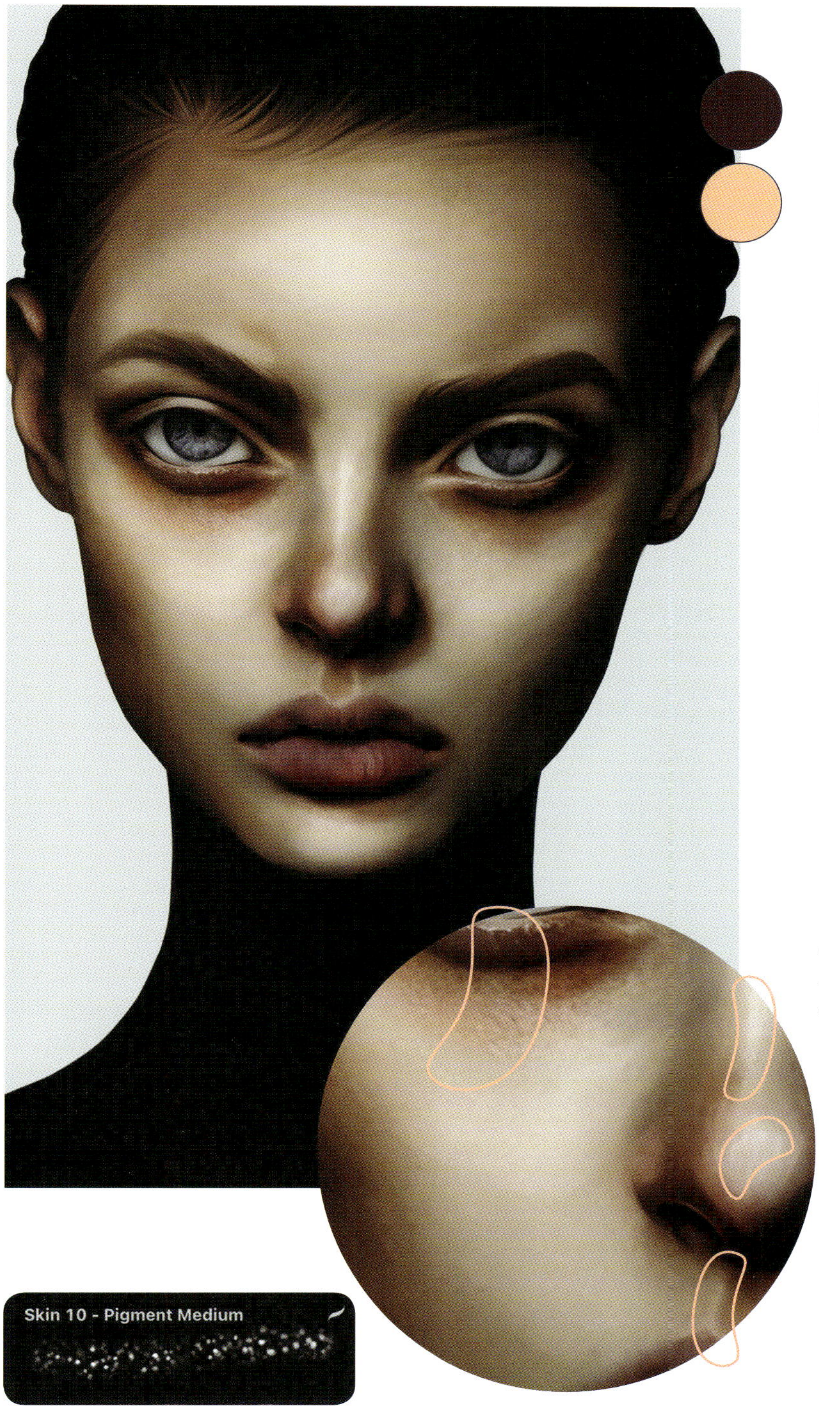

7.2 LIGHT BASE TEXTURE

Now let's repeat the last two steps with a new layer and grittier brushes. This time, we'll use lighter colors (see examples) and the layer effect **Overlay**.

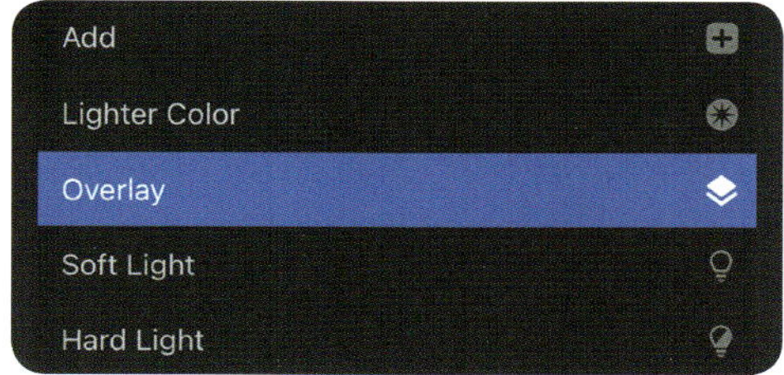

When combined with lighter colors, overlaying creates beautiful highlights that make the skin look shinier. Reduce the layer opacity if the effect is too strong.

7.3 PIGMENTATION

By using dark brown colors, it's easy to create natural-looking, uneven pigmentation or age spots with the same brushes (see forehead).

Repeat the previous steps with your chosen brushes until you're happy with the result. Try out the **Vivid Light** layer effect and **Add** for highlights. Since results vary with skin tone, different layer effects may give you better results.

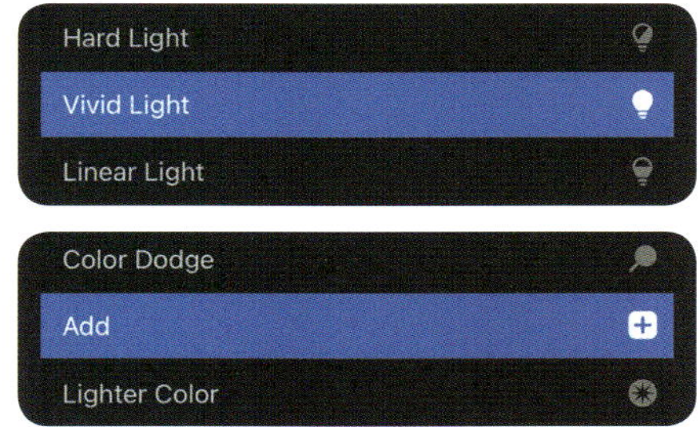

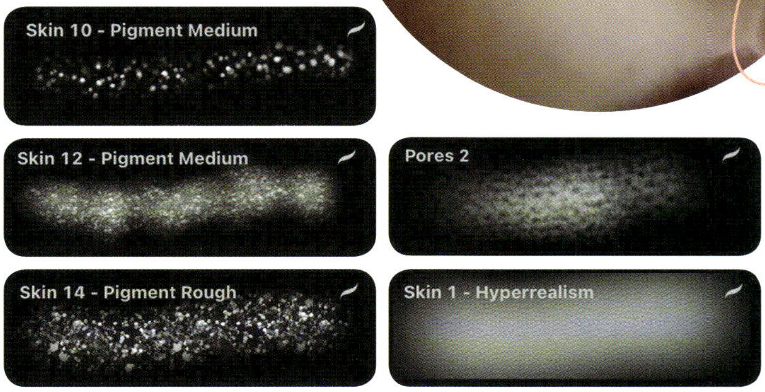

Skin 10 - Pigment Medium

Skin 12 - Pigment Medium

Pores 2

Skin 14 - Pigment Rough

Skin 1 - Hyperrealism

The changes to her skin texture are very subtle. To see the differences more clearly, pinch the pages of the book together, making both versions of the face touch.

7.4 BEAUTY MARKS & FRECKLES

If you're looking to add some freckles or moles, start with a new **Soft Light** layer. I like placing them on the outside of the eye area, or near the corners of the mouth.

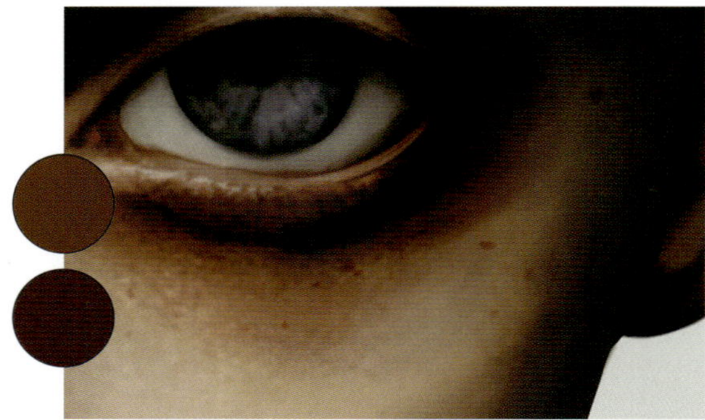

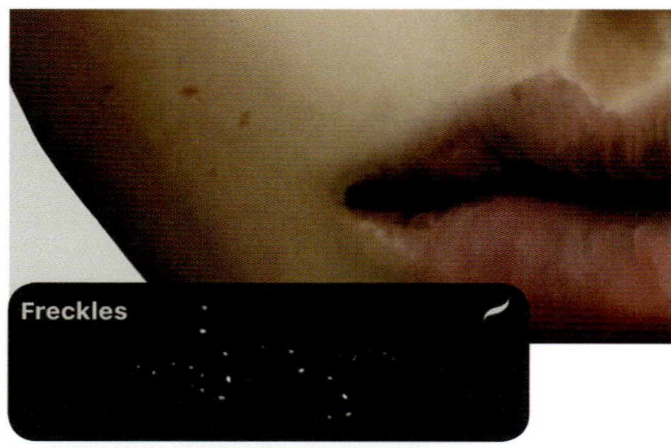

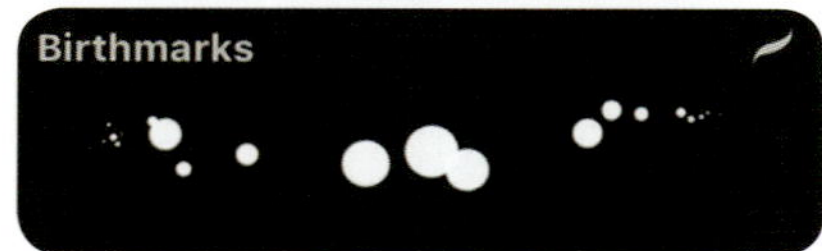

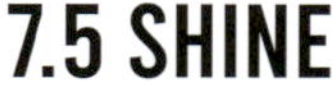

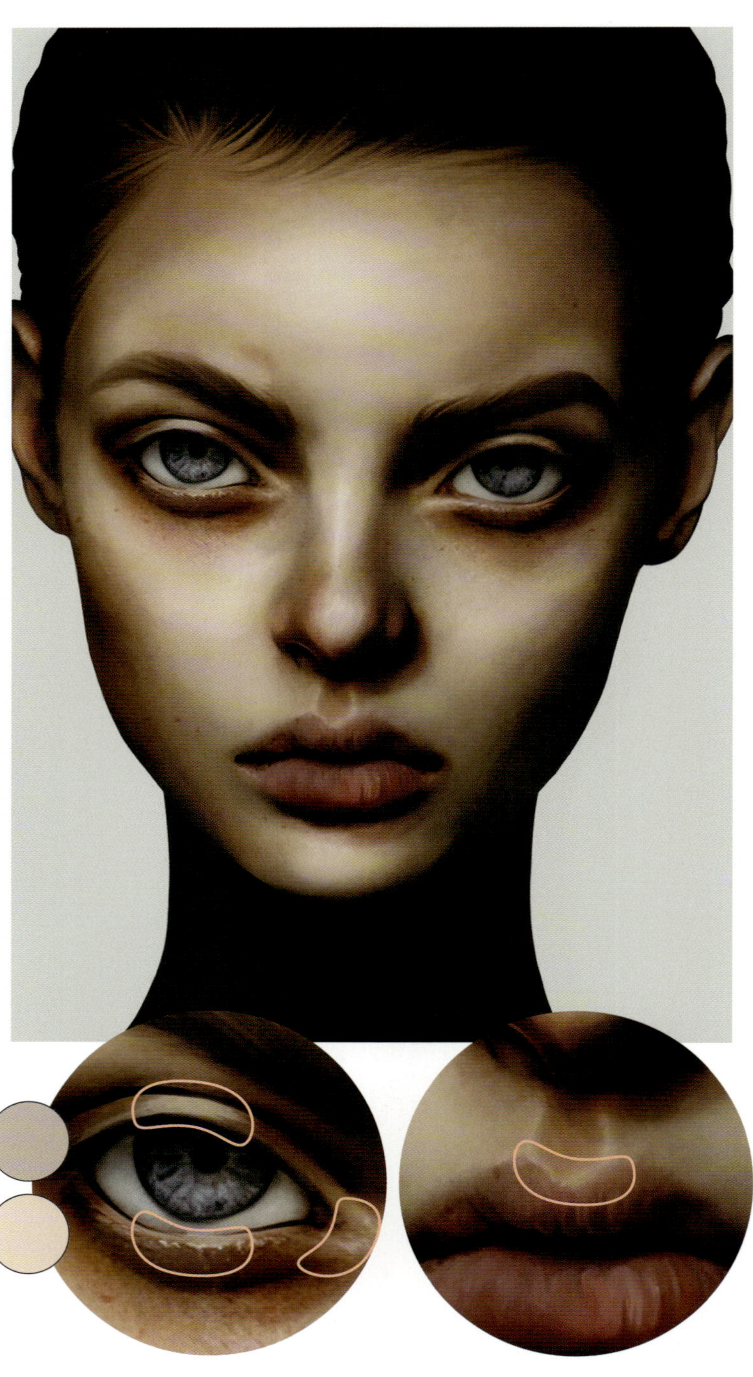

7.5 SHINE

Create a Normal layer and paint a few shiny areas using a very light skin color. I tend to place them where the top lip meets the philtrum, as well as the top and bottom eyelids.

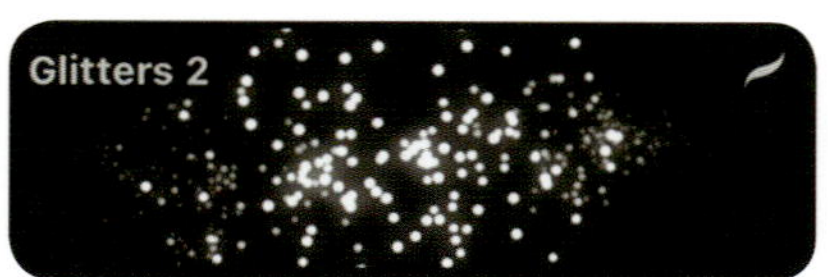

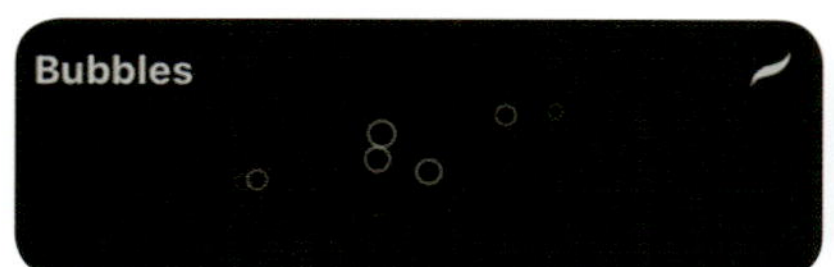

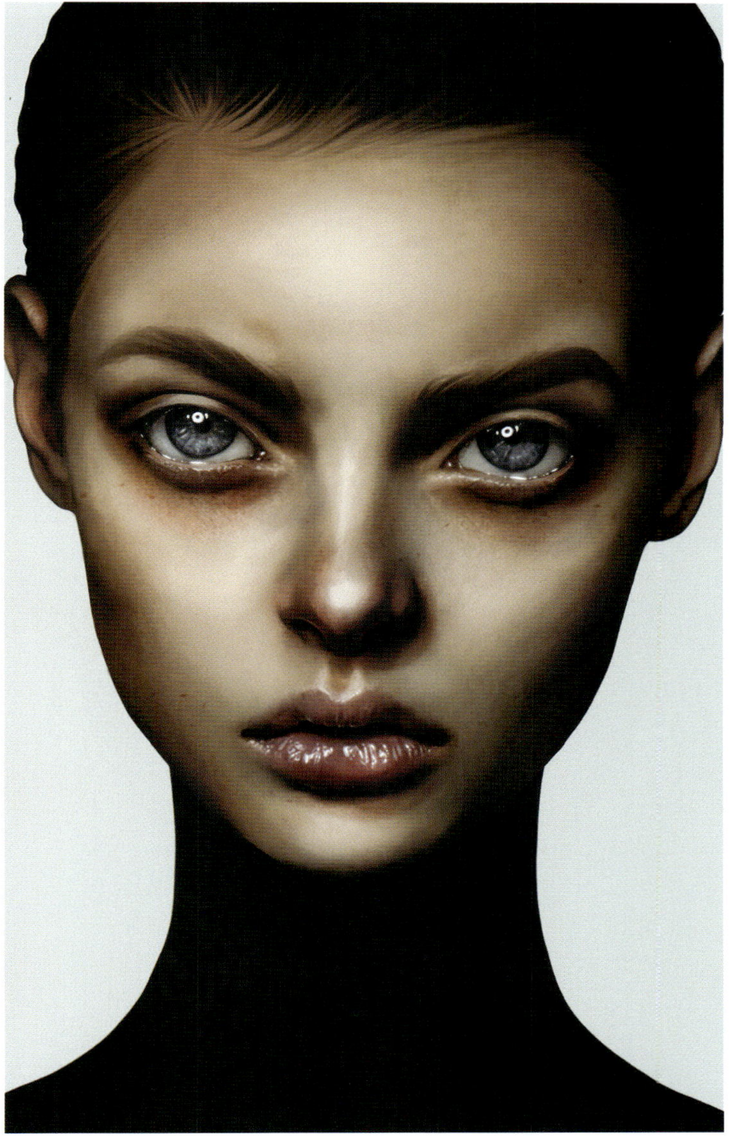

Adding highlights is my favorite part because it brings so much life to the character. I like when the eyes look a little over-the-top, but tone yours down if you prefer a more natural look.

7.6 SPECULAR

Create a new Normal layer for your specular highlights. Select white or a very light color.

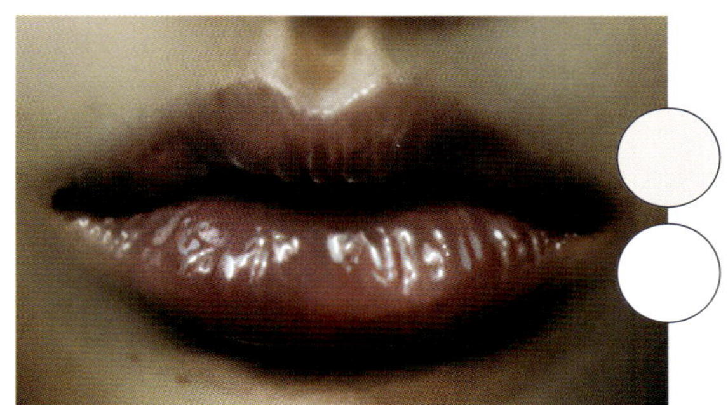

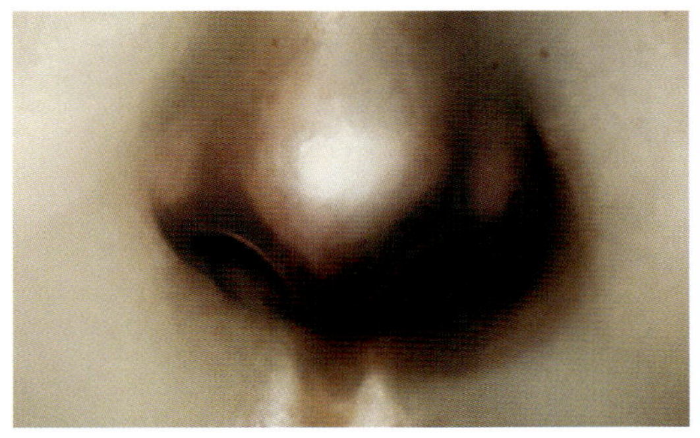

Basics 1

Glitters 2

Glow

Bubbles

You can make the sclera more realistic by adding a few highlights where it meets the bottom eyelid. A brush with the **Luminance Blending** setting and **Add** blend mode enabled works best for this!

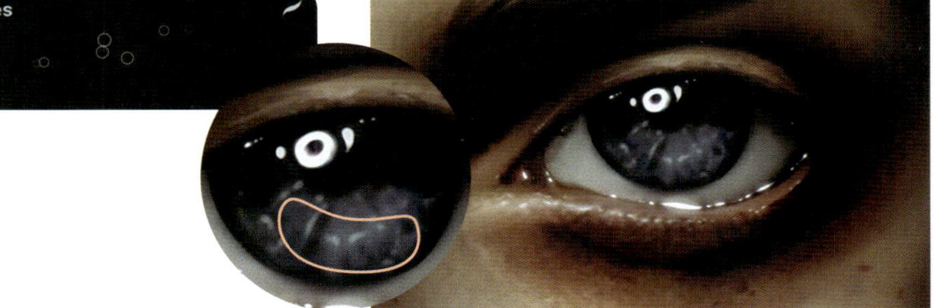

7.7. HAIR

Create a new Normal layer to paint the lashes and brows. You can paint right over the existing eyebrow to add detail. Pick a main hair color (dark brown, for instance) and use that for both the eyelashes and brows. Then bring in a lighter color to add a few reflective areas.

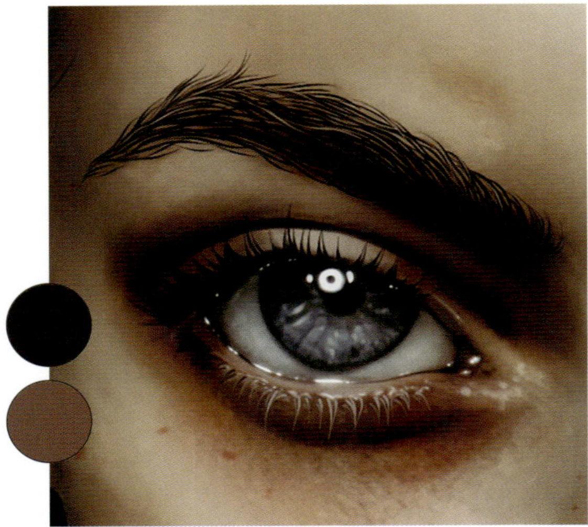

If your light is coming from above like it is here, then it's a good idea to lighten the eyelashes on the lower eyelid considerably.

This is what my layer looks like when isolated:

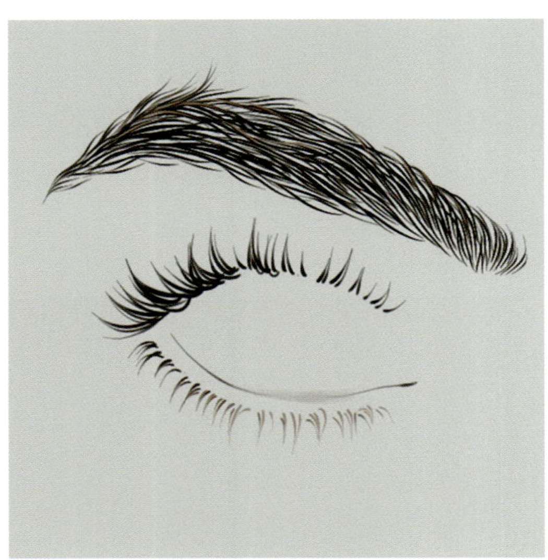

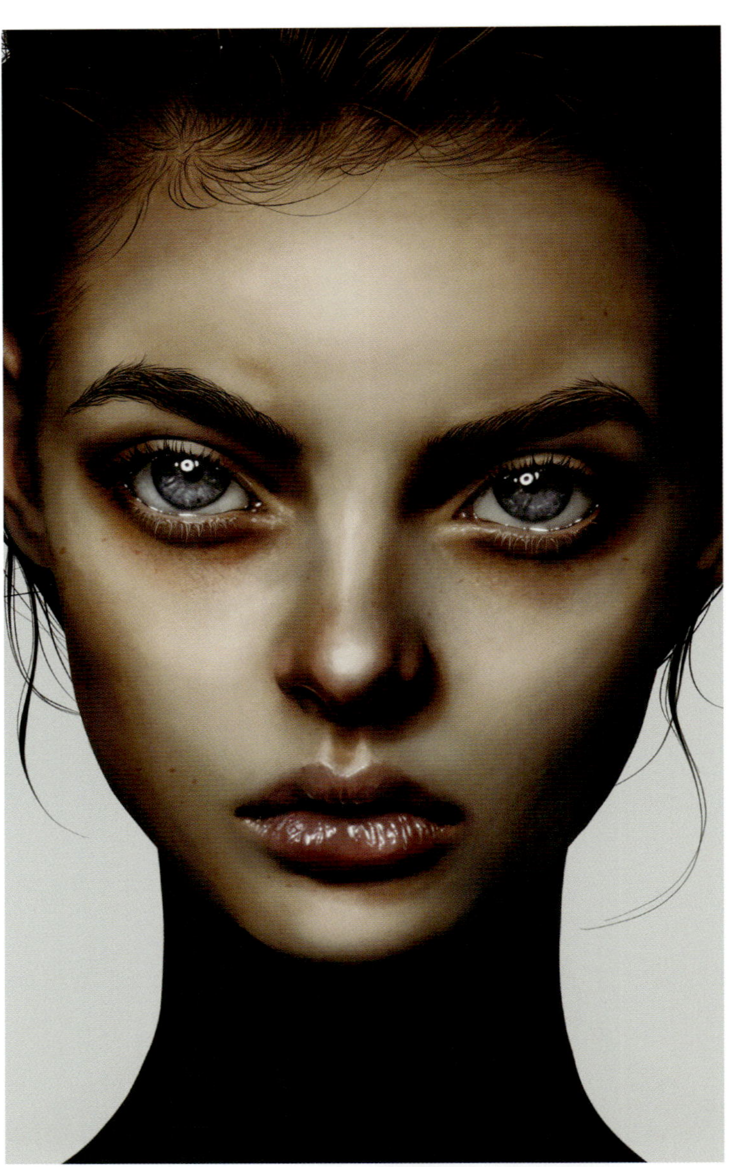

Thicken the roots of the lashes a little and group them into small clumps, as they're rarely separated perfectly.

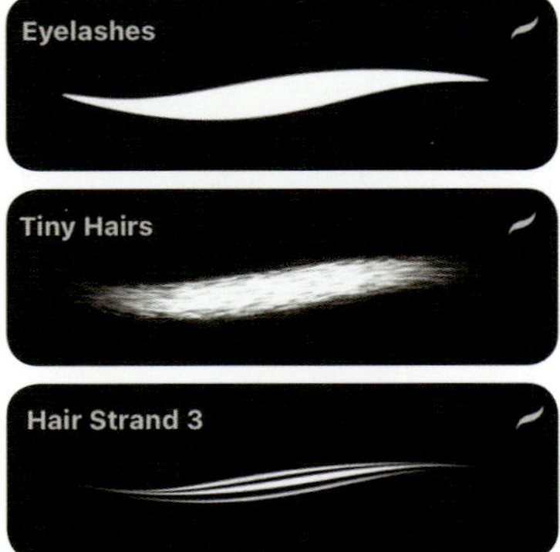

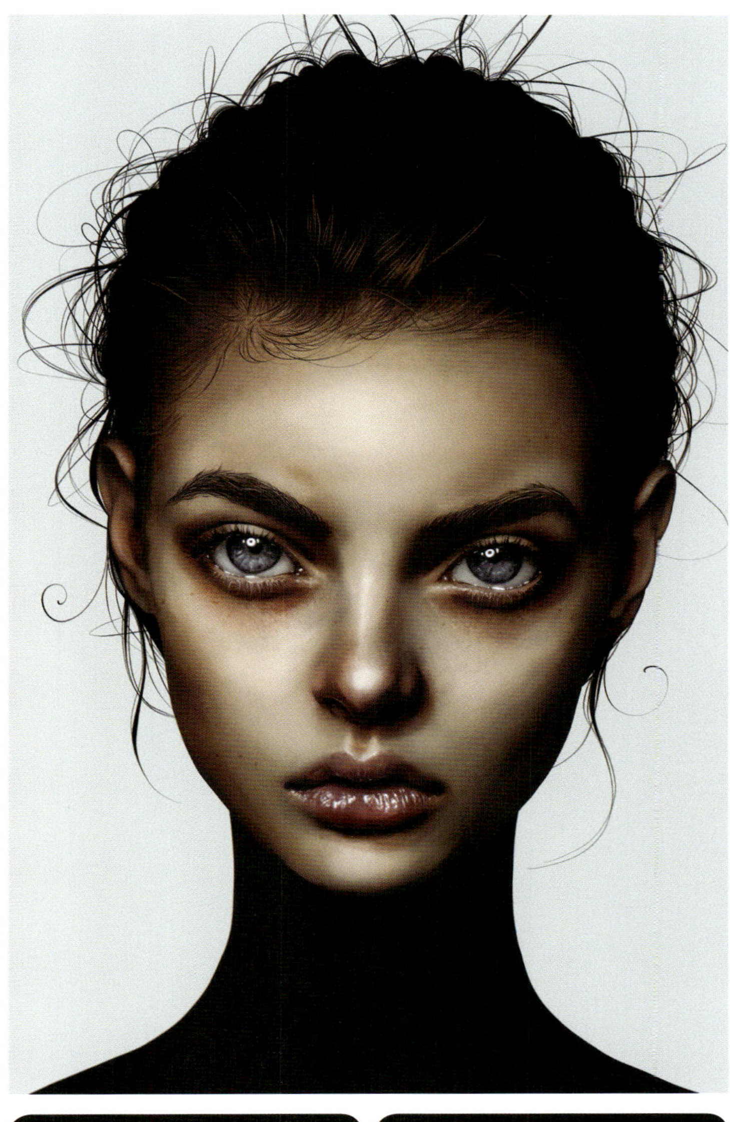

Paint the hair by starting with a base color and a slightly lighter color to create the illusion of shine/ light reflection.

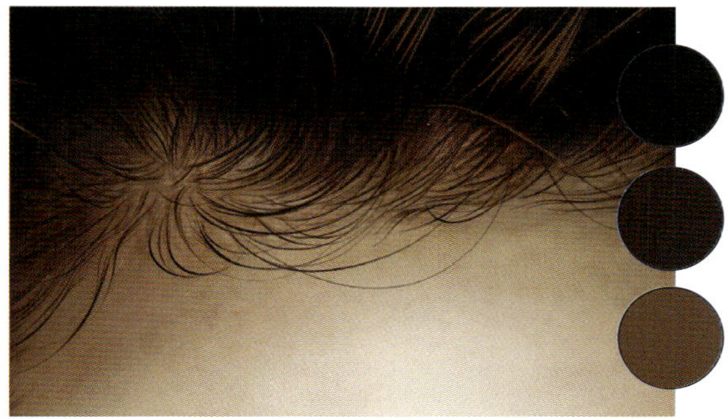

Paint the highlights with soft lines. It's best to use a brush that has a fade-in and fade-out bound to pen pressure.

Sneak in a few broken hairs for added realism:

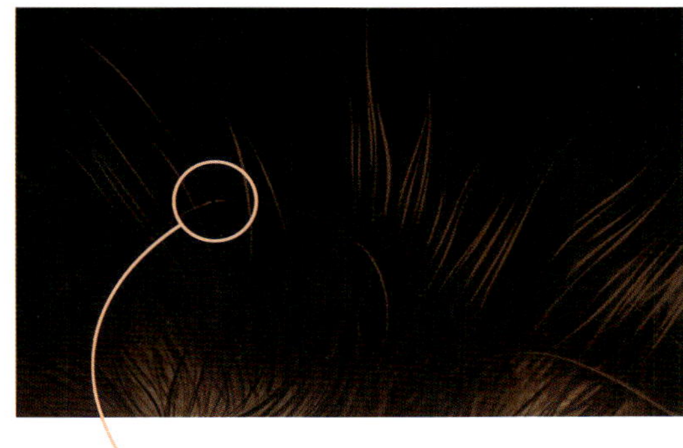

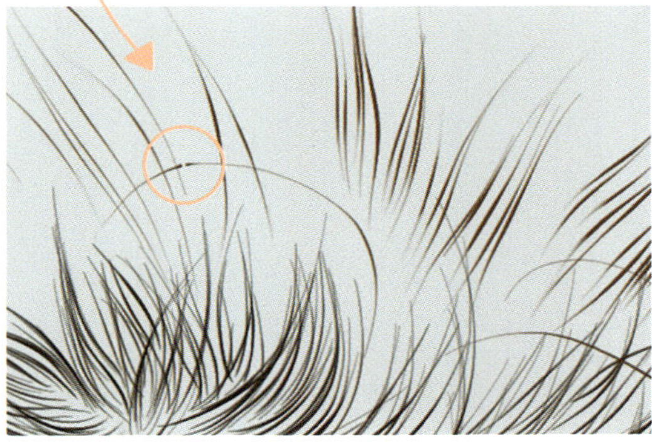

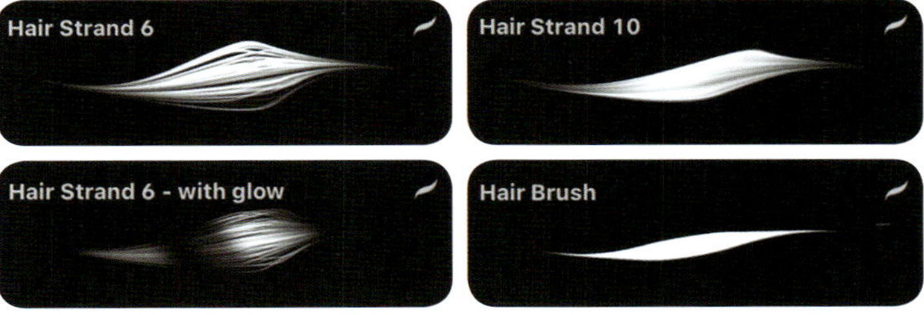

I like to give my characters a few Tim-Burton-esque locks. I think it adds a subtle sense of surrealism.

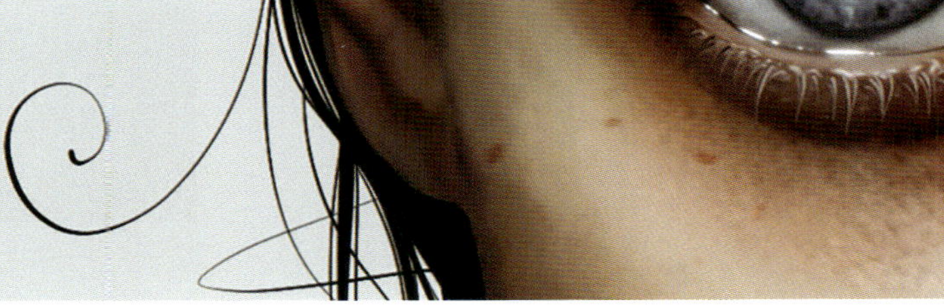

STEP8

MARBLE SCAR

Do you remember the image below from the mood board a few pages back? Now we'll use it to illustrate the name of my painting, as well as her peculiarity.

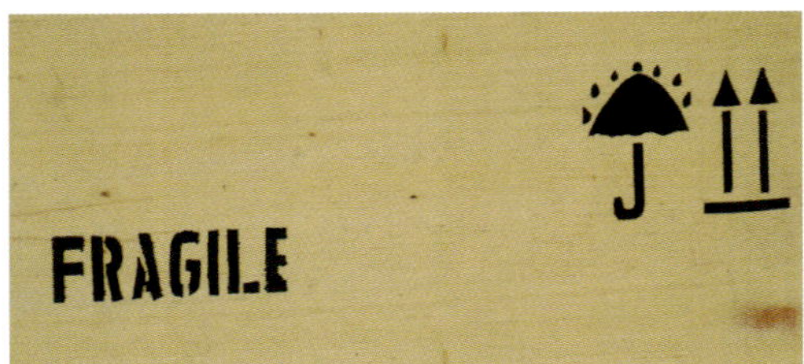

To emphasize the painting's name, I decided to give my character a scar. Not just a normal scar though; I'm going for the look of a fissure, like cracking marble.

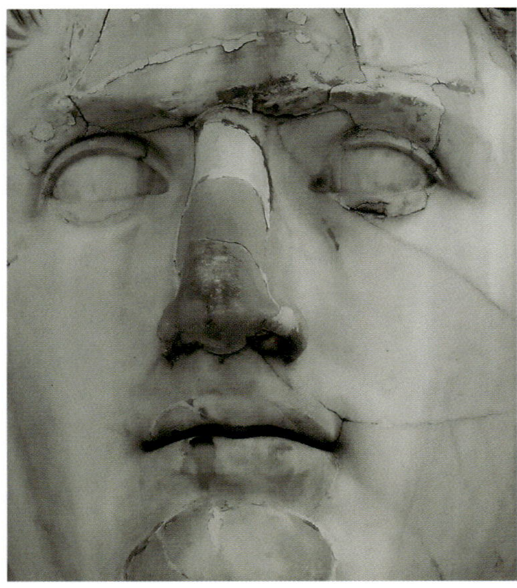

The viewer will just see a regular scar at first. Only on closer inspection will it become clear that it's not quite normal. If the character was a regular human, this scar would not be realistic. But maybe she's not a regular human after all...

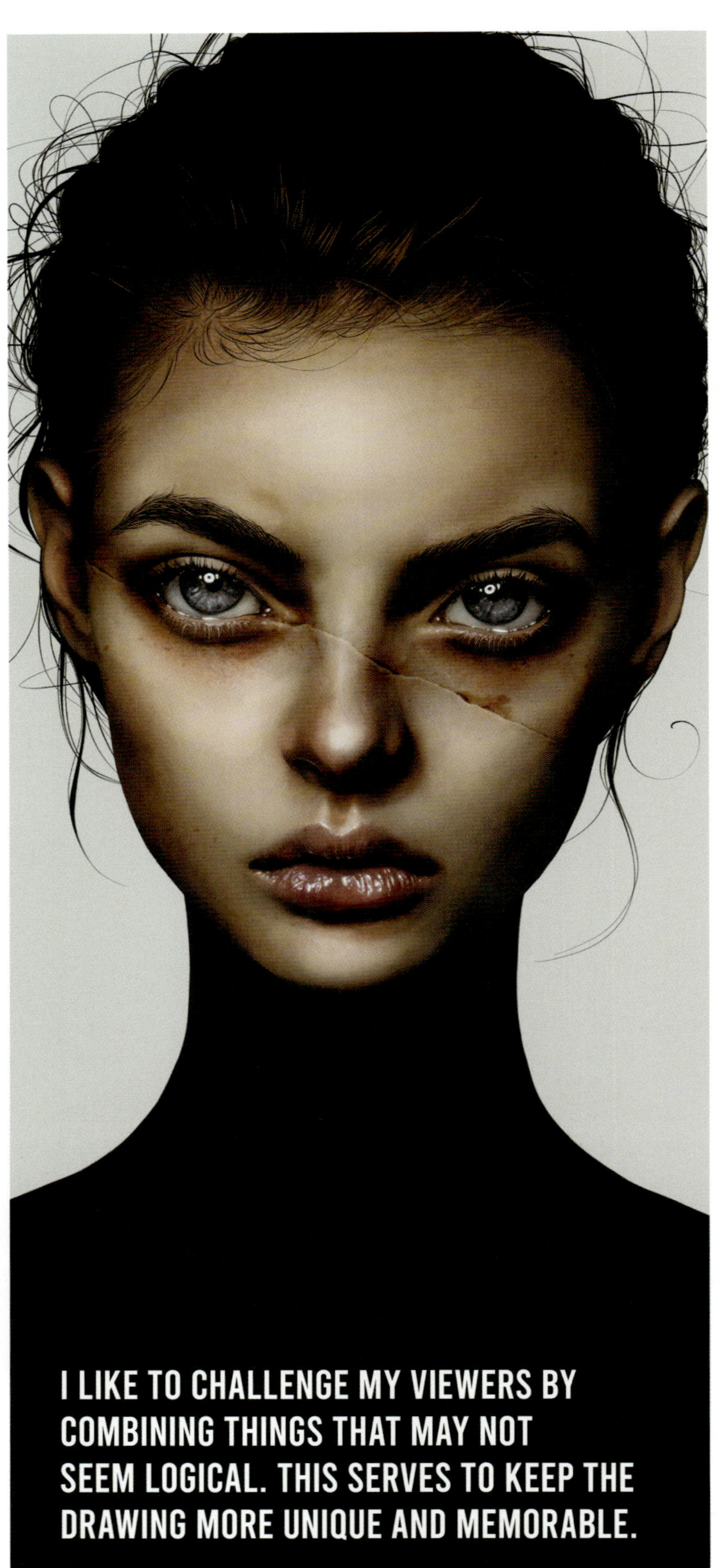

I LIKE TO CHALLENGE MY VIEWERS BY COMBINING THINGS THAT MAY NOT SEEM LOGICAL. THIS SERVES TO KEEP THE DRAWING MORE UNIQUE AND MEMORABLE.

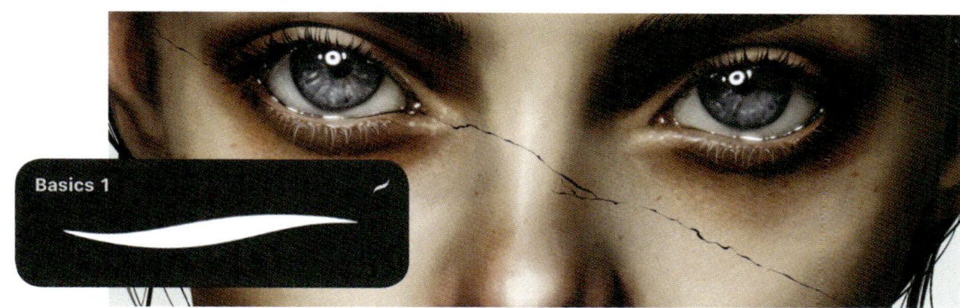

8.1 Draw a dark line where you want the scar to be located. Make the line thicker in some areas to indicate deeper laceration.

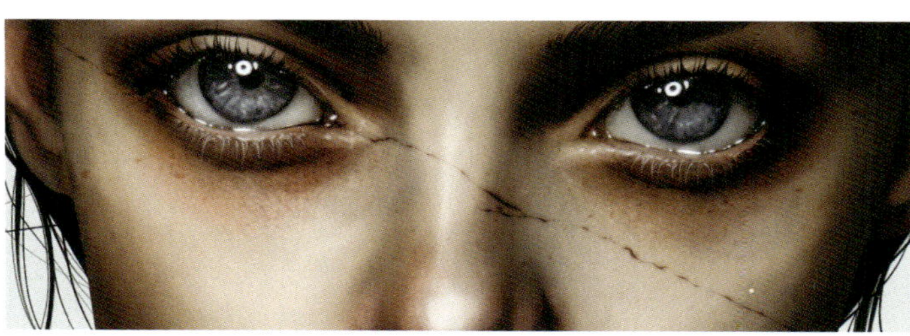

8.2 Duplicate the layer, go to the **Adjustments** menu and select **Gaussian Blur** to make your line a little softer. Merge both layers after you're done.

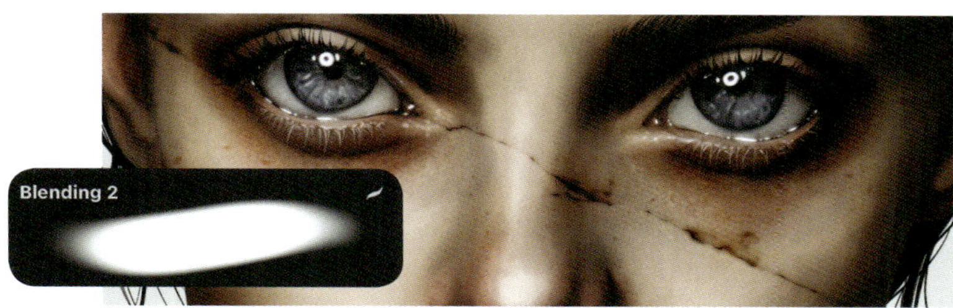

8.3 Pick a lighter color to add a few shadows to the deeper areas of your scar. Make sure to use a brush with soft edges for this.

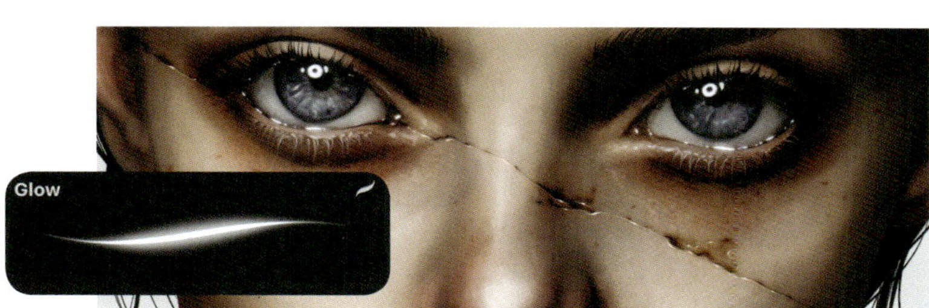

8.4 Create a new layer to add highlights with a lighter color. When you're done, use **Gaussian Blur** again to soften them a little.

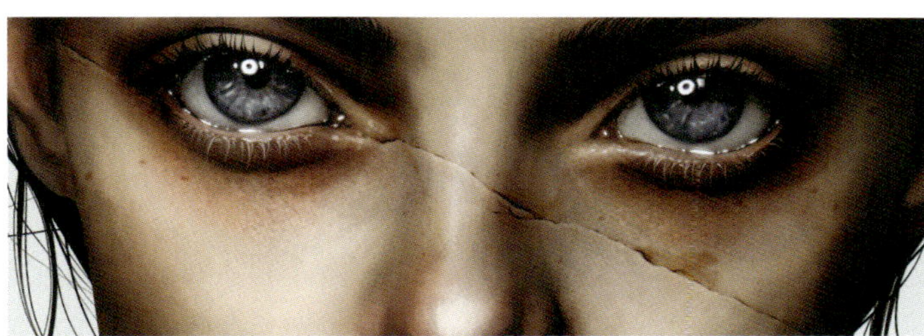

8.5 Merge your layers and change the layer effects from **Normal** to **Soft Light** or **Hard Light**, whichever looks better. If necessary, blur a few areas with the smudge tool.

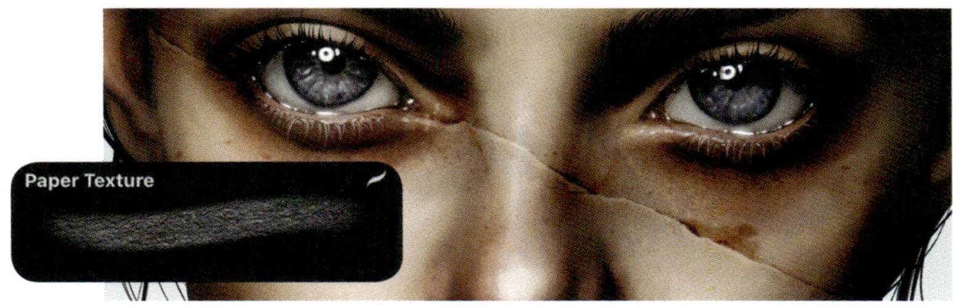

8.6 Use a grainy brush to add some roughness and a few irregularities.

STEP9

HEADDRESS

It's finally time for the headdress! I copy the dried leaves from my reference image 1:1. When working with repeated elements, it's possible to copy and paste a few of the individual leaf ends. However, unless you disguise them well, they might look too obvious. My suggestion is to draw most of them individually, only copy-pasting in places that aren't focal areas. Mirror your copied elements, or even **Distort/Warp** them to further change up the look.

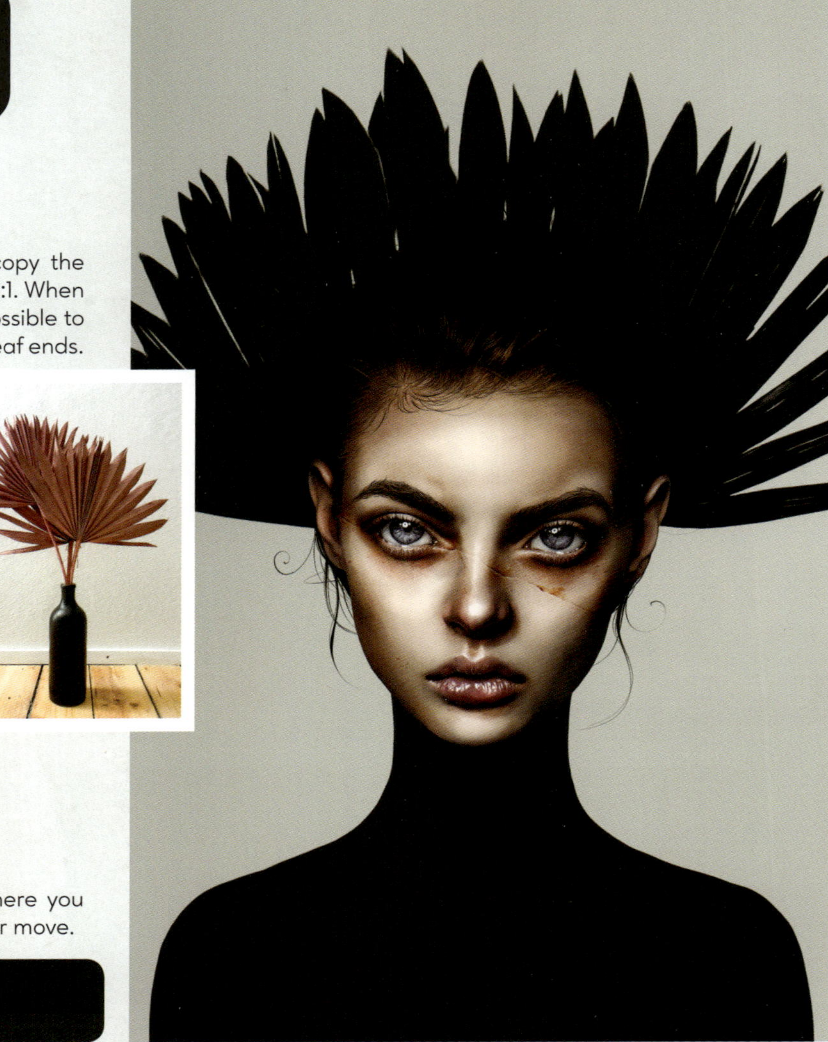

Use the **Select** tool to mark areas where you can cut, distort, warp, shrink, expand, or move.

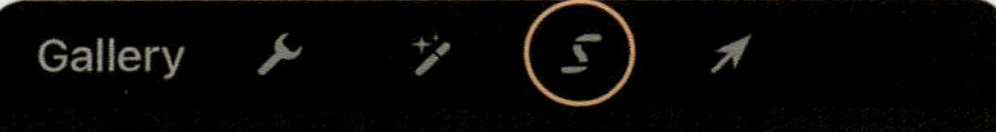

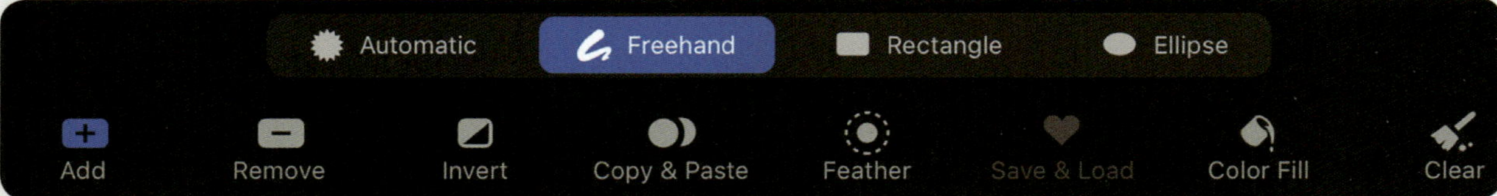

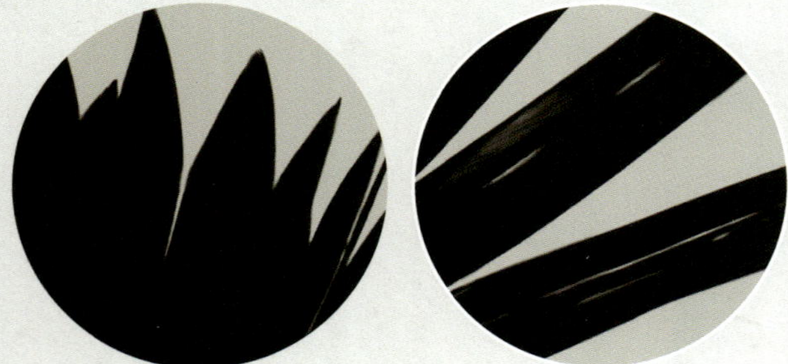

First, I paint the leaves...

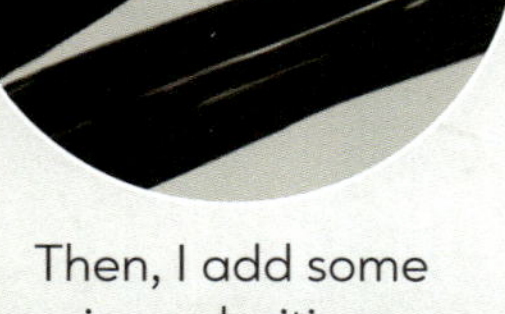

Then, I add some irregularities.

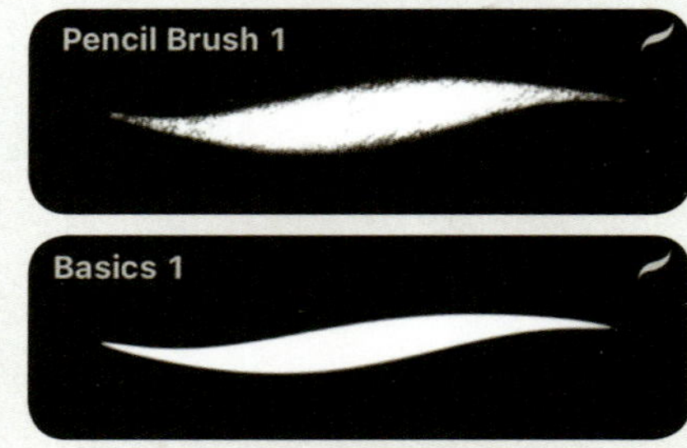

I add some wooden sticks that are held together by string. The sticks are supposed to break up the symmetry of the image. I don't want the headdress to look too neat and orderly.

I want the headdress to look a little more chaotic, so I add a few dried flowers. I don't place them randomly though; instead, I use the rule of thirds (you can find more information regarding composition on pages 80-81).

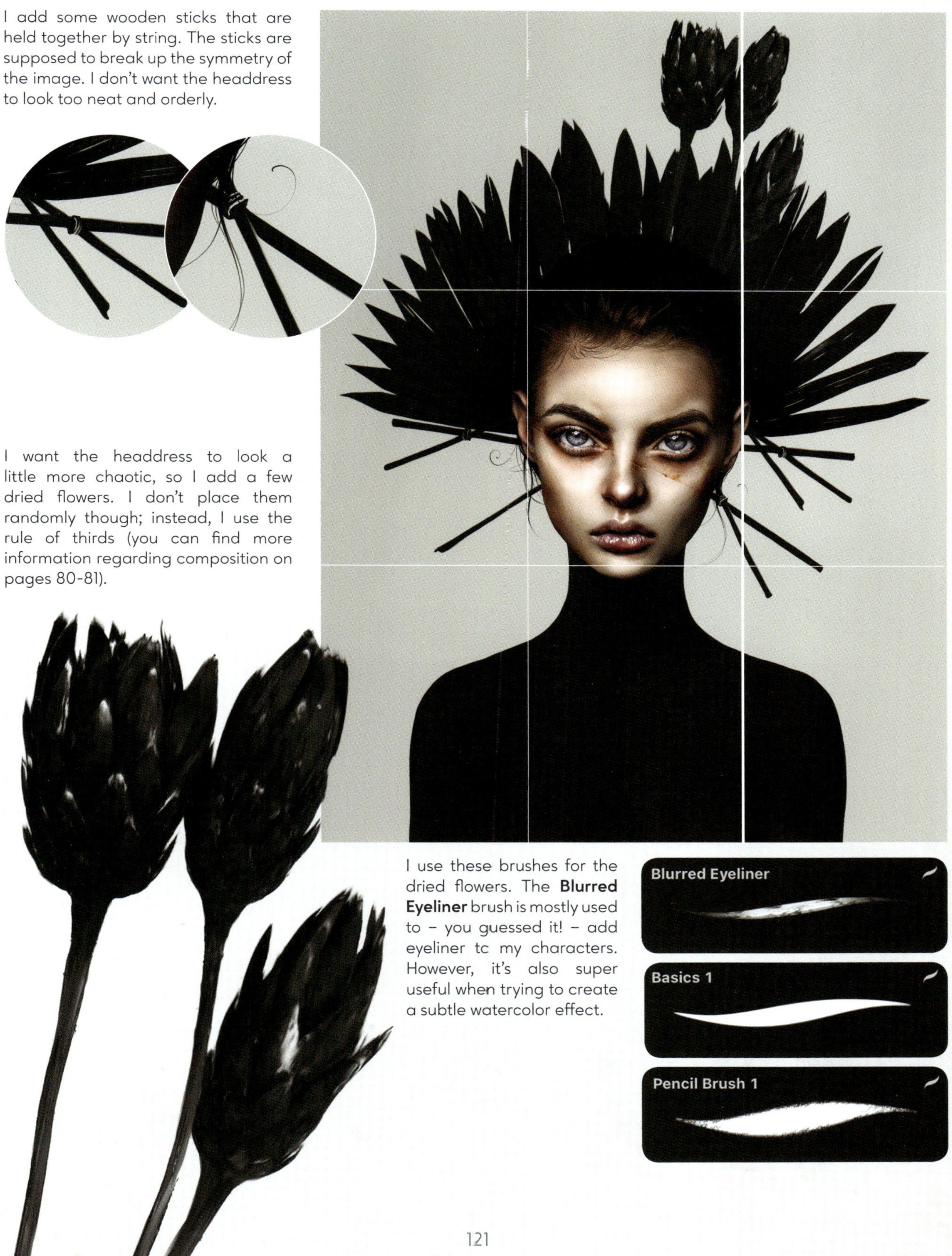

I use these brushes for the dried flowers. The **Blurred Eyeliner** brush is mostly used to – you guessed it! – add eyeliner to my characters. However, it's also super useful when trying to create a subtle watercolor effect.

STEP10

STRINGS

I add a few more elements, namely strings wrapping around the character's face and headdress. As my mood board reference seems too painful to me, I place my strings loosely so that they appear decorative... and not like a torture device.

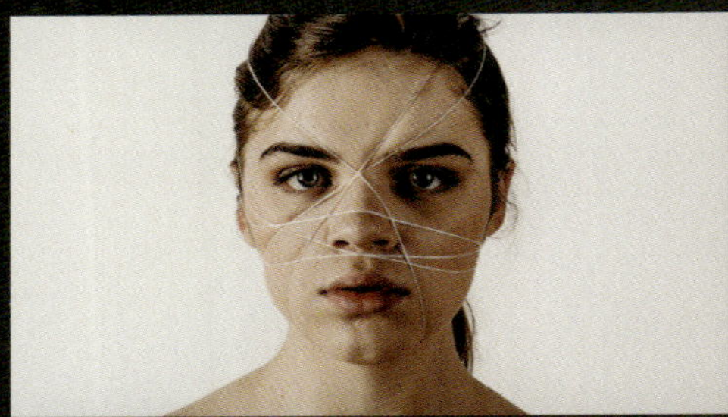

It's incredibly important to remember the strings cast shadows onto the skin:

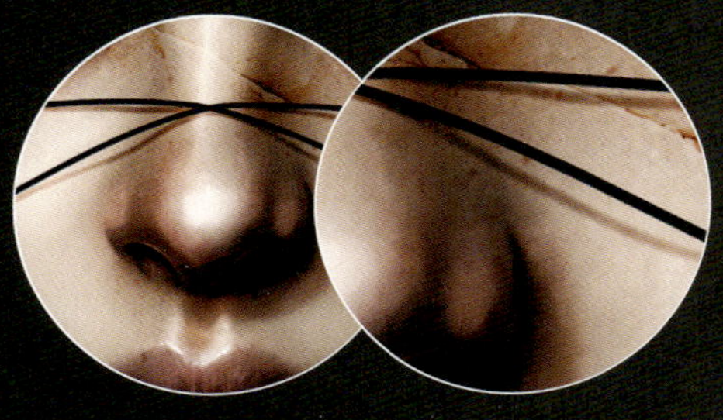

You can use the method we used in step 6.7 to create these shadows. Use one of the blending brushes in combination with a dark brown color, then set the layer to Soft Light or Hard Light, whichever looks better.

> If the object casting the shadow moves farther away from the skin, the shadow's opaqueness will lessen. Start with an opaque line, then mask out the areas that receive less shadow.

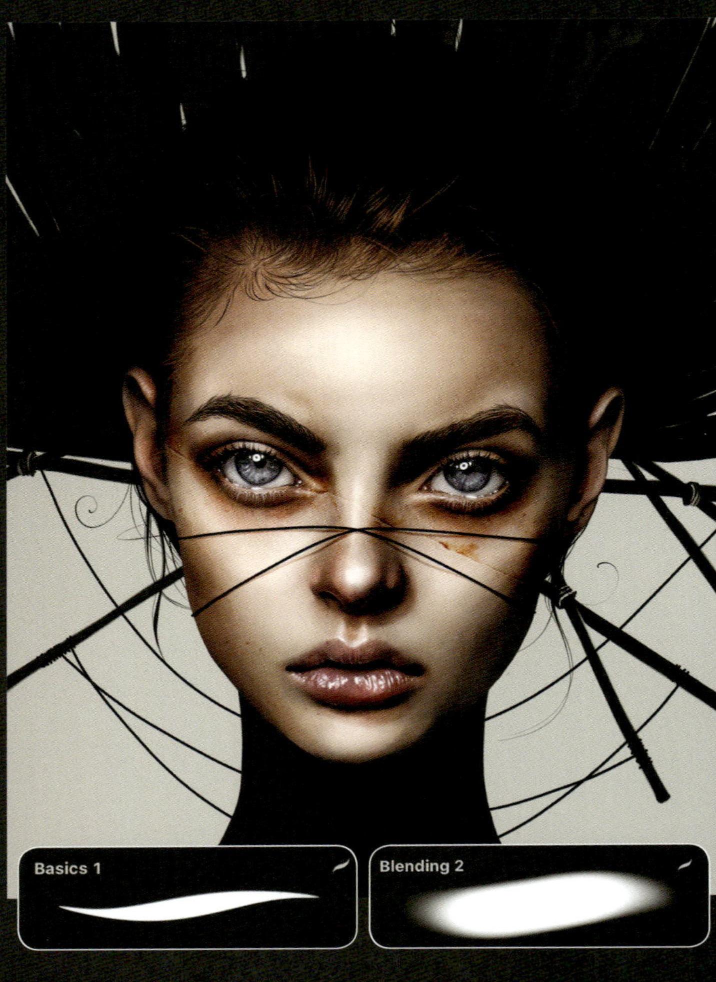

CREATE A LAYER MASK

Friendly reminder: layer masks are very important! Create one by tapping on your desired layer, followed by **Mask**. A new white layer (linked to your original layer) will appear. Layer masks let you render areas of your layer invisible, but it's easy to make them visible again. This process is non-destructive, so if you're unsure whether you want to delete something, always use a mask.

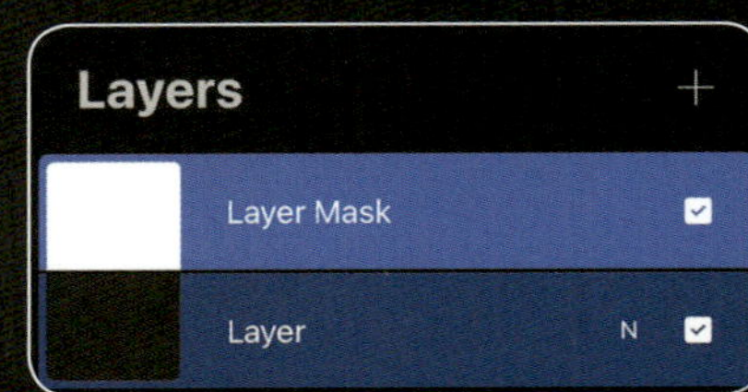

To turn an area invisible, use black to draw on the layer mask. To make it visible again, use white. If you want to reduce an area's opacity, use a shade of gray; the darker the gray, the less opaque it will appear.

Remember: we're drawing on the layer mask to make these adjustments, not the original layer.

STEP11

FINAL DETAILS

I add a few final touches, such as the septum piercing and the dark face-paint. Then I crop the image a little to improve the composition. It may seem like a waste to crop out areas that we painstakingly painted, but the character had too much empty room around her. Besides, your viewers won't know or care how much effort you put into those areas. It's better to make these decisions rationally rather than emotionally.

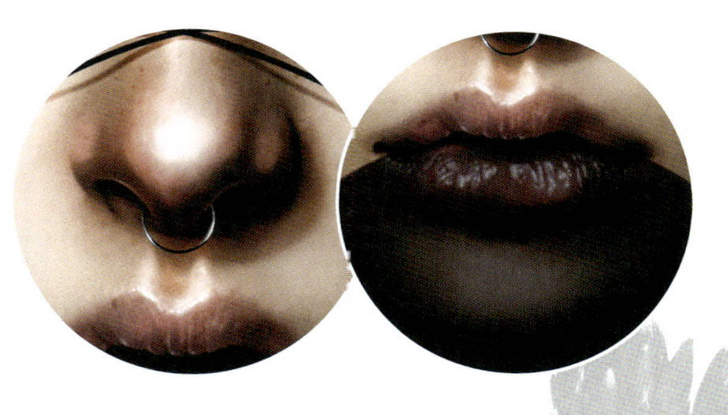

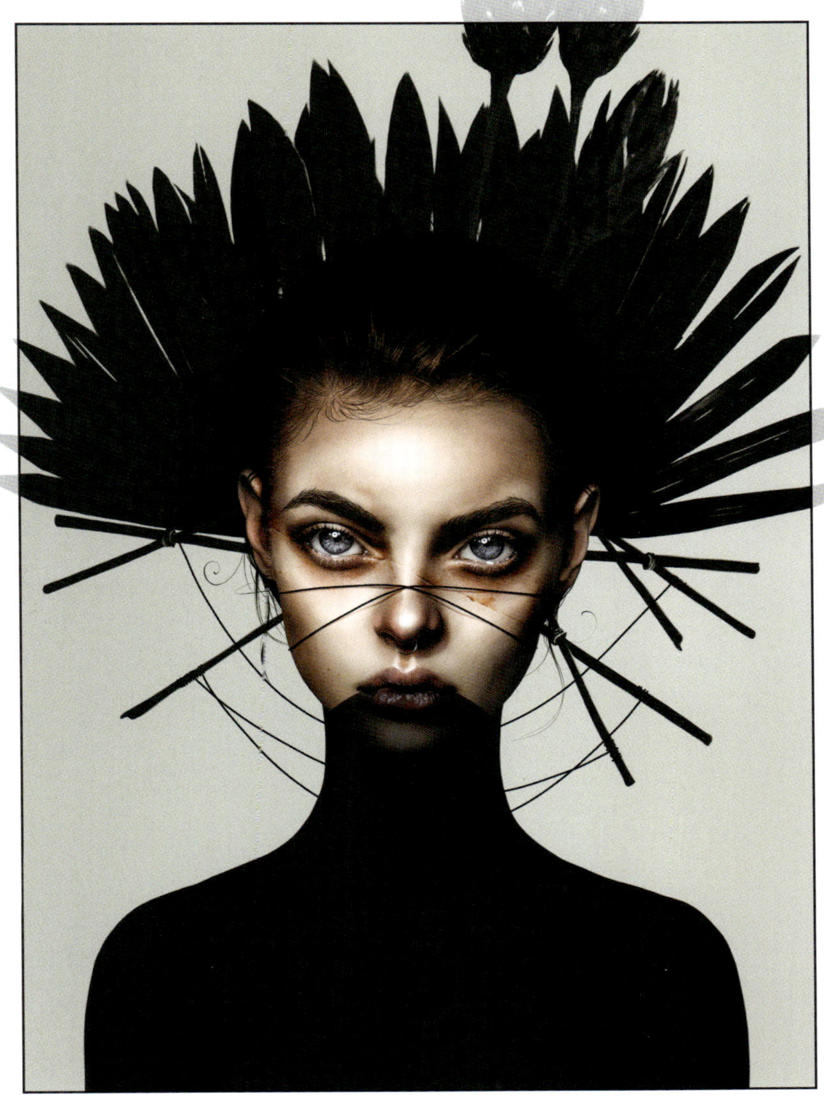

STEP12

12.1 COLOR GRADING

As you saw during the tutorial, Procreate gives its users many tools to fine-tune colors, such as **Color Balance**, **Curves**, **Gradient Maps**, and the **Hue**, **Saturation**, **Brightness** setting. They're all fairly straightforward, so I'd recommend simply playing around with them to understand their functions. For this painting, I choose to increase the saturation and contrast, as well as shift the color balance slightly toward the blues.

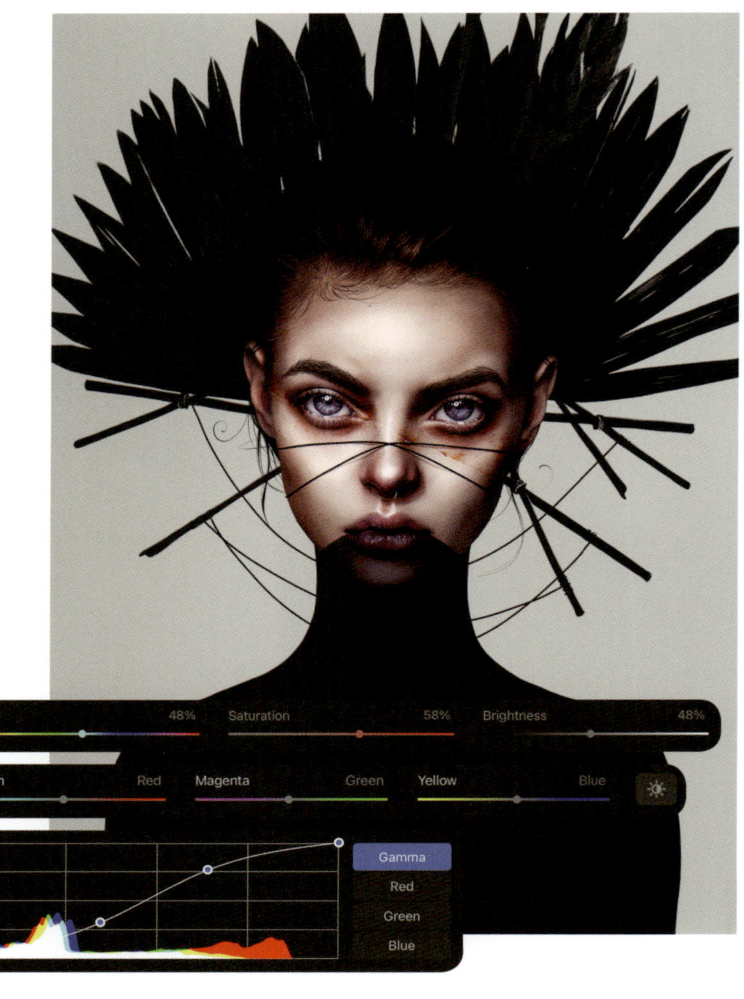

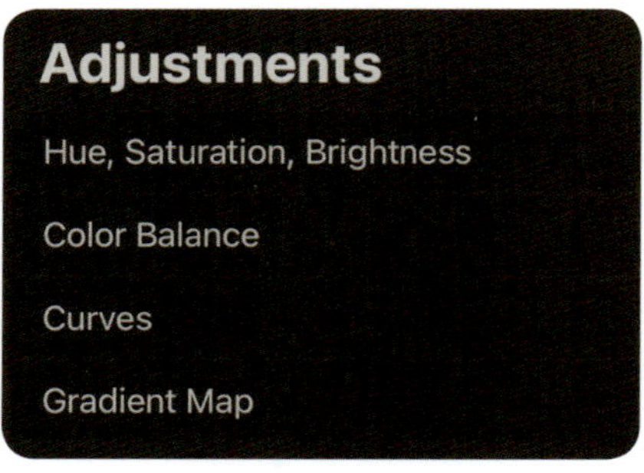

12.2 FINISHING

One of the last adjustments I make sure never to skip (even if I'm the only one who notices) is **Noise**. I add one final layer and fill the entire canvas with a Noise brush, then set the layer to **Add**. This creates an effect normally associated with photography and high ISO settings. For us, it adds a little more texture, and as a result, the illusion of more detail.

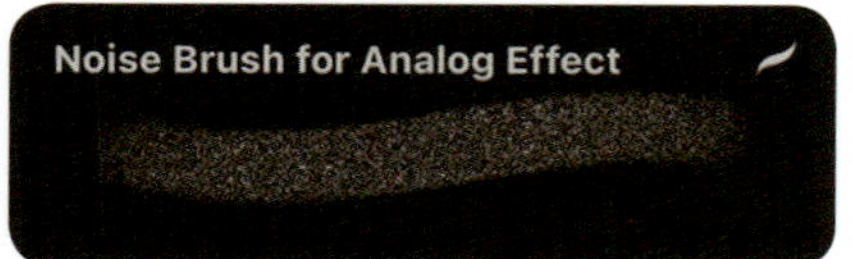

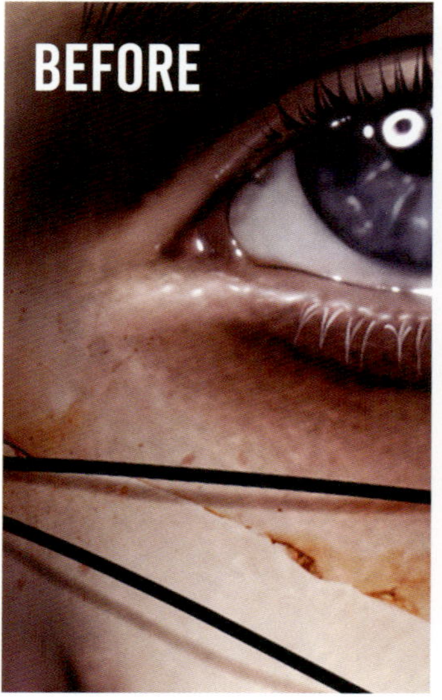

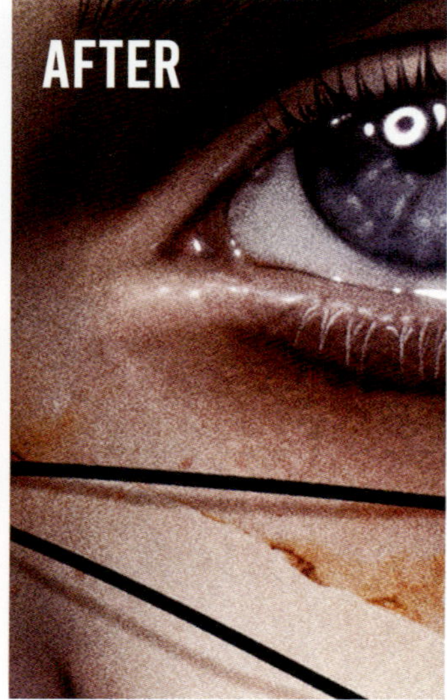

STEP13

LAST BUT NOT LEAST:

GIVE YOUR ARTWORK A NAME

The name you choose for your work can reinforce the piece's meaning or add background information and personality to your character. It can help your viewers understand what you're trying to say with your art. That's not to say that good art always needs to have deeper meaning – it's perfectly okay to pick a name just because it's pretty.

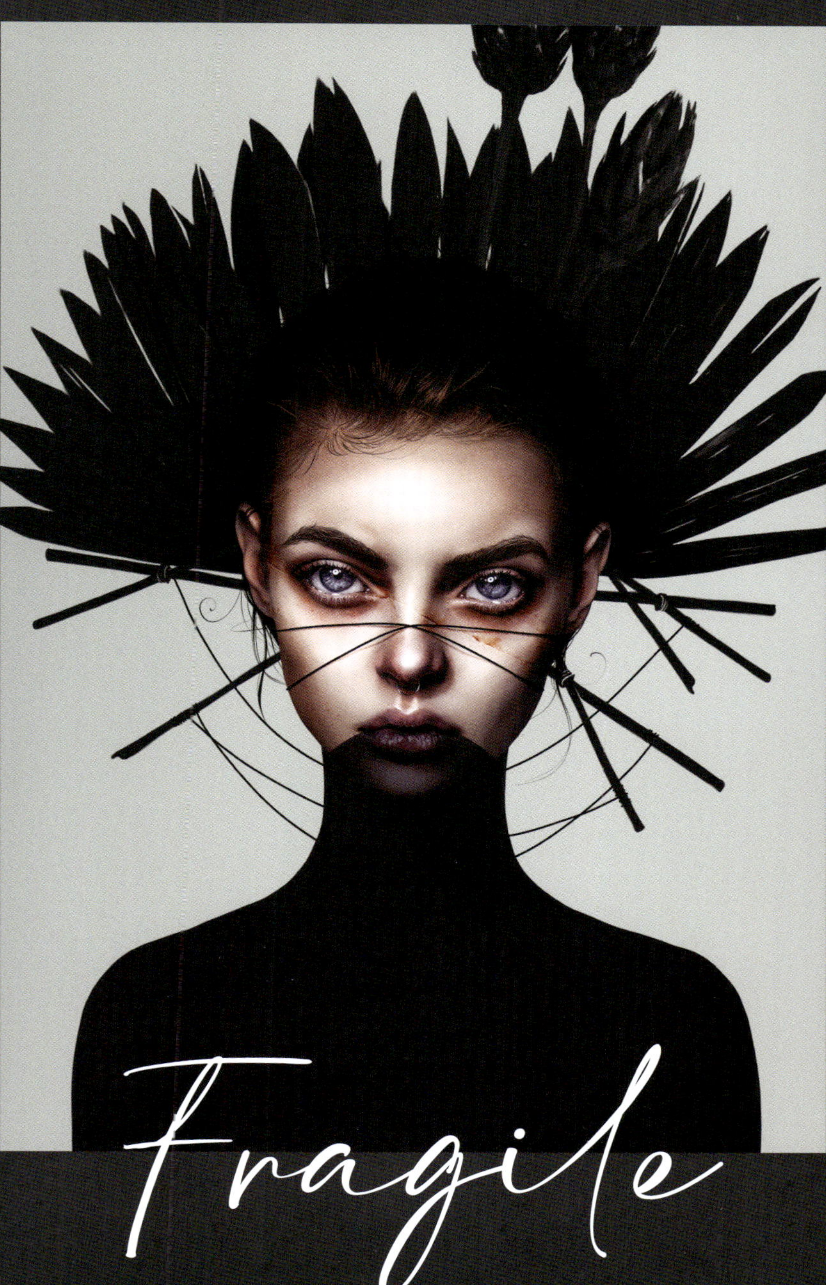

EXPORT SETTINGS

Now we're ready to export our finished painting! Tap on **Actions**, followed by **Share**. Here, you'll find a variety of file formats to pick from:

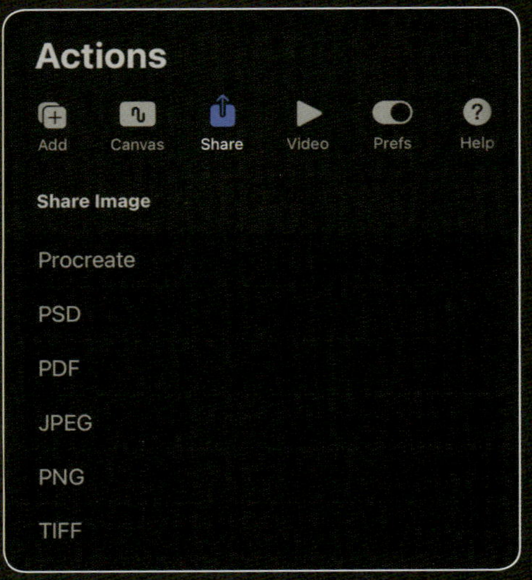

JPEG/JPG

The JPEG or JPG is the most common file format for image files. If you want to export your artwork as an image to use for social media, as an example, then JPG is the correct choice.

PNG

Images in the PNG format take up more space than JPG files, because they're lossless: you can re-open, edit, and re-save a PNG as much as you want without it degrading in quality. PNGs are also capable of containing an alpha channel, so it supports transparency. That said, it does not support CMYK color profiles, so it's not suitable for printing.

TIFF

Just like PNG, the TIFF file format is lossless, but it offers support for CMYK color profiles and layers. If you want to hand your file directly to a print shop, TIFF is the way to go.

PDF

PDFs are capable of storing vector graphics and text. As such, they are mostly used for documents containing both text and images. PDFs can be saved either lossless or lossy, so file size can vary greatly. For instance, if you want to send someone a resume with a portfolio section, PDFs are a good choice.

PSD

PSD is Photoshop's native file format. Photoshop has been the standard in image-editing software for decades and is frequently used in conjunction with Procreate. If you're planning on further refining your project in Photoshop, you can export it as a PSD. All your layers and layer effects will remain intact.

PROCREATE

The Procreate file format allows you to save your entire project, including all effects and layers. If you're trying to pass your artwork on to another artist for a collaboration, then it's a good choice to export in this file format.

VIDEO

If you switch over from the Share category to Video, you can export your own time-lapse video. Procreate automatically records every action you take and compiles it into a handy little time-lapse video.

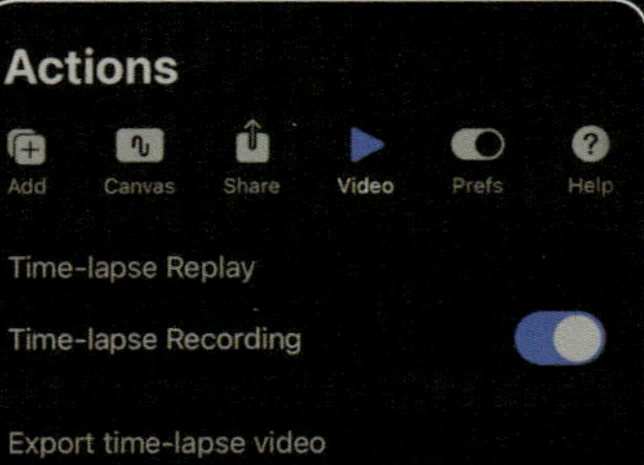

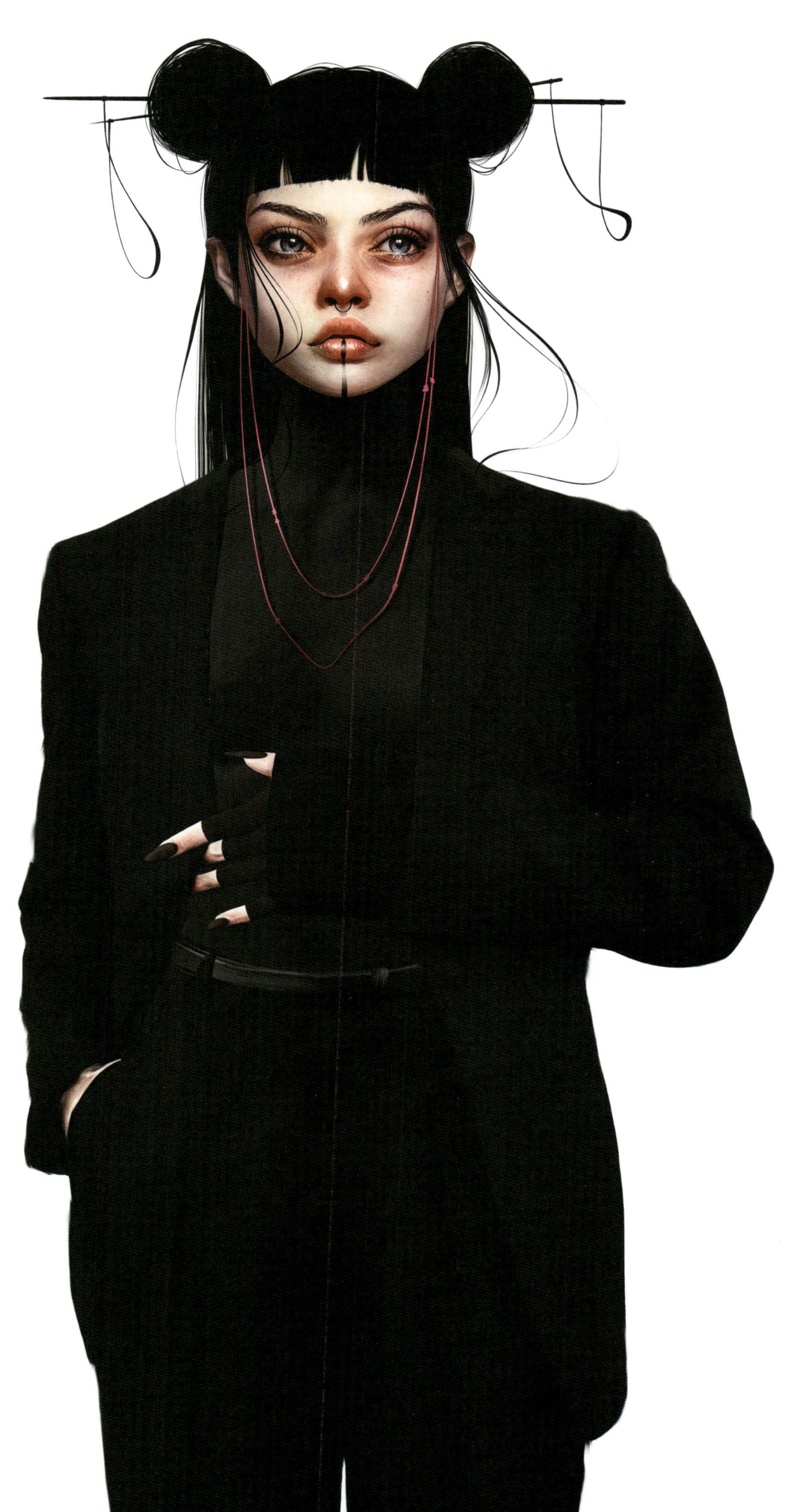

CHEAT SHEET

"IT'S SO FINE AND YET SO TERRIBLE TO STAND IN FRONT OF A BLANK CANVAS"

– Paul Cezanne

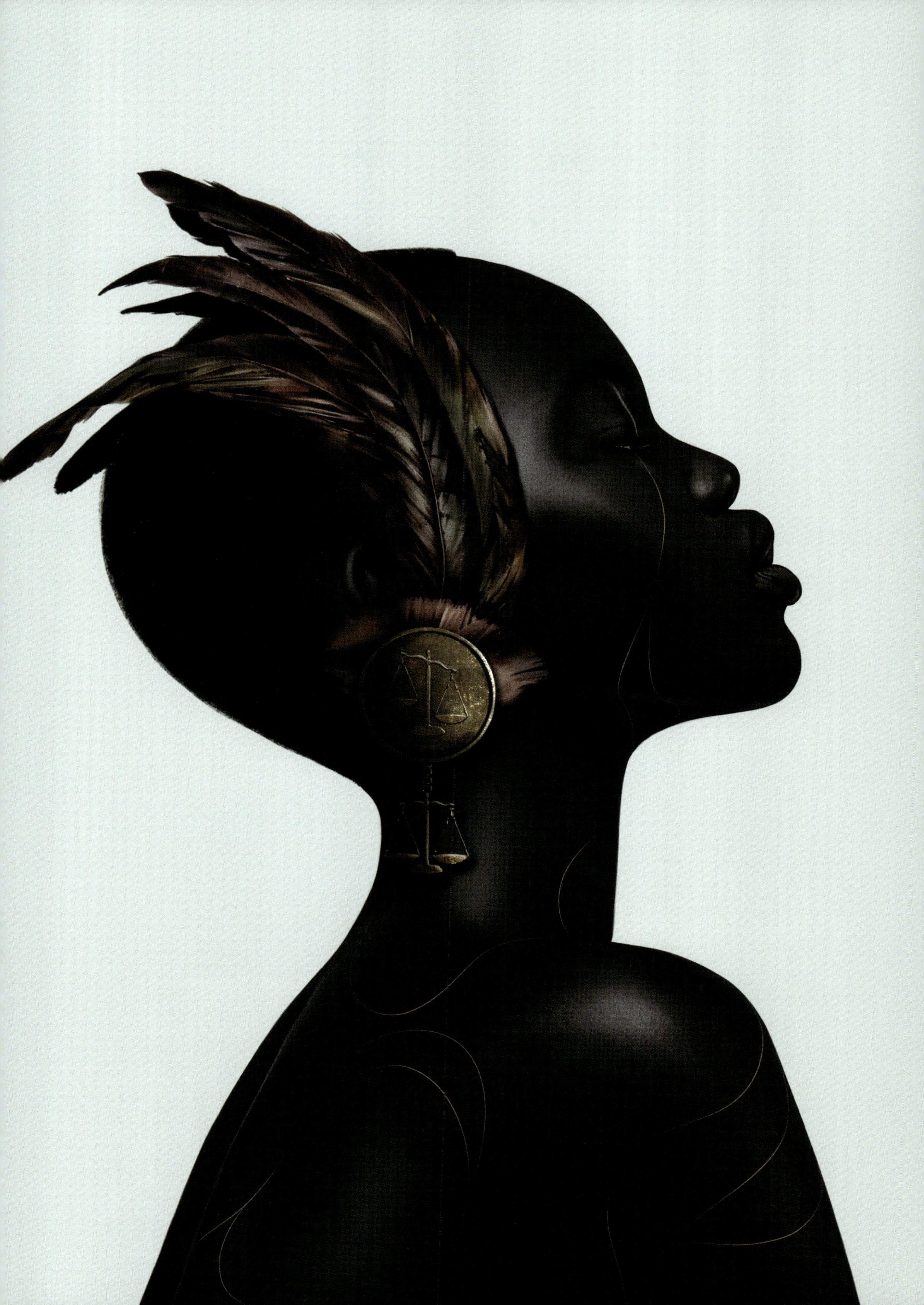

CHEAT SHEET

Here, you can find helpful tools and information that may improve your workflow. These are mostly things I learned over the course of many years and wish I'd known from the start!

Adjustments

Hue, Saturation, Brightness
Color Balance
Curves
Gradient Map

Gaussian Blur
Motion Blur
Perspective Blur

Noise
Sharpen
Bloom
Glitch
Halftone
Chromatic Aberration

Liquify
Clone

LIQUIFY TOOL

These days, you can find the Liquify tool in Procreate as well as many other image-editing programs. It liquifies your layer to make organic changes, such as nudging an asymmetric face in strategic spots to achieve symmetry, without having to repaint anything. The tool is easy to understand and use. You can find it under **Adjustments**. The settings at the bottom let you fine-tune the strength of the tool, as well as its specific function. You can move areas, rotate them, pinch, or expand them. To get a better idea of its functions, I recommend testing them on a photo.

REALISTIC PORTRAIT BRUSHES

Realistic-looking skin and hair brushes can really speed up your workflow. In this brush set, you can find 102 portrait brushes that imitate different skin types. It also houses a variety of hair, makeup, and texture brushes, and now even 21 fur brushes. You can find the link to the brushes on my website under Brushes & More.

www.laurahrubin.com

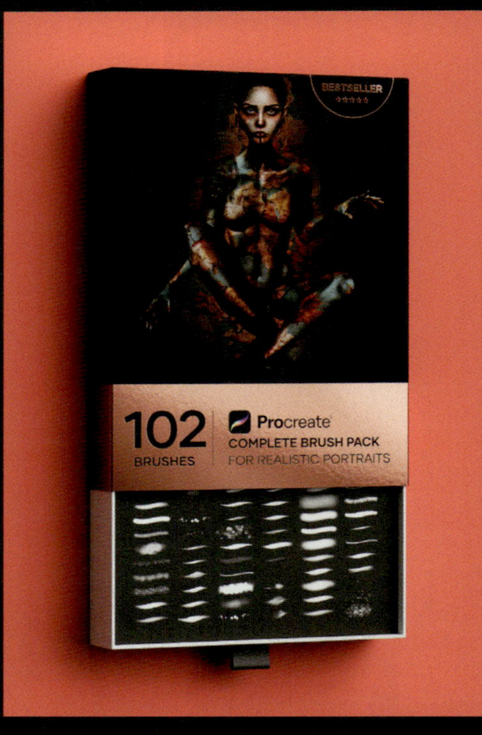

PROPORTION STAMPS & PERSPECTIVE STAMPS

If you're having issues creating realistic proportions or perspectives, you might find these stamp sets useful. You can find the link to the stamps on my website under Brushes & More.

www.laurahrubin.com

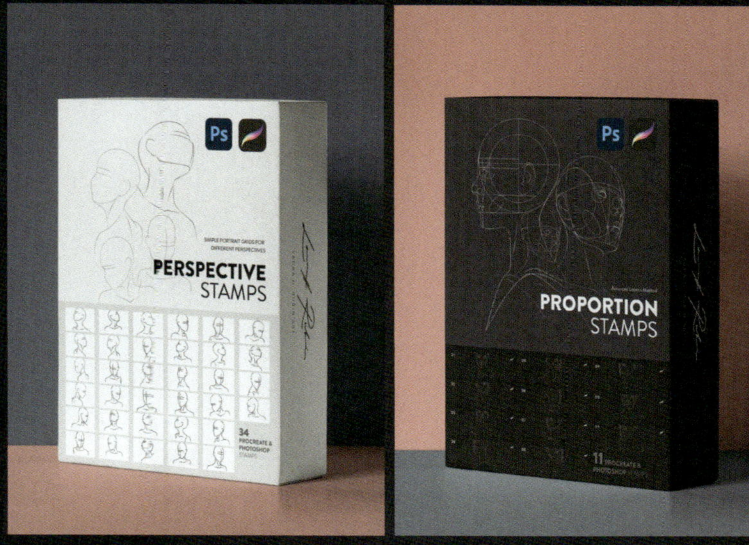

BASIC HEADS TO BUILD UPON

If you need more help with creating your characters, these head templates may come in handy. The set includes 66 busts from various perspectives, from which you can build your own character by drawing over the template. You can find the link to the head templates on my website under Brushes & More.

www.laurahrubin.com

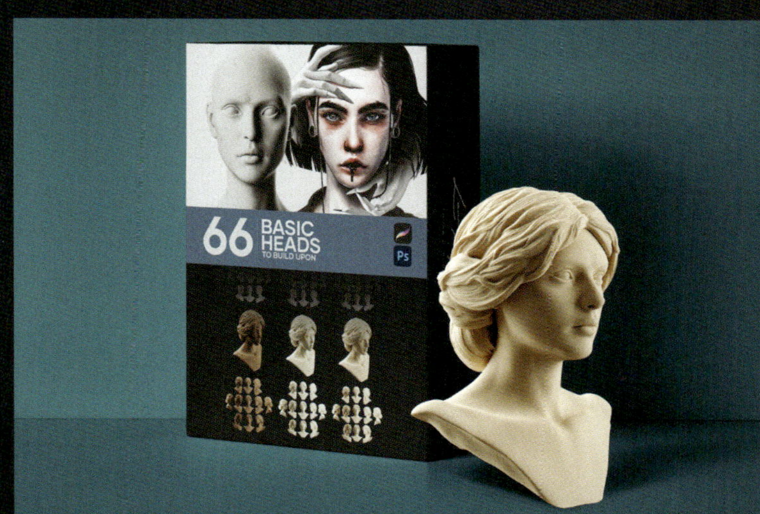

POSE APPS

You can use apps such as ArtPose or Magic Poser to create poses and choose perspectives in a 3D space. All you have to do is import the image directly into Procreate. The Magic Poser app is a little more expensive and only available by subscription, but it allows for additional functionality and presents a better user experience than ArtPose. Since I don't use complex poses that often, ArtPose has been good enough for me.

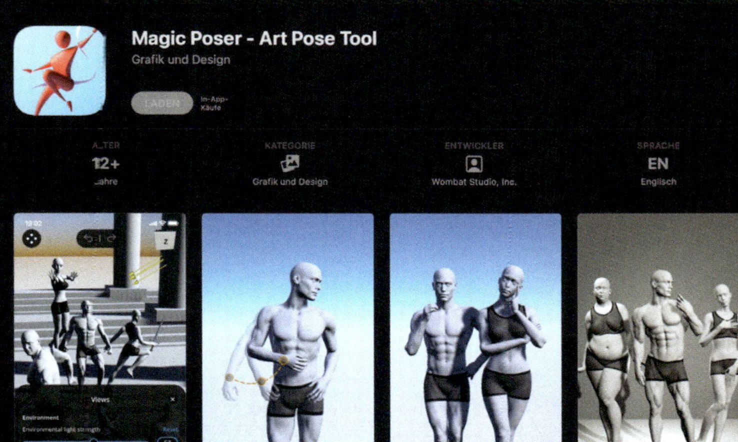

TOPAZ GIGAPIXEL AI

Topaz Gigapixel is an AI tool that can upscale images without compromising their quality. Most images look even better and more detailed than before. It is especially useful for those who want their images printed larger than the image resolution actually allows.

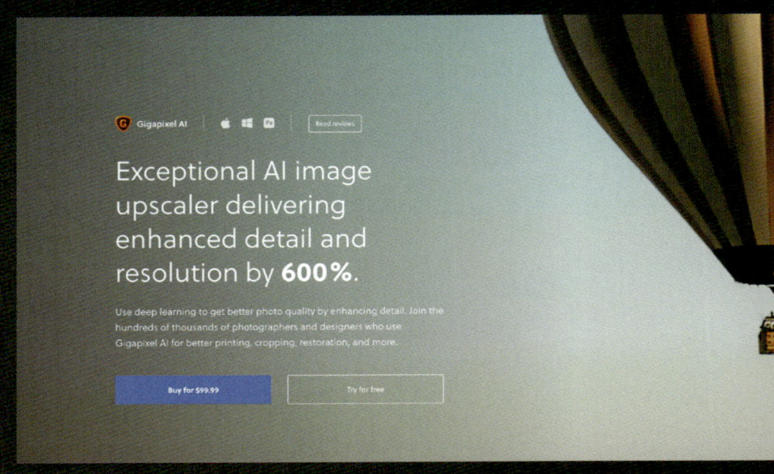

FACE GENERATOR

If you need inspiration for a new project, it may be worth trying an AI face generator. There are a few different ones available, and quality varies. I haven't been able to test it yet, but I've heard good things about the website https://generated.photos. Try generating a realistic face and using it as a reference!

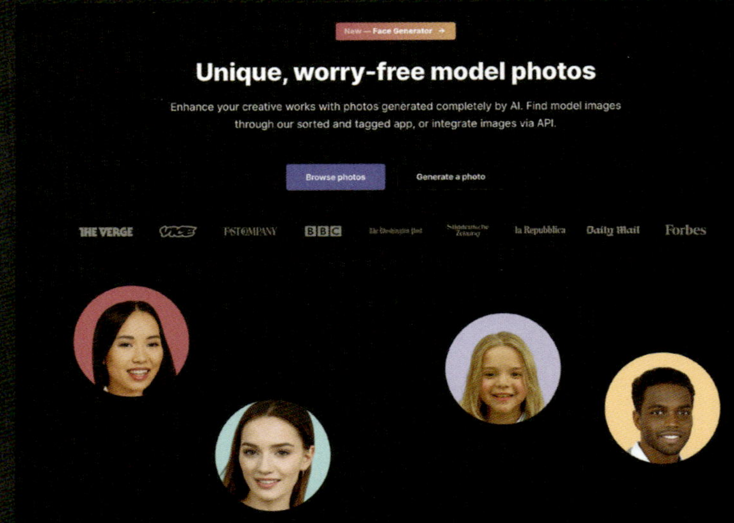

COLOR PALETTES

If at any point you're not happy with your generated color palettes, then you might find the palettes on my website useful. There's a variety of palettes for skin colors or general inspiration. You can find the link on my website under Brushes & More.

www.laurahrubin.com
#Freebie

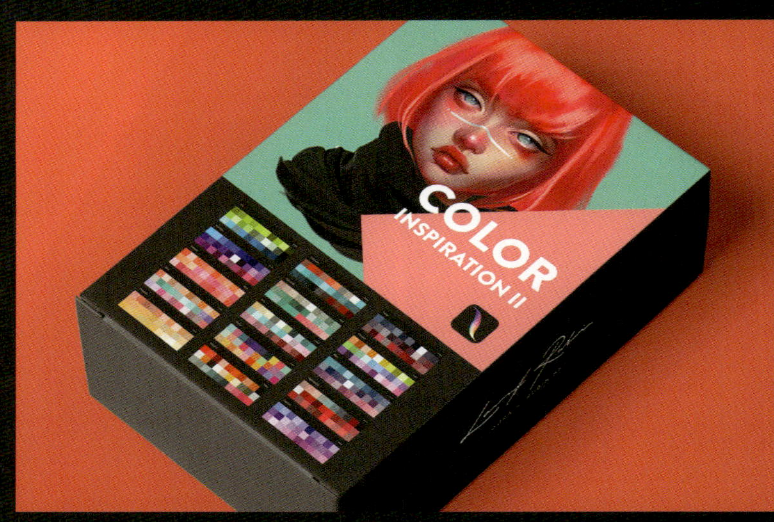

HELPING HANDS

If you find hands difficult to master, you can find a set of realistically painted hands on my website, including a construction grid. They are available under Brushes & More.

www.laurahrubin.com
#Freebie

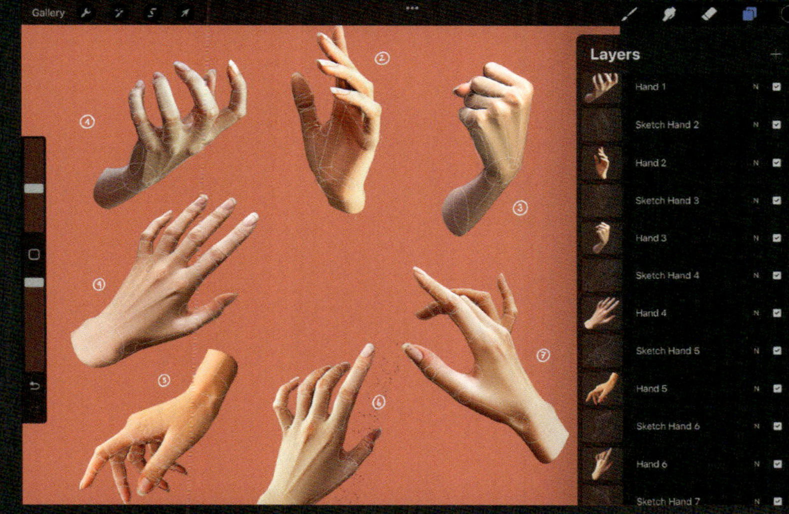

PAPER TEXTURES

If you're in a rush and don't have time to paint detailed skin textures, then using a sheet of paper (with visible grain texture) is a quick cheat. You can either photograph your own or download one online, then import the file into your project. Change the layer effect from **Normal** to **Multiply**, and you should be able to see the paper texture on the layers below, while the paper itself is invisible. The paper grain lends itself to a more or less realistic skin texture.

LAYER EFFECTS

Don't underestimate layer effects – you can save a lot of time if you use layer effects in strategic places. For instance, try importing a picture with a few bright flowers into your current project, and then change the layer effect (to whichever one you want; I'd try them all). Depending on which effect you pick, you can add a whole new flair to your image.

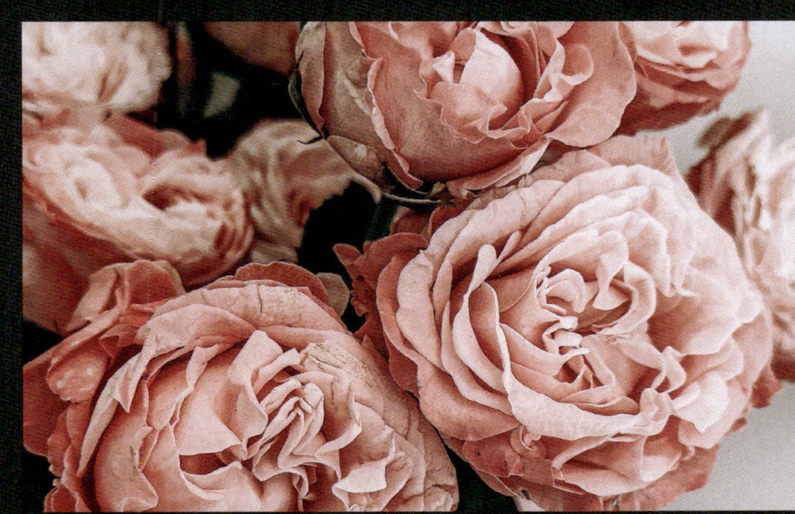

QUESTIONS & ANSWERS

"HOW YOU DRAW IS A REFLECTION OF HOW YOU FEEL ABOUT THE WORLD. YOU'RE NOT CAPTURING IT, YOU'RE INTERPRETING IT"

– Juliette Aristides

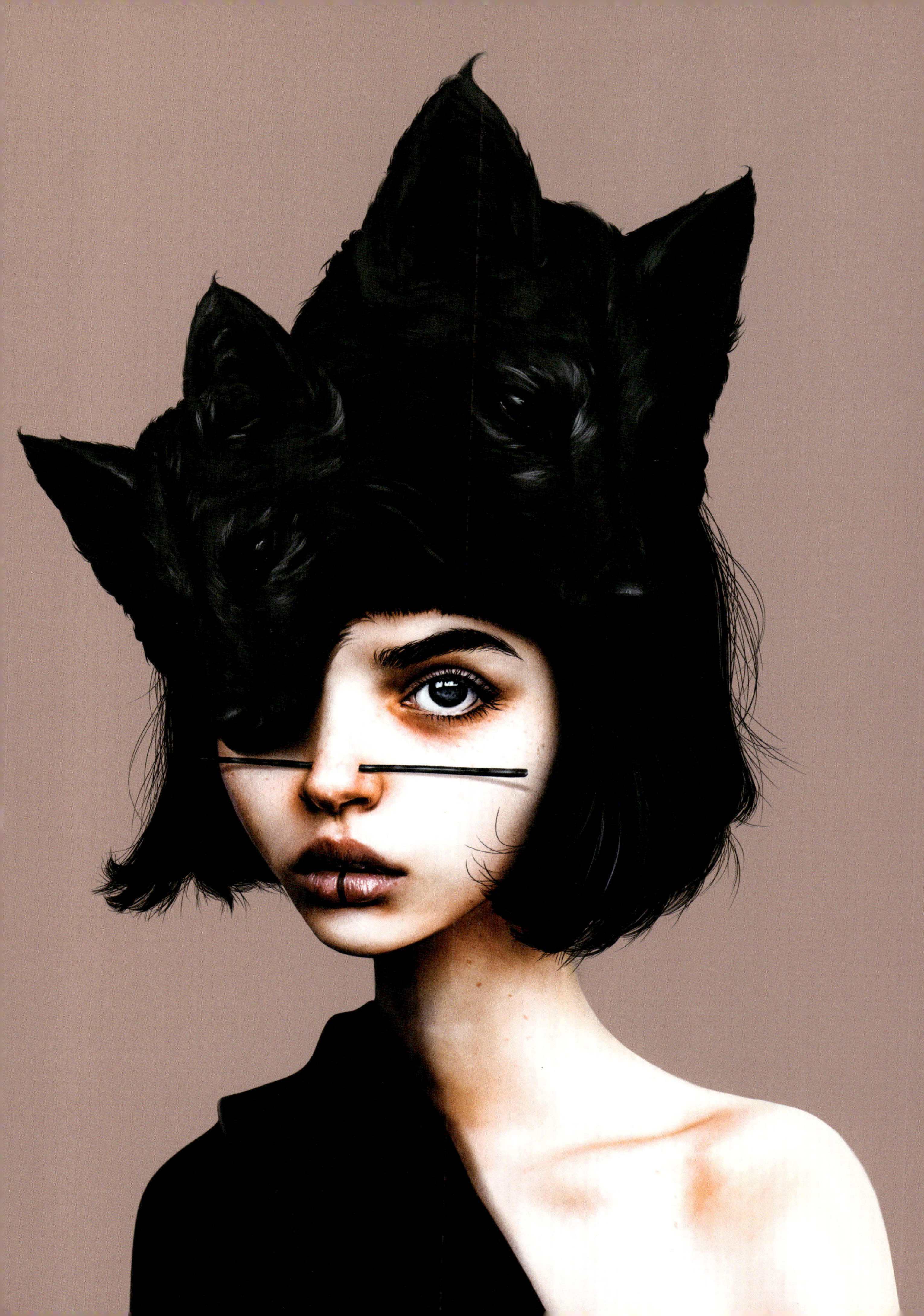

QUESTIONS & ANSWERS

WHAT DO YOU THINK OF NFTs?

Pros: It's a good source of income for digital artists, especially those specializing in art that may not be suitable for every living room (such as the stunning work by @Beeple_crap, who started the trend).

Cons: There's a staggering impact to the environent from blockchain technology.

Conclusion: We should avoid things that cause harm to our planet as much as possible. If you want to create an NFT, I'd suggest only doing so if you already have an interested party. Ninety-seven per cent of NFTs remain unsold and, as such, are unnecessarily integrated into the blockchain, rendering the environmental impact a complete waste.

WHO ARE SOME OF YOUR FAVORITE ARTISTS?

My favorite artists (among the living) are: Eva Gamayun, Nathaniel Gray, Korali Lopez, as well as Nikolay Ryazanskiy, Pablo Hurtado de Mendoza, Zeen Chin, João Ruas, and many more!

WHAT DO YOU LIKE TO DO WHEN YOU'RE NOT DRAWING?

I like to read, craft, and repair random items. I love caring for my plants, visiting quiet places in nature, playing video games, and collecting antique things.

HOW DO YOU DEAL WITH ART BLOCK?

I do something completely different. I try out new cuisines, watch a movie I've never seen before, go for a walk in a new place, or just generally expose myself to a new experience. Your brain is quick to respond to new inputs, and you'll find new inspirations in the process.

WHAT'S MOST DIFFICULT FOR YOU TO PAINT?

Honestly, there are very few things that I find easy to draw. Even though I have a lot of practice, I rarely know whether something will turn out well. That said, I think emotions are the most difficult thing to paint convincingly.

DO YOU EVER HAVE DOUBTS IN YOUR WORK?

Yes. I often see work by other artists and think, "Damn, why are they all better than I am?" It's okay to have some self-doubts, but it's not healthy to frequently compare yourself to others. I'm still learning this lesson myself.

HOW DO I FIND MY OWN STYLE?

By searching for it among the various styles of other artists. Look for artists whose work you love and let yourself be inspired by them. You'll automatically start combining and integrating various styles into your work, which will turn into your own style over time.

It was Picasso who said: "Good artists borrow, great artists steal." Of course, that doesn't mean you should literally steal someone else's work, but rather let yourself be inspired by it. If someone calls you a copycat, ignore them!

WHAT SORT OF EDUCATION IS NECESSARY TO BE ABLE TO LIVE OFF YOUR ART EVENTUALLY?

Here in Switzerland, there is no type of training to become an artist, by definition. However, there are creative jobs (which pay very well) that can help you become a graphic designer, photographer, VFX artist, and so much more. I would definitely recommend the SAE Institute, or training as a graphic designer. You will learn everything you need to know in these fields, and will most likely find suitable jobs. Once you have a degree, I would also recommend seeking employment somewhere for a few years to discover more about the industry and how to deal with clients. Along the way, you can pursue your work as an artist and eventually be self-employed (as soon as you feel confident enough).

DO ARTISTS EARN ENOUGH MONEY?

If you do it right and stay relevant (including on new social-media platforms), then yes! It's possible to earn a lot more than the average 9-5 job would provide.

HOW DID YOU MANAGE TO SCORE CONTRACTS WITH DISNEY AND SQUARE ENIX?

I think they noticed me through my social-media accounts. If your goal is to have big companies notice you, it's probably worth looking into how to use strategic hashtags.

HOW DID YOU START SELLING YOUR ARTWORK?

I first tried to set up a Shopify store, but that was a mistake. Nothing against it, but you have to pay them a monthly fee, even though you might not be earning very much at the start. That means there's a guaranteed expense, but not necessarily a guaranteed income. After that, I switched to Redbubble, Society6, and InPRNT. These vendors take a cut of your income, but do not charge a fee. If you don't sell anything, you don't pay anything either, which is preferable when you're just starting out. I haven't had a bad experience with these vendors, so I'm still using them to this day!

HOW DO I ACHIEVE A BIGGER REACH ON INSTAGRAM?

- Use strategic/current/relevant hashtags that describe your image.
- Tag some of the bigger art accounts or magazines to make them notice you.
- Keep up to date with current trends.
- Connect with other artists. Giveaways are a great way to offer something exciting to your followers.
- Know your target audience. You can achieve a lot with just making pretty art, but try sharing some walk-through clips or mini tutorials, so your followers can learn something while scrolling through their feed. Everything is content.
- Lastly: always be nice and helpful and stay away from drama! If you don't have anything nice or constructive to say, don't say anything at all. There are already enough trolls on the internet!

EVEN THOUGH I PRACTICE A LOT, MY STYLE DOESN'T SEEM TO GET REALISTIC ENOUGH. WHAT AM I DOING WRONG?

Be honest with yourself – have you ever spent 20–30 hours working intensely on a piece of art? Most likely your work isn't bad, it just isn't finished yet. Painting realistically takes a long time. Don't give up!

Or... it could be possible that your strength lies in another genre of art. Your work doesn't have to be realistic to be great!

YOUR THREE FAVORITE CAREER MOMENTS?

1. When Disney contacted me for a collaboration.
2. When I was told that my work will be part of the 2024 Lunar Codex Project and will be sent to the moon in a time capsule.
3. When I was approached to write my first and second books.

WHAT KIND OF MUSIC INSPIRES YOU?

It depends on my mood, but I tend to listen to a lot of alt rock/metal such as BMTH, or metal hip-hop/rap like Hyro the Hero. I'm also fond of contemporary classical music such as Ludovico Einaudi or Danny Elfman.

ARE THERE ANY OTHER PROGRAMS YOU CAN RECOMMEND FOR DRAWING AND PAINTING?

Paid: Adobe Photoshop, Clip Studio Paint, CorelDRAW, Affinity Photo (cheaper Photoshop alternative).

Free: Krita, MediBang Paint Pro, Adobe Fresco (free for six months).

HAVE YOU MADE ANY MISTAKES AS AN ARTIST, AND WERE THERE WAYS TO PREVENT THEM IN HINDSIGHT?

First: you'll never get everyone to love your art. Instead, try not to take every criticism to heart. Learn to accept and use constructive criticism – if you don't, you're only hindering your own growth as artist.

Second: never turn down an offer just because you're scared to make a mistake. It's okay to make mistakes, that's how you learn. You don't learn anything by not trying something in the first place.

ARE YOU MORE PARTIAL TO TRADITIONAL OR DIGITAL ART/ ARTISTS?

Both equally! Traditional art feels more real in a way... but digital art is my passion, and since I studied Film and VFX in college, I also love every type of animated art.

DO YOU HAVE A BIG DREAM/GOAL YOU'D LIKE TO MAKE A REALITY?

One day, I would love to create the main character for a video game. I was recently offered precisely that, but I'd never heard of the game studio, despite being an active gamer, so I had a bad feeling and declined the offer. I'm still not sure whether I made the right decision, but I hope that my hunch was right.

ARE YOU EVER BORED WHILE PAINTING?

Yeeeah, usually when it comes to painting hair or mind-numbing details like eyelashes and pores. I recently discovered a love for true-crime podcasts and find they really help to relieve my boredom when rendering details.

HOW LONG DOES IT TAKE YOU TO CREATE A REALISTIC PORTRAIT?

Roughly 15–25 hours.

HAVE YOU EVER HAD ISSUES WITH TROLLS? HOW DO YOU DEAL WITH IT?

Sure, everyone with an online presence has had problems with trolls.

The most important rule is: don't feed the trolls! They're not worth engaging with because they're not arguing in good faith.

If you don't want to or can't ignore the troll, then disarm them. An imaginary scenario:

"I hate this! Your art is unprofessional!"

You can't learn anything from this criticism, so the commenter only wrote it to make you feel bad. The best response is probably something like this:

"I'm sorry that my work upsets you so much! I'll try my best to do better next time."

This answer doesn't leave any room for further unconstructive criticism. You absolutely don't have to apologize for your work, but this isn't about being right or wrong, you're just trying to make the troll go away.

GALLERY

"ARTISTS ARE JUST CHILDREN WHO REFUSE TO PUT DOWN THEIR CRAYONS"

– Al Hirschfeld

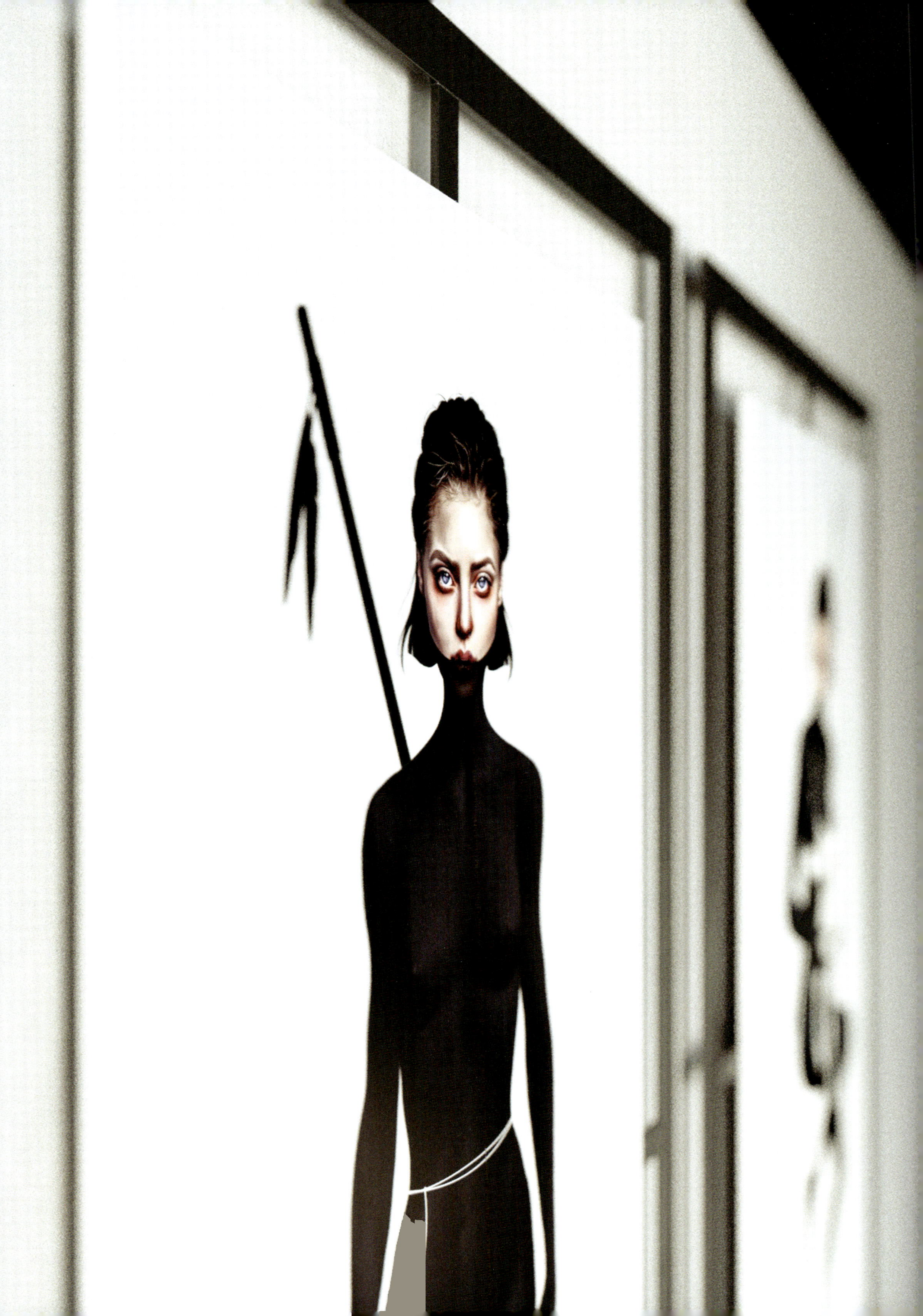

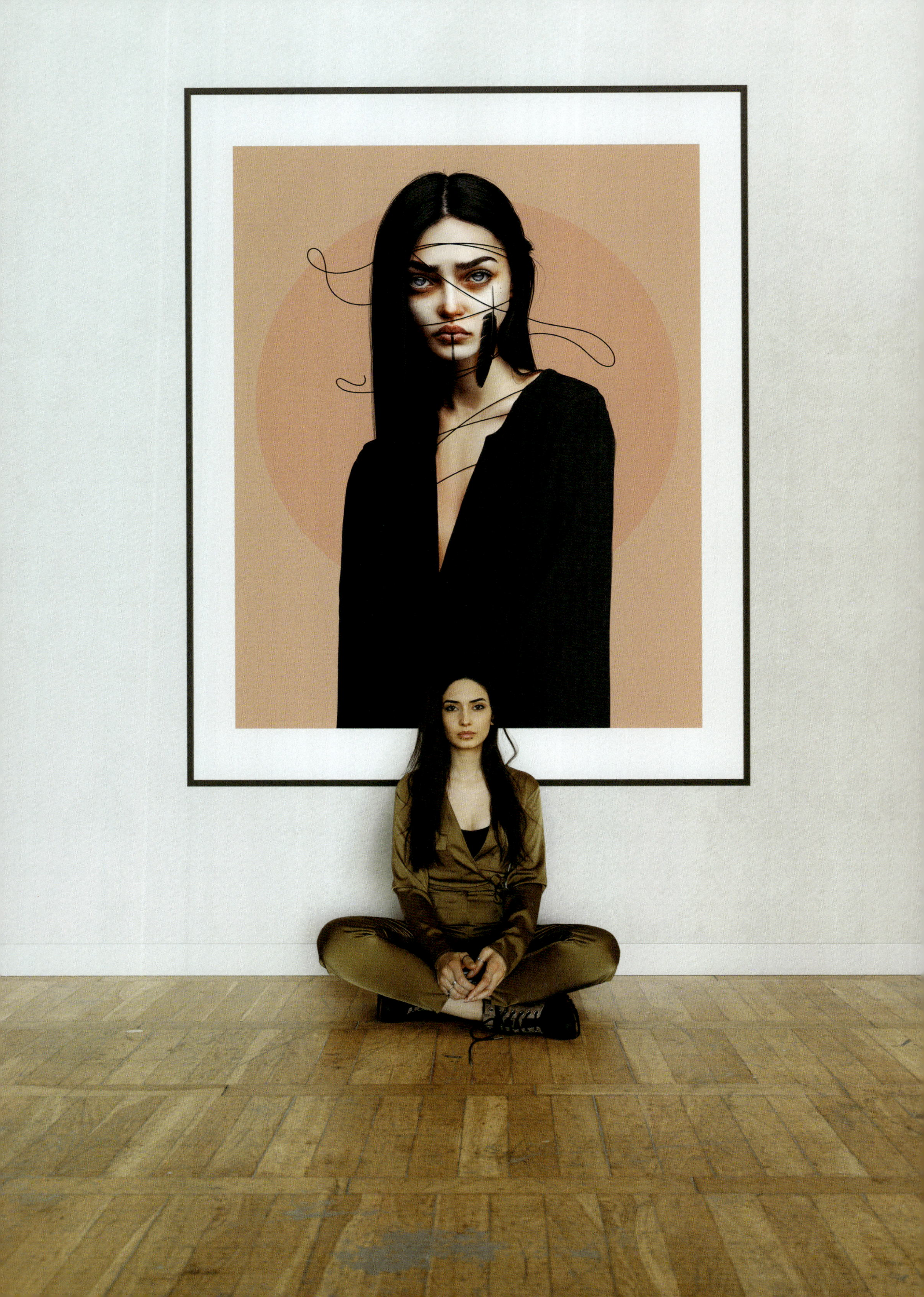

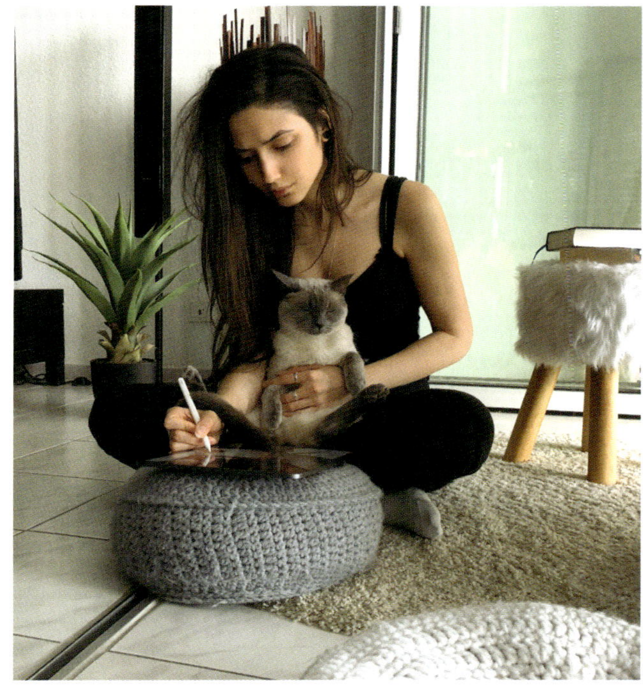
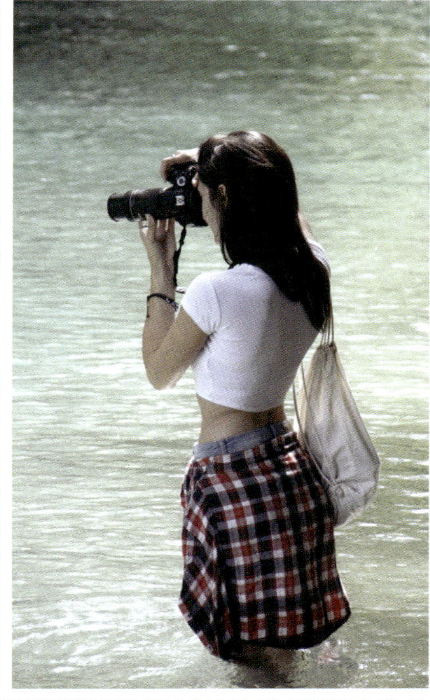
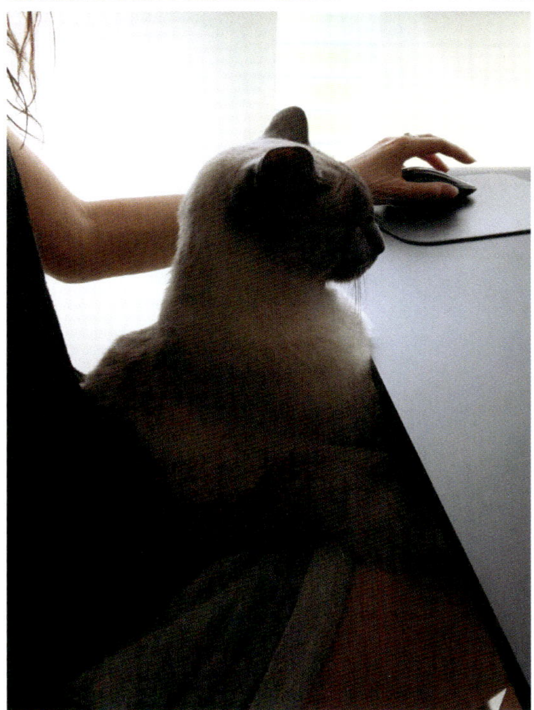
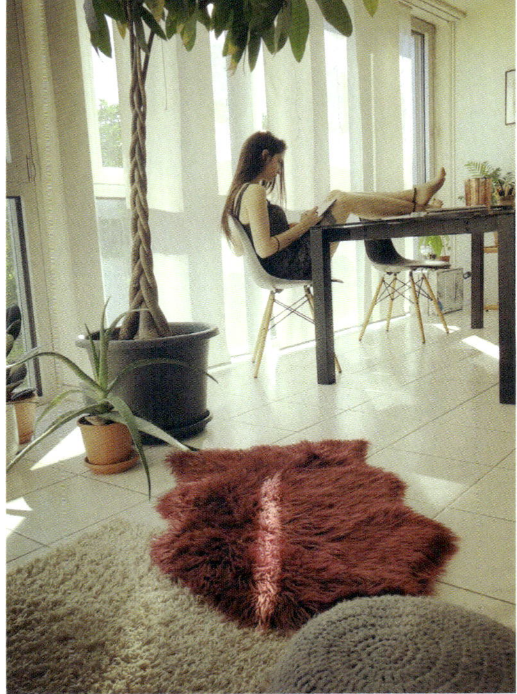

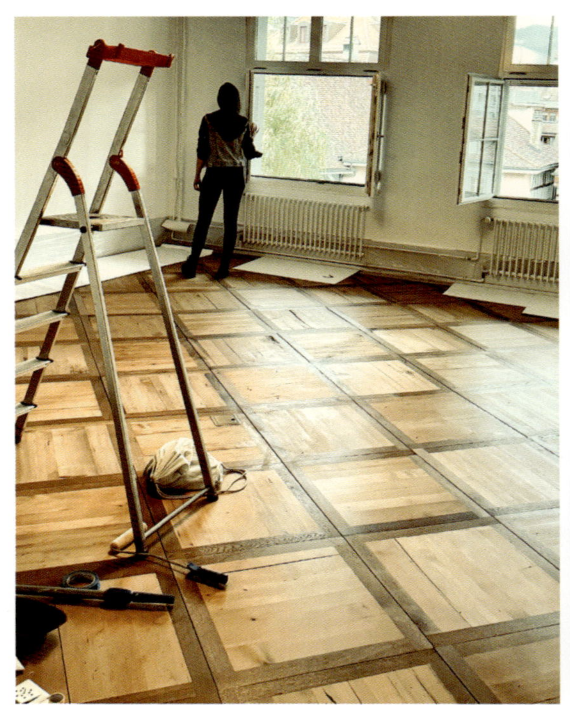
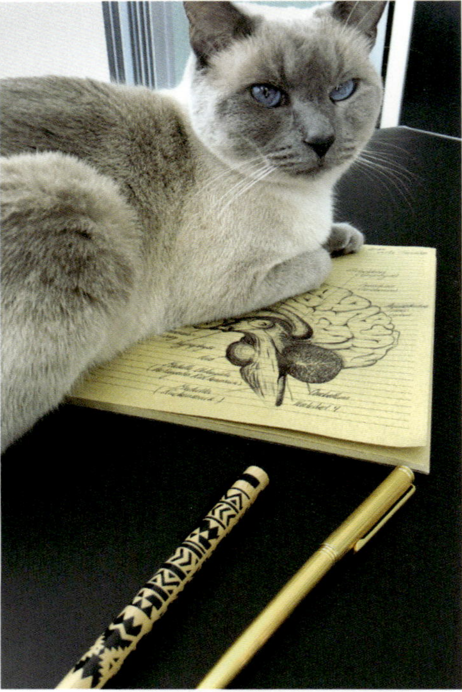
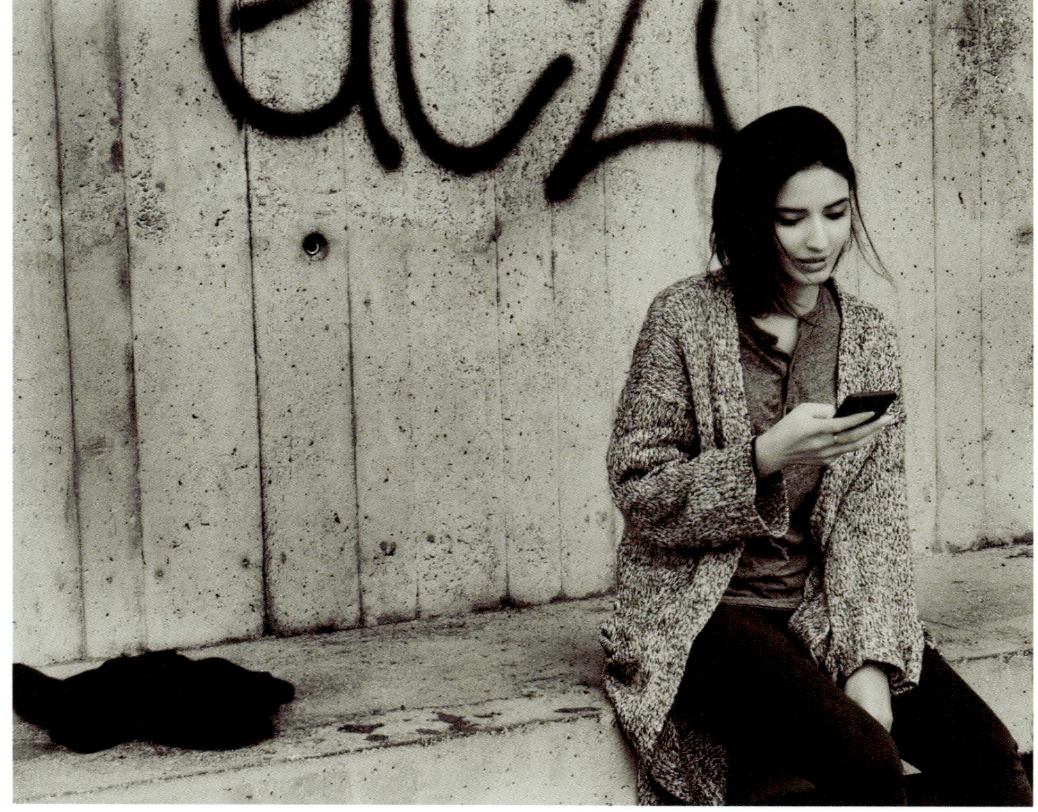

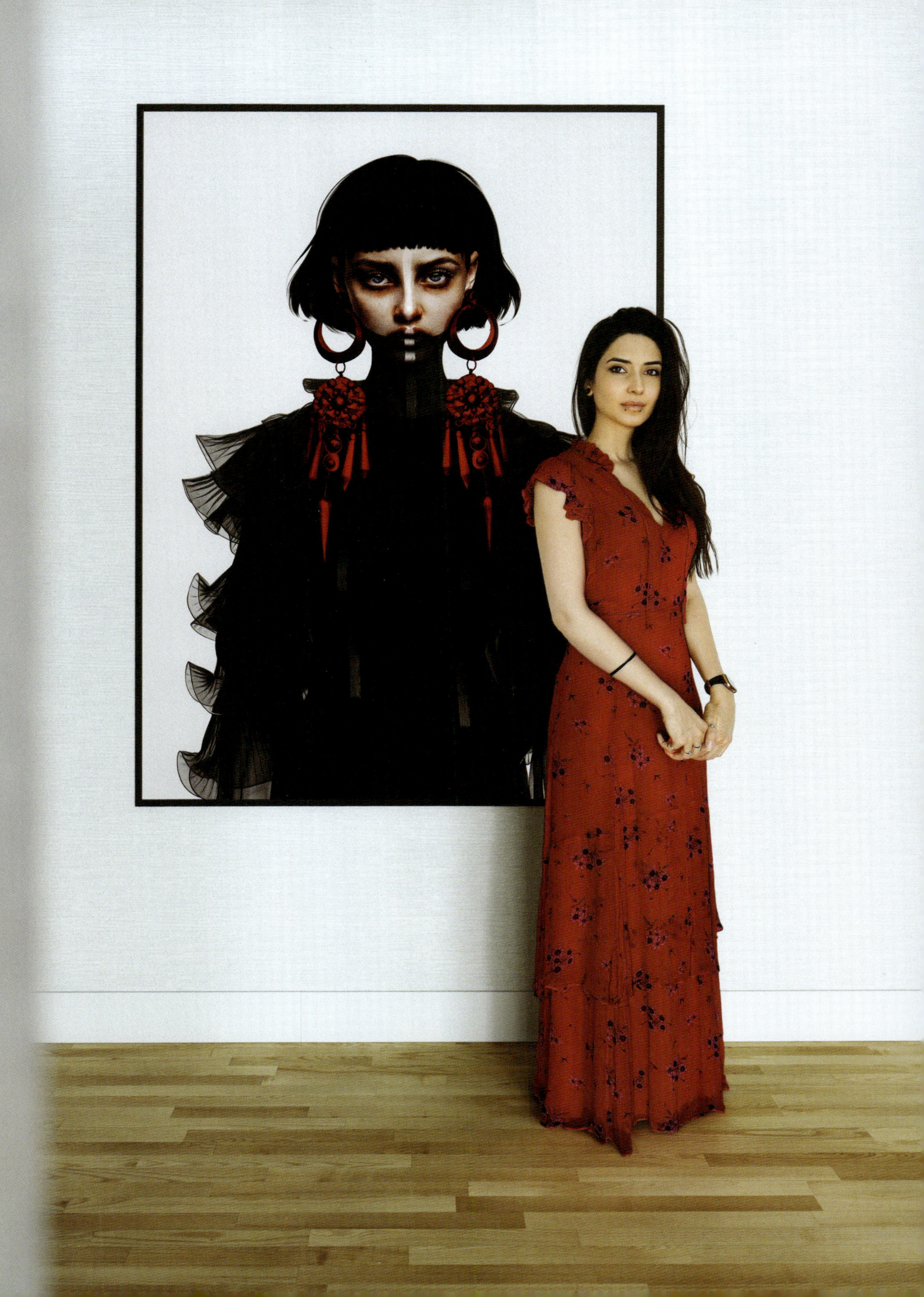

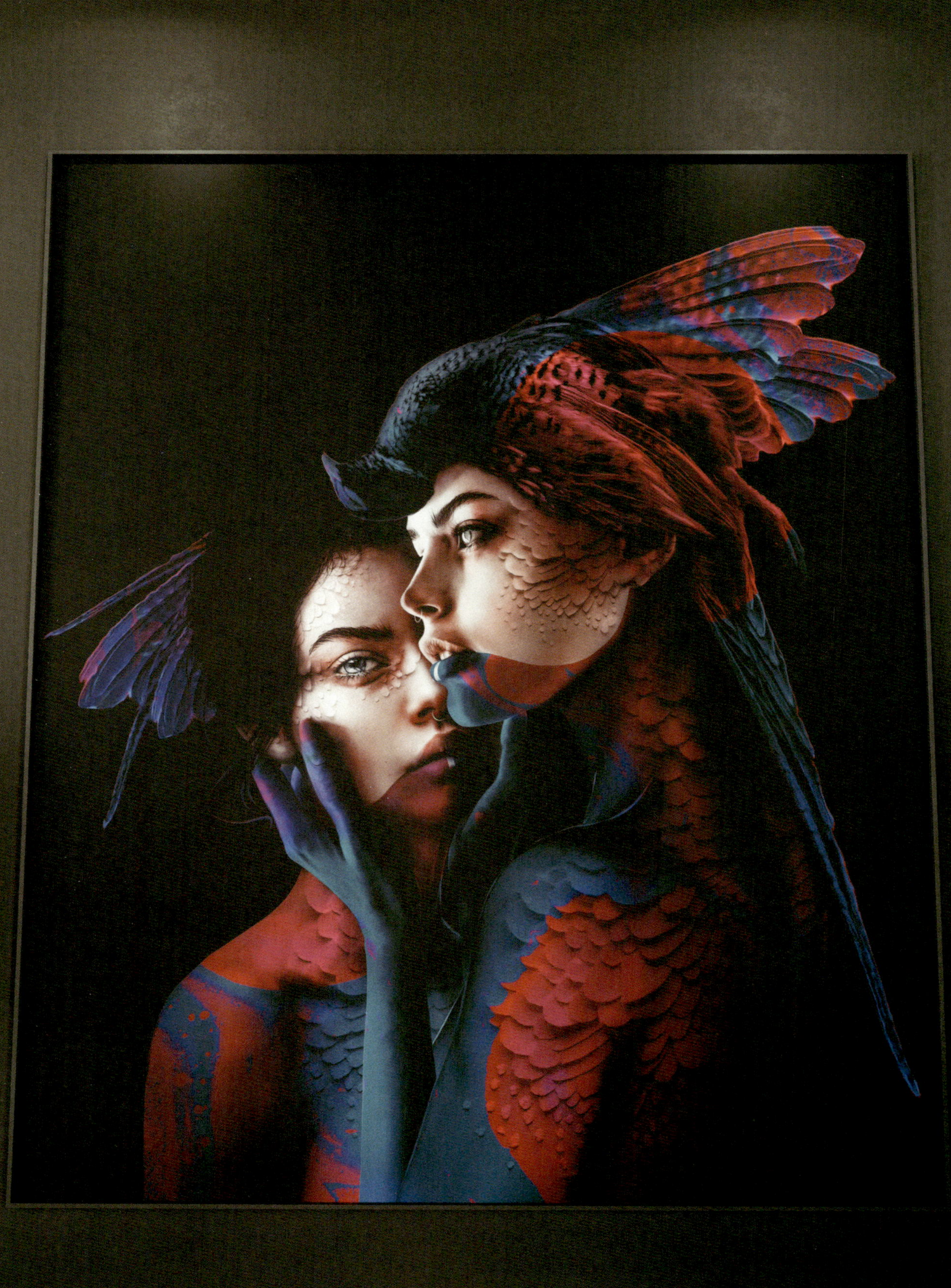
DIFFERENT
LAURA H. RUBIN

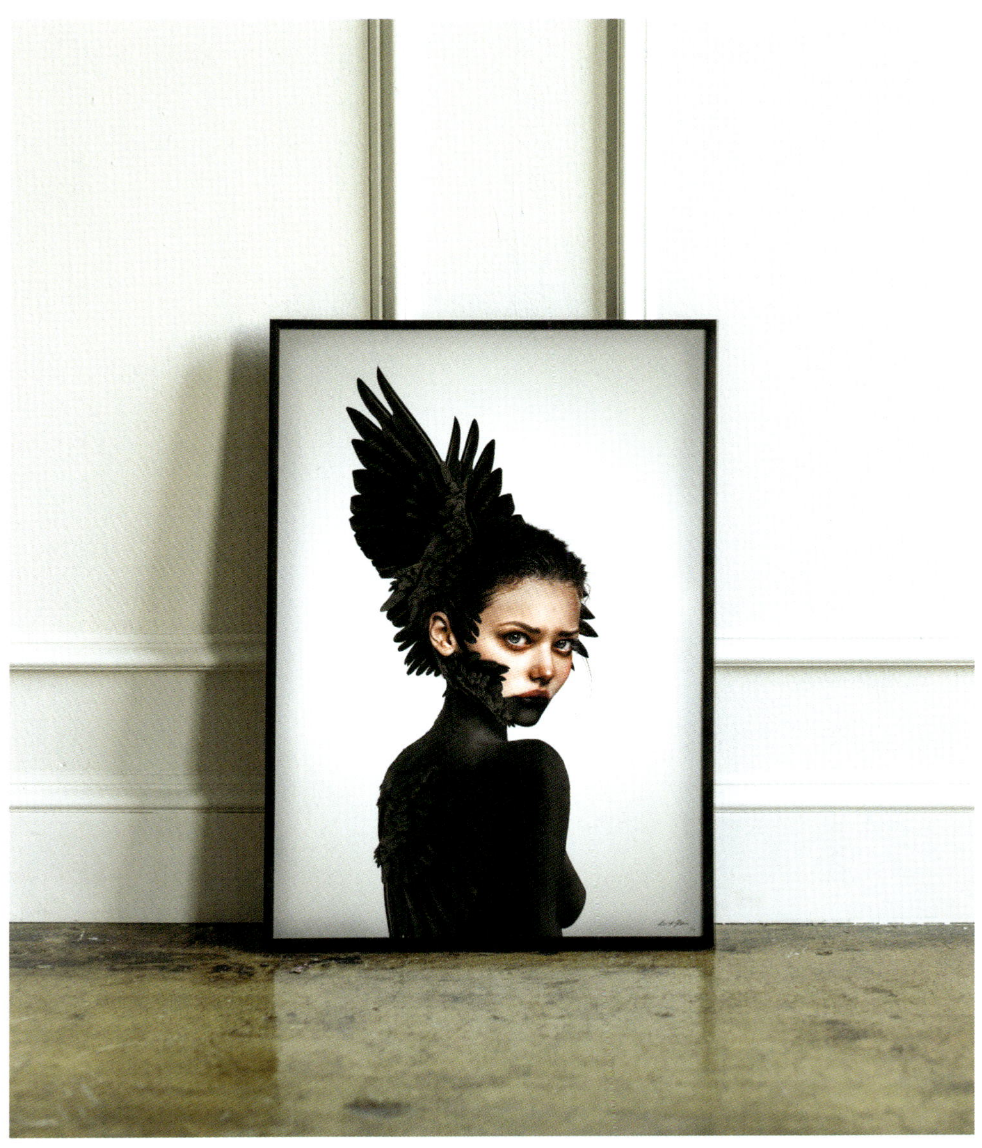

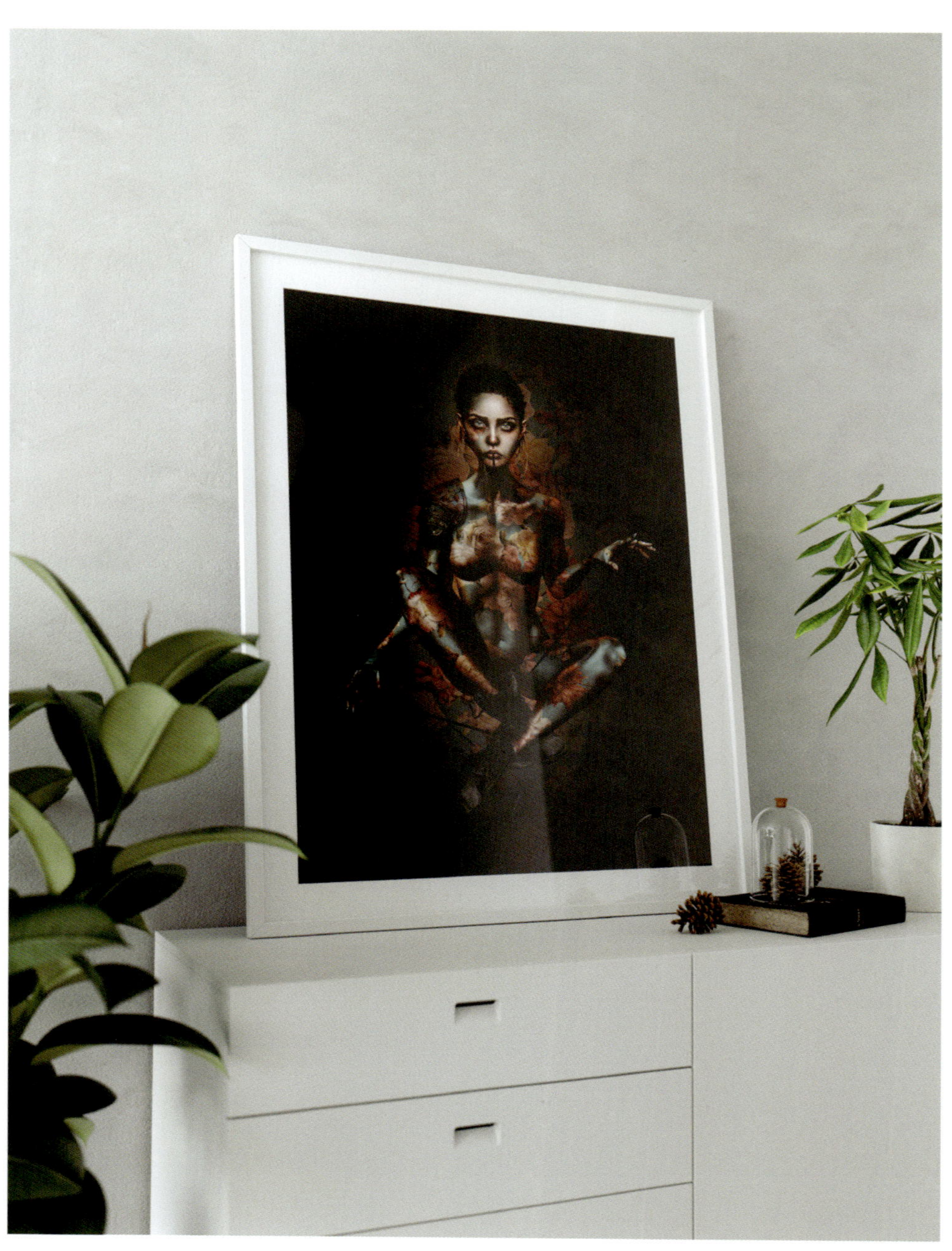

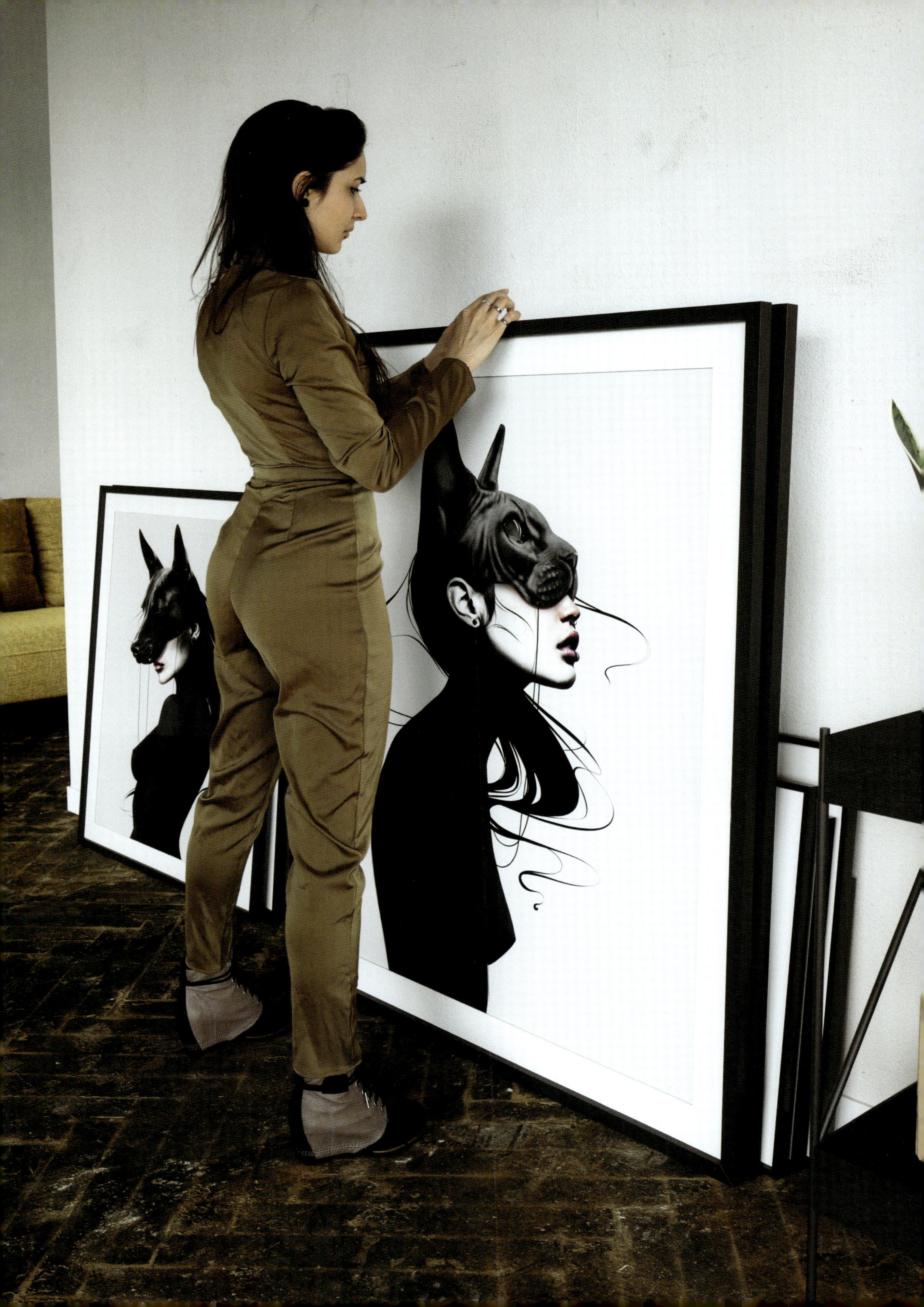

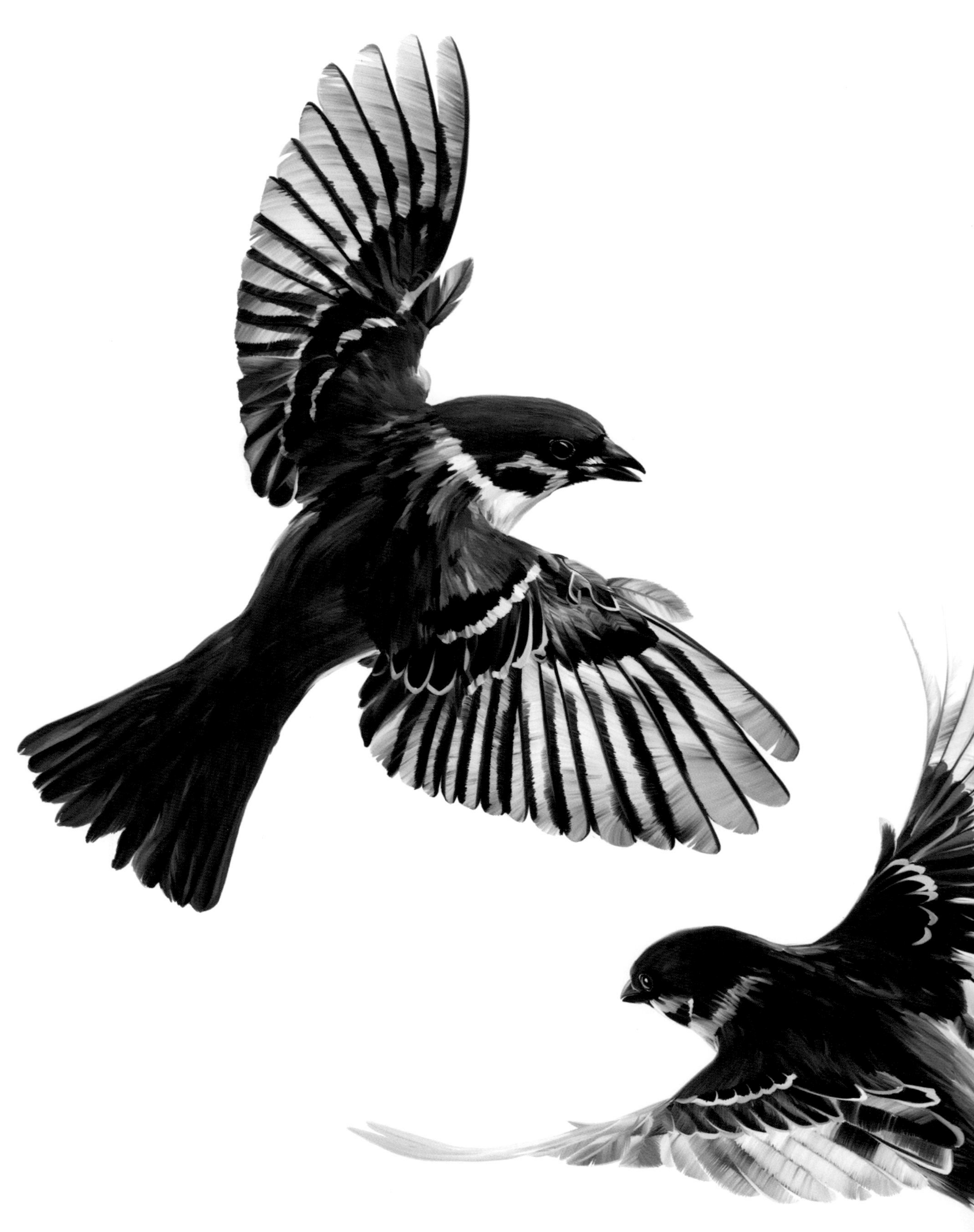

THANK YOU

A huge, huge THANK YOU to all my wonderful readers and my amazing publisher, especially Rhee, Joe, Sam & Simon. This book wouldn't have been possible without you and your support.

Thank you Oly, the best partner I could have wished for. I'm so grateful for your continuous, unconditional support in all endeavors I undertake!

A big thank you to Yu, my best friend. You listened tirelessly to me babble about tutorial chapters during our coffee dates every Monday, even though you've never used Procreate. Your wise words were integral to the making of this book: "I have no idea what you're talking about, but just add a lot of images, then everyone will understand!"

Thanks everyone, from the bottom of my heart!

xo

Lara

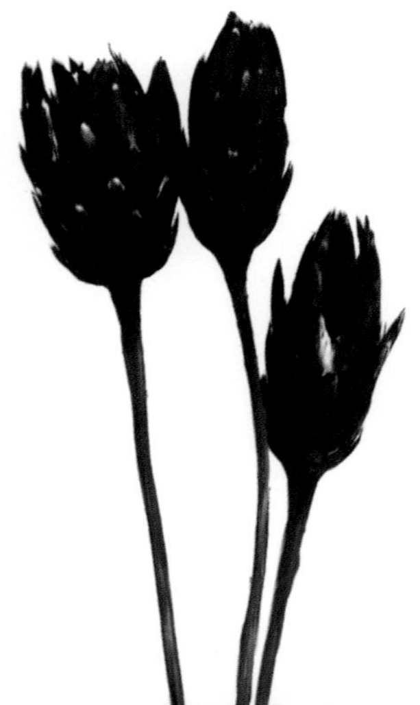